The Nowhere Men

Also By Michael Calvin

Family: Life, Death and Football
Life's a Pitch
Only Wind and Water

The Nowhere Men

Michael Calvin

CENTURY

Published by Century 2013

2 4 6 8 10 9 7 5 3 1

First published in Great Britain in 2013 by
Century
Random House, 20 Vauxhall Bridge Road,
London SW1V 2SA

www.randomhouse.co.uk

Addresses for companies within The Random House Group Limited can be
found at: www.randomhouse.co.uk

The Random House Group Limited Reg. No. 954009

A CIP catalogue record for this book
is available from the British Library

ISBN 9781780891071

The Random House Group Limited supports the Forest Stewardship Council®
(FSC®), the leading international forest-certification organisation. Our books
carrying the FSC label are printed on FSC®-certified paper. FSC is the only
forest-certification scheme supported by the leading environmental organisations,
including Greenpeace. Our paper procurement policy can be found at
www.randomhouse.co.uk/environment

Typeset in Minion by Palimpsest Book Production Limited,
Falkirk, Stirlingshire

Printed and bound in Great Britain by
CPI Group (UK) Ltd, Croydon, CR0 4YY

To my children, Nicholas, Aaron, William and Lydia.
Follow your dreams.

Acknowledgements

Scouts are never off duty. I've just come off the phone from Mel Johnson. I mentioned in passing that I am due to attend the final game at Underhill, Barnet's idiosyncratic little ground for the past 106 years. 'Ah' he said. 'You can do me a favour. They're playing Wycombe. Can you give me a report on their keeper? A lad called Ingham. He's 18, six two, six three, played about half a dozen games. I'm hearing good things. I'll try to watch him on the last day of the season.'

Coincidentally, I had spoken earlier to John Griffin. He told me Peter Taylor was scouting Charles Dunne, Wycombe's full back, for the England Under 20 squad, and raved about Matt Ingham's potential. 'We had him out at Oxford City for eight months, and he's only been in the first team for six weeks, but we are going to lose him' he said. 'I'm already digging in the dirt for the next one.'

Mel Johnson was described by Caroline Shea, PA to QPR's last 34 managers, as 'the nicest man in football' when she took me for a cup of tea before one of the countless interviews for this book. Griffin runs him close, but, in truth, there were few scouts to whom I did not warm. I thank everyone who gave me their time and their trust. I'm especially indebted to Jamie Johnson, Mel's son, who gave me the idea for this book during a casual conversation in the manager's office at Millwall. I hope my respect for their trade, and my interest in the tangential issues touched by the recruitment process, shines through.

You would not be reading this without the support I have received from Ben Dunn. I value his wisdom and foresight, which are unusual traits for a West Ham supporter. His team at Century are of Champions League quality. Thanks, so much, to Julia Twaites, Bela Cunha, Glenn O'Neill and Natalie Higgins. The legal advice of Duncan Calow was invaluable. My literary agent, Paul Moreton, has also been hugely supportive.

At one stage in the process, I was overwhelmed by the volume of information I had accumulated. Enter, stage left, my guardian angel, Caroline Flatley. My former PA at the English Institute of Sport was in the process of leaving the BBC for an executive role at British Cycling, but found time to transcribe the final 27 hours of interviews. A Northern lass like her, attempting to decipher the Bristolian burr of Gary Penrice, redefined culture shock.

I retreated to the Cornish village of Nancledra, and Smithy's Cottage, to shape the opening chapters. Thanks to Margaret and Mark Taylor, for tolerating this unshaven hermit, whose body clock had exploded. That's why, above all, I need to recognise the support of my family. Quite how my wife Lynn has lived with me during the gestation period of this book is beyond me. She has had more broken nights with me, in writing mode, than with any of our children, Nicholas, Aaron, William and Lydia.

I promise I won't put you through it again, until the next time.

Michael Calvin April 2013

Contents

1

The Initiation

Mel Johnson took his tea, without milk or sugar, and sat with his back to the wall, at the circular table closest to the door. His eyes moved quickly, constantly, as he completed his risk assessment. He was friendly and attentive, but there were 83 other scouts in the first-floor room at Staines Town. It was his business to know their business.

A wry grin. He noticed Bullshit Pete was sitting alone, chasing a piece of chicken around his plate. Buffet Billy was working his way through chips, rice and a curry which had the colour and consistency of melted caramel. The Ayatollah was in a conspiratorial huddle with his followers, whose synchronised glances offered clues about the nature and direction of their discussion.

Agents circulated, seeking the convertible currency of casual gossip and inside information. One, nonde-script in appearance apart from a lilac roll-neck sweater, was identified by Johnson as Billy Jennings, a striker who helped West Ham win the FA Cup in 1975. His bottle-blond mullet, a feature of my schoolboy scrapbook, had receded to a monkish semi-circle around the ears.

Emissaries from the international game – Brian Eastick, England's Under 20 coach, and Mark Wotte, Scotland's performance director – held court. The room hummed with conjecture and cautious conversation. It had the feel of a bookmaker's on an urban side street. The men, largely middle aged and uniformly watchful, had the pallor of too many such mid-winter nights on the road.

I had invited myself into their world, a place of light and shadow. They were the Nowhere Men, ubiquitous yet anonymous, members of football's hidden tribe. The elders, like Johnson, had paid their dues at the biggest clubs. Initiates were paid 40 pence a mile, and informed decisions on players worth £10 million or more. All were under threat from technology and the new religion of analytics.

Such men are central to the mythology of modern football. Scouts may be marginalised, professionally, but they possess the power of dreams. There is no textbook for them to follow, no diploma they can receive for their appreciation of the alchemy involved in the creation of a successful player. Their scrutiny is intimate, intense, and highly individual. They must balance nuances of character with aspects of pre-programmed ability, and fit them to the profile and culture of the clubs they represent.

Everyone knows what scouts do, but no one truly understands why they do it, and no one knows who they are. Their anonymity is anathema to the modern game, a gaudy global carousel which invites examination on its own, highly lucrative terms. Scouts supply the star system, but remain resistant to it. At best, they are indistinct figures, judged on false impressions like old-school golf caddies, who were assumed to drink heavily and sleep in hedges. They are an enclosed order, by circumstance rather than philosophy.

Anyone who has ever stood, shivering, on a touchline or sat, shouting, from the back of a stand thinks they can do their job. Whether the average football fan would want to commit to such a disconnected lifestyle is another matter entirely. Being paid for watching up to ten games a week might be the sort of fantasy which sustains a fourth former during an afternoon of algebra, but the hours are long, and family unfriendly. Scouts eat on the run, live on their nerves, and receive a relative pittance.

This may seem counter intuitive, but I resolved to study them, and to share their experiences, because I believed in the essential romanticism of their role. Over the course of more than a year on the road, I was seduced by the process of discovery. I saw boys whose precocity caused time to freeze, and young men, in

3

straightened circumstances, who seized a second chance to shine. I was there when the seeds of natural talent began to germinate; this may occur in a park, or on a non-league gluepot. It may be destined to flower in one of the cathedrals of the game, but it beckons only those who comprehend its potential.

Scouts are nowhere, and everywhere. They are rivals, but mix closely. They offered me an insight into the idiosyncrasies and insecurities of an incestuous community. Their judgements are severe, occasionally unkind, but they must be judged in the context of a game which has an unerring habit of brutalising its participants. What makes scouts different? Time and again Paul Newman's line, delivered in his role as Butch Cassidy, in the film *Butch Cassidy and the Sundance Kid*, came to mind:

'I got vision, and the rest of the world wears bifocals.'

On this particular Wednesday night, February 15, 2012, Chelsea were playing West Ham in the third round of the FA Youth Cup. Teenagers, courted and cosseted before adolescence, were accustomed to indulgences, such as being transported to Wheatsheaf Road in the first team's luxury coach. They filed, with studied indifference, through the tiny car park, past the picture window of a gymnasium which framed suburban wage slaves purging themselves on treadmills.

It was a big night for the Conference South club, even if its patron, TV astrologer Russell Grant, could not attend due to unforeseen circumstances. The surrounding streets were clogged with traffic, and the Staines Massive, the club's inevitably entitled support base, swelled beyond 1500. The following night's fund-raising quiz would struggle to make a quorum.

Chelsea were under pressure to justify an academy which had consumed in excess of £60 million, without producing a first team regular in its first eight years. The annual operational budget, £8 million, dwarfed that of many Football League clubs. A single youth team player, Brazilian striker Lucas Piazon, represented a £10 million investment. West Ham were quietly confident of nurturing a new golden generation, attuned to cherished principles and philosophies, but there were no guarantees.

For some, this Youth Cup run would be a career highlight. Around 10,000 boys are in the academy system. In the region of 1 per cent will make a living out of the game. Two-thirds of those given a professional contract at 18 are out of professional football by the time they are 21. The scouts were there to scavenge; it was their job to be in a position to take advantage of a coach's lack of foresight, or a club's lack of patience. They were looking for signs, hints of undervalued talent that others might miss.

Johnson, Liverpool's principal scout in the South of England, was reassessing players with development potential. His son, Jamie, Millwall's chief scout, was one of many representatives of Football League clubs looking at long-term loan targets. Dean Austin, newly employed on a part-time basis by Bolton Wanderers, sought youngsters with resale value.

Austin, the former Spurs full back, was working through his angst at the interruption to his coaching career, which had surprisingly stalled. He managed in the Conference, and combined coaching with player recruitment at Southend before becoming Brendan Rodgers' assistant manager at Watford and Reading. He had been seeking a manager's role, since leaving Crystal Palace in May 2011, and was prepared to keep head-butting a glass ceiling. 'He's my angry young man' said Johnson, affectionately. 'I just love getting out there, on that training field' said Austin, with convincing force.

Mark Anderson arrived from another dawn shift as a senior site manager for a construction company. Football was his release, the Liver Bird on his quilted jacket a badge of honour, even if wearing it on duty defied convention. He was proud of his association with a club of Liverpool's stature, as a youth scout, and radiated unfulfilled ambition. He, too, was determined to get back into the game on a full-time basis.

Steve Gritt was in his first year as Bournemouth's chief scout. While Alan Curbishley, his former managerial partner, endured the purgatory of punditry, he was sustaining a career defined by spells in charge at

Charlton, Brighton and Millwall. His most recent post, as director of Charlton's Academy, had relevance, but he remained in culture shock.

'When I first started in management with Curbs, twenty years ago, the managers went out scouting' he said, tightening the draw-strings on the fur-lined hood of his quilted coat. 'That's not the case these days. So many rely on the judgements of their scouts. Funny, that, because they are the ones who pay, if those judgements are wrong. This job is a bit of an eye-opener, to be honest. Even managers don't really realise what scouts do, how hard they work. They are out in all weathers, at all hours. They don't get the credit they deserve.'

The scouts sat where they could, in a 300-seater main stand. They didn't share the laughter as balls disappeared into adjoining gardens. They were blind to the idiosyncrasies of the setting. Closely planted Leylandii, evergreen symbols of Middle England, stood guard behind one goal. Newly built houses, as neat and symmetrical as loaves of bread on a baker's shelf, were vulnerable to stray shots at the other end.

During lulls in play, Anderson delivered despatches from football's dirty war. Scouts were having their car tyres slashed, on suspicion of poaching young players from smaller clubs, who were aggrieved by what was perceived to be the institutionalised greed of the Premier League's Elite Player Performance Plan. 'There's a lot of aggro out there,' he reported. 'It's getting naughty. A lot of clubs won't have us on the premises.'

Representatives of six Premier League teams, including Arsenal, Manchester United and Chelsea, drafted the plan, which created four categories of academy. It was, essentially, a self-selecting process since those in the top category were required to under-write an annual budget of £2.3m and employ at least 18 full-time staff. Wealthier clubs were freed from the need to recruit young players within a 90 minute radius, in terms of travel time, from their bases.

Naked self-interest is excused when an outstanding 14-year-old has a bounty of up to £2 million on his head. EP3, as it is known in the trade, was reportedly forced through when the Premier League threatened to withdraw £5.4 million in so-called 'Solidarity funding' from Football League clubs if they did not sanction its adoption. Their resistance, understandable because it gave an open invitation for scouts to pilfer boys as young as nine for small change, was futile.

Young footballers are on the menu, and the price list is set. Instead of paying seven-figure sums, the biggest clubs need only to pay £3,000 for every year a newly recruited boy has spent at another club's academy between the ages of 9 and 11. As little as £12,000 compensation is required, for every year he has been nurtured, elsewhere, between the ages of 12 and 16. Premier League clubs, who had accumulated debts of

£361 million from a collective income of £2.3 billion, had a vested interest in portraying anarchy as opportunity. Johnson, a man of ritual and restraint, busied himself with his paperwork. He had folded a sheet of A4 into quarters, and recorded the players' names and numbers, in formation, in blue and red ink. It would be stored, like thousands of others, in a series of suitcases in his garage. Occasionally, in shorthand designed to offer a mental image, he wrote 'looks like' next to a name. Thus Taylor Miles, scorer of West Ham's 43rd minute equaliser, was linked in perpetuity to Craig Bellamy. He lacked the Liverpool player's default mode of an enraged ferret, but shared his energy and eye for goal.

Whenever Johnson spoke, he instinctively held the official team sheet over his mouth with his right hand, to prevent strangers overhearing. His voice was soft, yet insistent. 'You're very much on your own in this job,' he said. 'It can be very lonely. You don't really have friends, you have your fellow scout acquaintances, but they're not really friends. It's a bit of a secret world. We try not to tell each other who we're watching, but most of the time it's quite obvious.'

Two young men behind us, one apparently preoccupied with his iPad, another saucer-eyed from texting from his smart phone, caught his attention. 'You can tell the agents,' he said, with a barely decipherable flick of the head. 'They're the ones who are on the phone all the time. They don't watch the game at all. They're here to work the rooms, to see and be seen.'

His son, Jamie, was initially impressed by John Swift, Chelsea's elegant, straight-backed central midfield player. He made good angles, picked clever passes and was sufficiently adept, technically, to be comfortable on the ball in tight areas. 'A young one, a Gary Gardner type, Dad,' he said, referring to another midfield tyro, at Aston Villa. 'Good footballer but an academy player,' came the reply. 'Ask yourself the question: will he keep me in a job if I take him for a Championship or League One club? No. He'll get you the sack.' Swift duly faded into insignificance.

The older man was examining body shape, the probabilities of genetic inheritance. 'Look at Elliot Lee – Rob's son. Chip off the old block, isn't he? But a big arse. Not an athlete.' Few words were wasted, and judgements were harsh: 'Look at the goalkeepers. One's a great size, but a coward. The other's a great shot stopper but too small. Their mistakes prey on your mind.'

I was struck by Chelsea's Todd Kane, a full back in the modern idiom. He was strong, adventurous and aggressive, and his delivery from wide areas caused problems. 'He could have a career, him. My first thought is Brentford. He's a Nicky Shorey type. He does what it says on the tin. Problem is his size – can't see him defending at the far post at top level. He'll be a proper pro though.'

There was logic to Johnson's caution, borne out of 27 years' experience. 'The window of opportunity isn't open for long, and they're out there flicking and farting around. It is a cruel world. They have only one chance to impress. There are too many games, too many players, to spend long on them. When you are working for Liverpool, a lot of the time you are crossing names off your list.'

Islam Feruz, a small support striker blessed with extreme pace, earned a reprieve by scoring a goal of sublime quality. He picked up the ball midway in the opposition half, surged past four challenges into the heart of the penalty area, and dinked a shot over the advancing West Ham goalkeeper. 'Blimey!' exclaimed Johnson. 'Didn't see that coming. That was Diego Maradona.'

Feruz was a child of his times. The only son in a family of Somalian refugees which relocated to Glasgow after fleeing to London from Tanzania, he was saved from deportation, at the age of 12, by the advocacy of Celtic's youth coach, the late Tommy Burns. He made his first team debut at the age of 14, in a memorial match for Burns, a man of immense integrity in a game of shallow expedience.

Within 18 months, Chelsea had taken advantage of a loophole in the system to spirit him south. Conscious of competition from Manchester City, they installed the family in a flat near their Cobham training ground.

The boy was reportedly being paid £10,000 a month, and had his own website, which proclaimed: 'Islam Feruz will be famous.' Wotte, who might have been expected to be a little more circumspect, promptly compared him to Romario.

With five minutes remaining, and the scores level at 2–2, most of the scouts had seen enough. Only Anderson stayed to witness Chelsea's win, on penalties, after the game had ended 3–3 after extra time. 'What have I got to go home to?' he said with a mischievous smile. 'I'll be here helping them sweep up.' He would make himself busy, networking with agents, parents and coaches. He could talk for England, but, crucially, he was a good listener. He, too, worked a room, like a bee collecting pollen.

Johnson scurried to his car, in the company of Steve McCall, Ipswich's chief scout. His small talk – 'that Nat Chalobah, he's got Chelsea-itis. Got all the tools, but a laid-back Larry' – was tellingly deceptive. It was several months before he revealed he had logged the defender's speed of thought, intelligent movement and ease on the ball. He recommended him, as the putative holding midfield player Liverpool were seeking.

Johnson had been taken to Anfield by Damien Comolli, with whom he worked, as chief scout, for Tottenham. He recruited Gareth Bale from Southampton, but was a victim of regime change under Harry Redknapp. It was the first time he had been 'moved on' since he began scouting, as a self-confessed 'football fanatic', in 1985. The following year, on Good Friday, he recommended Norwich City sign an 11-year-old midfield player he had spotted playing for Ridgeway Rovers in the Canaries Cup.

David Beckham was duly invited for trials at Carrow Road, but joined Tottenham's School of Excellence before Manchester United, and corporate canonisation, beckoned. Since Leyton Orient, the boy's local club, were also unfulfilled suitors at that time, there was an appropriate symmetry to Johnson's next tutorial, an Under 19 international between England and the Czech Republic at Brisbane Road.

Johnson parked in the terraced streets surrounding the ground, and popped into a newsagent to buy a local paper. 'Everyone canes me for it, even Damien,' he said, with a self-deprecating chuckle. 'But I always buy one for the titbits. You never know what you'll find out.' He returned to his car, and studied the Czech squad on his iPad for an hour, before he entered the Olympic Suite, 35 minutes from kick-off.

The scouts were devouring ham and mustard sandwiches, with the obligatory chips, as they retold tall tales of ducking and diving. My favourite revealed the ingenuity and duplicity of one solid citizen, who monitored youth football for Portsmouth, did first team match assessments for Newcastle United, and covered non-League football for Wolverhampton Wanderers. All three clubs were ignorant of his involvement with the others.

Johnson preferred the company of Tottenham coach Clive Allen. 'He was good to me at Spurs,' he explained. 'He kept phoning to see how I was after they outed me. You don't forget things like that.' They discussed striker Harry Kane. He was excelling on loan at Millwall, whose manager Kenny Jackett had worked with Johnson at Watford and QPR. The one doubt, about his pace at the highest level, was neutralised by memories of Teddy Sheringham, a player whose game intelligence compensated for a slight lack of speed.

'I love this place,' Johnson reflected, as we looked out on to a museum piece, the deserted old main stand. 'The fans are the funniest around. I was here once when they started chanting "we can see you washing up" at the inhabitants of the flats in the corner. It's a proper club, with some great people.' Memories of the old John Chiedozie tea bar, and the fabled eccentricity of former manager John Sitton, stirred a smile.

Stuart Pearce, who was to make a cameo appearance as England caretaker manager against Holland at Wembley the following night, nodded as he bustled past with his retinue. Johnson had talked football with him the previous week, in Jackett's office at the Den, but his perspective shifted suddenly, as the teams, and his sheet of A4, came out. 'We know the England boys so well,' he rationalised. 'This is my chance to look at the

Czechs. They've beaten some top sides.' He quickly concentrated on goalkeeper Lukas Zima, a tall, slightly built fashion victim in tangerine kit, and predominantly orange boots. All that remained was for him to address the error of my ways.

'Don't look at the game, look at the man,' Johnson instructed. 'You are following play just like the coaches who come out with me. Scouts study their man. I blank the other players out, although if the ball is at the other end of the pitch I'll watch out of the corner of my eye, just in case I get asked for an opinion. You cannot follow the ball in this job.'

I felt self-conscious at first, but it was simple, and startlingly effective. Watching Zima so intensely had a strange intimacy. He morphed from an unknown name on a team sheet to a definable human being. His mannerisms became familiar, and the complexities of his character emerged. He unwittingly evoked sympathy and understanding. Johnson was enthused: 'Look at him. Good concentration. Keeps communicating. Attention to detail. He's alert, thinking. A good size. I like him. I like his bravery. He's been out at people's feet a couple of times. I know he punches, but all the foreign ones do, especially at youth level.'

As he spoke, England broke quickly from an ill-judged Czech attack. Harry Kane chested the ball down inside his own half, fed Ross Barkley on the right, and sprinted to receive a return ball on the edge of the penalty area before scoring with a low shot into the corner. Johnson spoke with proprietorial authority and concern: 'There was nothing the keeper could do. He's got nothing in front of him. That Celtic boy, the left-sided centre half, is struggling for his life. It's not the keeper's fault they keep getting caught out by balls over the top.'

The consensus at half-time was that the Czechs were 'crap'. Lil Fuccillo, Luton's technical director, was telling anyone who would listen: 'it's Barça this, Barça that. I'm getting sick of it. We've got to play to our strengths in this country.' Rather than enlist in the Bedfordshire branch of the Flat Earth Society, Johnson gravitated towards Dave Holden, the veteran Arsenal scout, who was instrumental in the recruitment of Alex Oxlade-Chamberlain.

There was an easy rapport between the pair – 'not a lot out there is there?' – and each knew not to read too much into the small talk. They strayed beyond the immediacy of the match, to engage in a discussion about the best culture in which to inculcate young players. Holden, a former school teacher who had retained a broad Geordie accent, insisted: 'Players recognise the best players. They'll have a young one in the group if they see something in him. Players also challenge coaches. They know if the coach isn't good enough, the outstanding player in the group will regress to the level of the others.'

The gossip was global. Jaap Stam was making a

positive impact as Manchester United's Brazilian scout, and was pushing hard for Dede, the Vasco da Gama central defender. Barcelona had taken out first options on 39 young players at Boca Juniors. Glenn Rocder, the former Newcastle manager, had been added to Aston Villa's scouting staff. By the time the litany of opportunity was complete, the second half was underway.

We were joined by Anderson, Liverpool's youth scout, who exclaimed 'there's our boy again!' when Todd Kane delivered a cross on the run that enabled Chelsea colleague Patrick Bamford to extend England's lead with a stooping header. Johnson's other duty involved monitoring winger Nathan Redmond, who was introduced as a substitute, midway through the half. 'Watch him,' he counselled. 'He won't really be trying. He'll be more worried about playing for Birmingham on Saturday, and in the Cup replay against Chelsea next week.' Sure enough, Redmond was measured, to the point of indolence. He contributed little, apart from a languid flick and brief bursts of pace in insignificant areas. Another early departure was entirely excusable.

Again, Johnson had rationed his intelligence. No one had detected his interest in the goalkeeper. 'The trick in this game is never to let people know what you are thinking, or how you are working. There are plenty out there happy to feed off your knowledge.' His report on Zima, who had been signed by Genoa from Slavia

Prague, was on the Anfield system by 2 a.m., with a recommendation that he be watched by Liverpool's Italian scout.

It was one of 200 such reports, submitted that week. Whether it would receive the attention it deserved was another matter entirely.

2

Billy's Boys

The whiff of cordite was disguised by the sweet scent of fresh lilies, which saturated the lobby at the Melwood training ground, where an honour guard of men in late middle age cradled scrapbooks sanctified by the scrawl of superstars and superannuated under-achievers. A bronze bust and an inscription, set in polished granite and extending from floor to ceiling, demanded due homage to the heroic contradictions of Liverpool Football Club.

The inscription read: 'Above all, I would like to be remembered as a man who was selfless, who strove and worried so that others could share the glory, and who built up a family of people who could hold their heads up high and say: "We are Liverpool".' It was signed, in spidery copperplate, 'Billy Shankly'.

Behind the façade of unanimity, that family was dysfunctional. It appeared divided by doomed romanticism, emotional incontinence and institutionalised ignorance. The football club which enshrined the socialist philosophies of the Ayrshire mining community that shaped Shankly's character now existed only in the imagination of its followers. It was, like Nye Bevan's NHS, an unsustainable ideal, a relic of cultural change.

Social circumstances were forbidding. Merseyside was a predictable prisoner of recession. A derelict site, opposite the entrance where the men congregated on a bright, cold day, was boarded up. Melwood was protected by three strands of barbed wire, stretched above walls consisting of rectangular slabs of pre-stressed concrete. Pallid, three-storey blocks of flats, the residue of 1960s planning policies, had signs relaying the bleak message: 'Ball games prohibited.'

Mel Johnson visited infrequently, but understood the dynamics of the situation. He respected manager Kenny Dalglish, and revered the doctrines of the Anfield Boot Room. Yet he represented modernity, and the influence of Sporting Director Damien Comolli, whose 4 a.m. emails signalled the start of many working days. 'Damien expects you to work as hard as he does,' said Johnson. 'That means you have to be prepared for silly hours, and silly trips, but you want to do as well as you can for the fella.'

This was not a universal consideration. Comolli has been seen as a polarising figure. Though knowledgeable and discerning, he was accused of overstating his influence at Arsenal. He recruited well at Tottenham, but had a difficult relationship with manager Martin Jol. He had his critics at Saint Etienne, a club riven by internal politics. However, Liverpool's new American owners were convinced by the authenticity of his links to Billy Beane, the patron saint of *Moneyball*, whom he had first met as a student. The fault lines between tradition and innovation were widening, imperceptibly, but inevitably.

Moneyball was a game changer for a certain type of owner, enticed into English football by the commercial potential of its globalisation. They wished to match Beane's success, in turning the Oakland Athletics into baseball's most conspicuous overachievers through a novel recruitment strategy based upon the analysis of previously unconsidered statistics, and the defiance of conventional wisdom. Comolli was in on the deal, long before Hollywood turned Michael Lewis' book, which gave the analytic movement its brand name, into a vehicle for Brad Pitt.

Comolli was waiting at the head of the open-plan stairs which led to the inner sanctum. His chameleon qualities were immediately apparent: his suit matched the corporate grey of the landing carpet, and his open-necked striped shirt, offset by Paul Smith cufflinks, was expensively mundane. Here was a self-contained man, accustomed to revealing as little as possible of himself. His overriding instinct involved placing everything in the context of past achievement, rather than unsubstantiated or inconvenient opinion.

His office reflected his character and lifestyle. A carry-on suitcase in the corner testified to his recent schedule: he had returned from Europe that morning, after watching six matches in five countries in the previous five days. There were few signs of human warmth, apart from two small family photographs, taken on a beach holiday, but hidden behind an incongruous, commemorative football. A French book, *Le But* ('The Goal'), sat on a coffee table before a plush leather sofa. A framed copy of the two-page press release announcing his arrival at Anfield was on the wall. The Academy Performance Plan, 2012–13, nestled at the top of a neatly stacked in-tray.

He wore his authority well. He exercised strategic control of Liverpool's recruitment policy, and organised a weekly conference call involving six key figures in recruitment. Domestic policy was carried out by Johnson, in the South of England, and Alan Harper, the former Everton midfield player, in the North. Steve Hitchen, based in Le Mans, had a global role, which included responsibility for a network of European scouts. Academy recruitment was overseen by Frank McParland and Stuart Webber, supported by David Moss, the former Luton winger. All had their own networks of scouts, contacts and informants.

Comolli spoke in a Eurodrawl which had eerie

similarities to that of former Liverpool manager Gerard Houllier. He explained: 'It is a mix of being humble enough to say I don't know everything and I can be wrong, and being self-confident enough to be comfortable with the decision I am going to make. It is a balance. That is something I took from my experience at Spurs. At one point I isolated myself too much from the scouting staff. I wasn't listening sufficiently. That is a mistake I won't make again. In the end you are the one who is going to be responsible. You are the one who is going to get criticism. You have to have thick skin. But I don't have a problem with that. I don't care what is said about me. People need to understand that when we make a decision on the successful player we go through the same process with a player who is a failure. There could be ten thousand reasons he went wrong, and one reason why the other player went right. The professionalism, the way we look at it, is exactly the same, whether it is a failure or a success.

'There are no rules in scouting because you are dealing with human beings. Emotional intelligence is very important, but it is not the only thing you need. It is a business which challenges everything about you. We review our system every six months. Have we got the right strategy in place? Have we got the right people? Do we need to adjust? What about the type of players we are looking at? Is our coverage in South America good enough? Is our coverage in Asia good enough?

Everybody works differently. You have directors of football who don't travel to games, but I do, and I watch a lot of games on video. I am at the very end of the process. It is very pre-remedial.

'The local scout sees a player: either he says "I am convinced" or "I would like to have another opinion." Then someone else goes. If it is abroad it is Steve. If Steve tells me "I am convinced" I go to watch, and decide. Sometimes he says "I want you to look." I don't think trust is the whole thing, but it is part of it. If Mel goes to see a player that three other scouts are recommending, and I think he is good enough, but Mel tells me he isn't, I will listen to him, and understand why. It is about challenge, and being challenged. Talking to Arsene, he said to me a fantastic thing: "The more I am in football the less I understand it." And that is Arsene Wenger. So who am I, you know, not to be humble? I cannot afford not to show humility. It is impossible. I can only talk about football, but that is probably true of successful people in any sphere.'

They were fine words, shiny sentiments which required the sandpaper of scrutiny. There was a compelling logic to the conventional wisdom, whispered in tea rooms and corridors, that Comolli's reputation, as a data evangelist, had set him on collision course with Dalglish, headmaster of old school football management. Both men portrayed their differences as strengths, and argued that they operated well, in an atmosphere of mutual trust and respect, but such statements of faith are rarely taken at face value in such a cynical environment as professional football.

Alex Smithies was one of the guardians of the club's conscience. He had been a fixture at Liverpool since being employed by Bob Paisley in 1979, and understood the accumulated weight of wisdom, acquired over 50 years in the game. He was based in Newcastle and specialised in assessing impending opposition, but his status, as Dalglish's most trusted scout, involved making a final check on principal transfer targets. He operated on the front line, where statisticians were regarded as armchair generals: 'I was at a meeting with Kenny the other day, when one of the whizz kids tried to get clever. Kenny told him: "At this club we rely only on our eyes and our ears."'

Those twelve words defined the battleground. Dalglish had been brought up to believe in the subjective judgement of a football man's eye and the timeless quality of peer recognition. Comolli, by instinct and inclination, believed in the objectivity of raw data, and the complementary expertise of a new generation of technically adept, university educated analysts like Liverpool's Michael Edwards, who blended mathematical algorithms with flesh, blood and bruises. He was too politically conscious to fail to detect the obvious challenge of my artful description of Dalglish as 'a traditional British manager'.

To be honest, it didn't take much to break the code. 'I don't like the definition,' he said, leaning forward, utilising equally obvious body language to emphasise the point. 'Kenny is extremely progressive and very, very open minded to everything which is new. When he left management I'm not sure he'd ever had a fitness coach. Now he is back we have five. He has bought into it. He trusts people. The scouting is the same. He said, "Before I didn't need scouts. I didn't need anybody abroad. Now it is global." The real Kenny is not traditional. He is progressive.'

Anfield was a place of whispers and moans; an overt challenge to Dalglish's fundamental faith in British players, who carried a forbidding financial premium in an overheated transfer market, was out of the question because of his legendary status. Yet the numbers didn't appear to add up. The £85 million paid for Andy Carroll, Jordan Henderson, Charlie Adam and Stewart Downing compounded problems created by the profligacy of the Rafa Benitez era. The deals didn't conform to the rigour of the *Moneyball* model, although Comolli argued, with some justification, that they had to be judged over a three or four year period. Liverpool's immediate future depended on an uneasy compromise, and an unusual outbreak of patience and perspective.

Though the endgame had still to be played out, Comolli had a missionary's ebullience: 'For the people who are open minded enough, the revolution has already happened. It can only keep growing and growing. We are at the point where we are advanced enough, in terms of what we can look at in the data, to make real progress. At the moment there are eight clubs in the Premier League who are either using statisticians or appointing them. Whether that will increase is very difficult to predict. You have dynamics within clubs, politics. You might have a statistician. But at what level does he operate? What interaction has he with the people who make those decisions? I know some of those details, but not all.

'When Michael Edwards was in America, he was not alone. Fulham were there. Everton were there. West Brom were there. That's why I speak with Michael every day. The first time I went to see Billy Beane in Oakland I had my biggest lesson. I realised then how much you can, and should, know your players. You look at fitness data, tactical and technical data. For first team recruitment you have two aspects: availability and money. If we know there is a top player somewhere, but not in a position we need, or not of the style we are looking for at this moment in time, we still monitor him on a regular basis. But the reality is we concentrate only on the ones who are going to come in and make an impact in the first team.

'There are not many players in the world that can get you into the Champions League, or can excel in the Premier League for a club of Liverpool's heritage and ambition. We can pretty much afford anyone we want, but how many of those players are available? You can write off those at United, City, Barcelona, Real Madrid. You will have difficulties getting them out of Chelsea or Arsenal. What's left, on the open market? That's why we must have a massive database. The management of the knowledge is a challenge in itself. Michael has helped us tremendously in organising it. He has prevented us drowning in the data.

'With senior players you assess the tactical, technical, physical and mental aspects of performance. Once you look at those four does he fit into your team philosophy? Is that what your manager wants? In a way you do not know what you are getting when you sign someone, but there are times when you are able to spend quality time with the player. You assess his background, his family and his agent. I often say, tell me who your agent is and I'll tell you who you are. We are nowhere near to being psychologists, but when you have been doing this job for quite a while you manage to read the player's personality. What you don't know is whether he will thrive under pressure, or whether he will collapse under the weight of a big club. The best way to solve that riddle, to make an educated guess about what the player can become, is by doing what they do with the draft in the US, where they psychologically test players. That will never happen here because you are dealing with someone else's property.'

And someone's son. Everyone involved affected to

ignore the moral ambivalence of the manic search for the best young talent. Competition was fierce, and minimal advantage, in an incestuous environment, was maximised. MK Dons manager Karl Robinson, who spent eight years as a Liverpool Academy coach, played a pivotal role in persuading Sheyi Ojo to sign for his old club instead of Chelsea, who assumed their £1.5 million bid for the schoolboy was sufficient. It cost Liverpool half that sum to lure Jerome Sinclair, another 14-year-old striker, from West Bromwich Albion's Academy.

Mel Johnson used his friendship with Wycombe Wanderers manager Gary Waddock, with whom he had worked at QPR, to secure another prodigy, Jordon Ibe. He was tipped off the night before the 15-year-old made his first team debut against Sheffield Wednesday, and made a late switch to see the boy get booked for celebrating his goal with his parents, in the main stand. Johnson had a head start on suitors from Tottenham and Manchester United, and immediately recommended him to Comolli. He watched each of his 11 games with increasing trepidation before Liverpool made a £500,000 down payment on Ibe's potential.

Yet one name at Melwood was spoken in hushed tones, as if reverence would spare its owner the random cruelties of fate: Raheem Sterling. Liverpool is a club, and a city, in thrall to the compelling possibilities of an underdog's story, and I had not known such anticipation for more than two decades. Then, at a social function whose purpose has long since been lost in time, I had sat next to Ian St John, and listened, rapt, to tales of a 12-year-old known simply as 'Michael'.

Michael Owen's was a straightforward story. He was the son of a former footballer, who represented the values of a tightly knit family with middle-class pretensions. Sterling's was more edgy, that of a ghetto child who owed everything to the wisdom and love of a mother, Nadine, who brought four children up on her own in the most difficult circumstances. Owen coped with his commoditisation, but no one knew if Sterling had the maturity to deal with the apparent inevitability of celebrity.

His journey began in Maverley, one of Jamaica's most marginalised communities, where gun crime is rife, and drug gangs dispense summary justice. He played street scrimmage, an anarchic form of football with fluid rules, on the ominously named Reaper Road, before, at the age of six, he emigrated, with his family. He was transplanted into a similar culture on the St Raphael's estate, in the shadow of Wembley Stadium.

The St Raphz Soldiers, a so-called Blood gang aligned to the Mozart Crew, fought the Suspect Gang from the adjoining Stonebridge estate. Violence escalated, with police reporting that Yardie drug barons had ordered hit-men, imported from Jamaica, to put a murderous end to factional fighting among crack-cocaine dealers in the area. Sterling failed to settle in a mainstream primary school, because of behavioural problems, but found salvation at the Vernon House Special School and in the Alpha and Omega youth team.

He gradually overcame anger management issues, and the stigma of being labelled by social services as having special educational needs was neutralised by his footballing ability. The game consumed him; it high-lighted his work ethic and underpinned his fragile self-esteem. His mother successfully taught him the importance of personal and mutual respect. He joined Queens Park Rangers' Centre of Excellence at the age of 11, and within three years was starring for the Under 18s. His pace and directness were matched by a surreal, almost balletic, quality on the ball. Crowds swelled from 50 to 500.

Mark Anderson, Liverpool's youth scout, was alerted to the phenomenon by his brother Lee. He first saw Sterling play against Crystal Palace. 'I couldn't believe my eyes,' he said. 'There were some raw edges, but he was the best thing I'd ever seen. I flagged him up imme-diately, and watched him countless times. He produced something special in every game, showed me every-thing.' Frank McParland, Liverpool's Academy Director, responded identically, and the chase was on.

Chelsea, Arsenal and Manchester City were also inter-ested, yet there was a strange innocence about Sterling. He omitted to tell QPR he had been taken informally under the wing of Tom Walley, a veteran youth coach

who produced such England internationals as Ashley
Cole and David James. Walley had no ulterior motive;
he was in thrall to the purity of the boy's talent. 'I was
looking for a bit of purple, a bit of quality,' he remembered. 'I found it.' The tipping point came one afternoon
in Cassiobury Park, Watford, where Sterling played one
on one against his friend, my nephew, Jamie. They literally used jumpers for goalposts. The coach called my
brother David, Jamie's father, with a simple entreaty:
"Get down here, quick. This is something special."'

Sterling was a regular in pick-up games organised by
Walley on a pitch marked out in the back garden of the
home of Tim Sherwood, Tottenham's technical co-
ordinator. A trial game was arranged, between Tottenham
Under 15s and a Brent Schools select, featuring Sterling,
who was thought to be available for £200,000. Remarkably, Spurs turned him down, because academy
coaches were split about his long-term potential and
the challenges of his background. Fulham were convinced
they were about to sign him. 'We had Raheem in the
building, and were totally blown away when Liverpool
came in for the boy,' admitted Barry Simmonds, their
chief scout. Anderson and McParland had successfully
lobbied Sterling's family, and close friends, that Raheem's
best interests would be served by a £1 million move to
Merseyside. A month before his 15th birthday, he was
billeted with 'house parents' and installed in the fifth
form at Rainhill School in St Helens.

Comolli, who admitted his reluctance to recruit players with definable social problems, exhibited an intriguing sense of detachment: 'We are happy to take risks on young talent. Time will tell whether young players tick all the boxes. We don't use statistics with them, because we haven't got any data. So we purely rely on the scout's eyes. It was the same with Gareth Bale when he came to Tottenham. We were relying on Mel's eyes, my eyes. Obviously I am involved to a degree, but when it comes to big signings, high profile young players, I don't go to see them. When they walk into the place most of the time I don't know them, but I trust the people I work with. Mel and Frank would have seen them. So would five or six other scouts.

'When we are really keen and think we are going to do it, I challenge people a little bit: "How does he compare to so and so? What's the deal? Is it expensive? Have you checked his background?" Then Frank comes to me, and says this is the deal. I then say yes or no. When you talk about young players we think we have a playing philosophy here which can be summarised very simply. We have a pass and move style. We want to have possession of the ball. We want talented players who are going to fit that system, who are going to make the difference individually in the final third. So if you talk about Raheem, or Jordon for that matter, that is exactly what they are.'

His aloofness defied the emotional intensity of the

game, and of the club which was going through an intermittent bout of self-analysis. Did he never experience that eureka moment of recognition, or that postcoital glow of sheer satisfaction? At last, a smile: 'Once, with Cristiano Ronaldo. I was with Arsenal. I was the only scout at the Montaigu tournament in France. It is the best under sixteen tournament in Europe. Portugal were playing Japan on a Thursday afternoon. At half time I called my contact in Portugal and said, "I have just seen something unbelievable, I need to know everything about him." It was incredible . . .'

He was wistful, almost lovestruck in tone, but it was a fleeting indulgence. 'Personal development is massive,' he announced, in a more familiar, businesslike tone. 'I am not the same person, not the same scout in practice, that I was fifteen years ago. It is an accumulation of experience that makes you intelligent, or more intelligent, I should say. There are things I look at now that I never used to look at. I had this understanding with Arsène. I knew exactly how he worked. I knew exactly how he thought. I knew exactly how he wanted to play, what type of player he wanted.

'Take Robin Van Persie, as an example. When we signed him for Arsenal he had generally been used as a substitute. Steve Rowley, the chief scout, and myself used to go and see ten minutes, fifteen minutes twenty minutes. We were absolutely astonished by his talent. We pushed and we pushed and we pushed for Arsenal to sign him. For peanuts. And of course he had deficiencies. He had disciplinary issues. He had this and that, but I always thought if we give this player to Arsène, he's gonna make him something special. What I hate in scouting is strict rules. Clubs tell me we do that and we do that and then we do that. I hate that, because there are no rules, absolutely no rules.

'I watched Robert Pires fourteen times, and he convinced me on the fourteenth time. I watched him home and away. In the national team and for his club. When it was cold, when it was hot. On the right, on the left, central. Everything you can think of. The only doubt we had about him was his mental toughness. I went to see him the day before my first daughter was born. When I came back home I had to take my wife straight to hospital. I almost missed the birth of my first child. Robert was playing for Marseille at Sedan. If Marseille lost, they were going down to the Second Division. You can imagine the pressure – that would be like Man United going down. He was absolutely outstanding. He carried the team on his shoulders. He was fantastic. The next day from the hospital, waiting for my child to arrive, I called Arsène and told him: "I have two pieces of news. One we are in the hospital. My child is on the way. Two Pires – sign him."'

His tone was measured, but it was, nevertheless, a stream of consciousness. The contradictions of Comolli's character had emerged without warning, like a sudden storm at sea. His knowledge was unimpeachable, extensive, but he felt the need for self-justification. It was as if he, the über-professional, had been overcome by vanity. The mask was off.

'I am not a man of rules,' he insisted. 'People talk of value. Value? You can find it everywhere. Did we find and create value by buying Luis Suarez for twenty-two million euros? Of course we did. He was an obvious one for everybody, but we took the plunge. We were the ones who decided to do something about it. Billy Beane is like all the people I have met in sports who are very successful. He has an incredible drive. Nothing can stop him. I am determined that our structure will not change.

'We will still need the scout with the flat cap. I don't agree with those who say all a football club needs is some kids with a laptop. They are missing the point. They went to see *Moneyball* at the cinema, or they read the book. The best users of statistics are the ones who have a highly qualified and competent scouting network and a highly qualified and competent analysis department. It is definitely a mix of the two. The best baseball teams use both. That's what people don't get.

'The Yankees have got twenty-one statisticians but they also have a very competitive, competent scouting network. The Red Sox are employing Bill James, the guru. They have statisticians in-house. They are very, very bright people. But they have fifty scouts all over the world. I was amazed. They cover Asia, the West Indies and Australia. They have a scout in Europe who covers Holland. That breadth of coverage is very, very important. Using both aspects will help us optimise our investments and reduce the risk of making a mistake. I don't believe in a single use of scouting, or a single use of data. It limits the options.'

The emotional squall was over. It was time to cross the city of Liverpool, and leave the club that Billy Shankly created, but Billy Beane was reshaping, *in absentia*. Shankly wove dreams, while Beane crunched numbers. Liverpool, under Comolli's direction, were spending extravagantly, while the Oakland Athletics excelled because they became masters of financial control. As Comolli spoke, Dalglish was holding court in Melwood's Media Centre. He proclaimed that it would 'take one hell of a player' to improve his squad.

Something had to give.

3

The Secret Room

David Moyes is not a man to cross on a moment's whim. He has a finely developed sense of respect. His trust, once earned, is of immeasurable importance. His professionalism is unimpeachable. His eye for detail is acute. His work ethic is prodigious and his wrath is best avoided. Had he walked into Finch Farm training complex, that bleak, wet Wednesday morning, he would have been distinctly unimpressed.

It was bad enough that a stranger should saunter through the heavy door, marked 'with permission only', which led to a sequence of four offices which symbolised the continuity of Everton's decade under the Scot's control. To allow someone of my calling into the nerve centre of a club which consistently overachieves in the face of financial restraint was positively heretical. My guide, James Smith, revealed the compelling simplicity of a system which many seek to emulate.

Appropriately, given the nature of my visit, Moyes was on a scouting mission in Europe. Thankfully, given my vulnerability, Duncan Ferguson, who has previous in dealing with unwanted intruders, was unaware of my presence. He was flicking yellow-flighted darts into a royal blue board in the players' dining room around the corner. Smith, Everton's head of technical scouting, was free to reveal the science behind the School of Science.

Smith has worked for Moyes since 2003. A sports science graduate from South Bank University in London who coached in the United States and worked his way up from Coventry City's Community Scheme, he was among the first wave of performance analysts who seeped into professional football in the early years of the last decade. He was promoted after five years, when Moyes had the foresight to recognise the value of an integrated approach to recruitment, which embraced technology and made a virtue out of necessity.

'I think he was the only manager outside the Premier League to use performance analysis software when he was at Preston,' Smith recalled. 'It's not unlike him to want to have the best things and to be ahead of the game. Managers don't let people in very easily – so much of the job is about relationships and confidentiality, because you are working very closely with them. He was not looking to overhaul recruitment exactly, but drag it forward a bit. He wanted someone with more of an academic background, as we stepped things up.'

Smith operates from the recruitment room. Its contents are cherished and highly classified. They represent Everton's most valuable intellectual property. Moyes' entire transfer strategy is mapped out on a succession of whiteboards which cover all four walls. This is the visualisation of a principle, the distillation of a philosophy. It underlines the collegiate nature of his approach and the clinical brilliance of his management skills. Everything is self-contained, yet inter-reliant.

Smith has 5,000 reports stored online, on around 1,000 potential targets. They conform to a blueprint, which matches the club's culture, aspirations and financial status. 'Maybe we're quite an extreme example because we really don't spend much money,' he reflected. 'Everything is motivated and directed by the way the manager's mind works and the way he transmits the core message – we can't afford to get it wrong. If Manchester City waste twenty million, which they've actually done at times, it doesn't really matter in the big scheme of things. So twenty on Jo, twenty on Roque Santa Cruz. No problem. But if Everton waste twenty million, we'll wait a long time to get anything like that again. David Moyes spends the money like it's his own.

'It is absolutely crucial that we've got a clear idea what, or who, we are looking for. The pool of players that could potentially play for Everton is huge – it's in the thousands, so we need some way of tapering it down. There are a series of filters that extract the ones you don't want. The first thing, of course, is that they've got to be good enough to play for a team that wants to be in the top half of the Premier League. So straight away you've ruled out most of the world's footballers. But at the same time they haven't got to be so good that they don't want to play for Everton.

'We know if they are potentially going to Manchester United, City, Arsenal or Chelsea, then they're not for us. We won't worry about a David Silva, and we dropped out of Gary Cahill quite early on because he was obviously going on to somewhere bigger. The next factor is age; that is massive because we're very conscious of resale value. We wouldn't typically buy someone over the age of twenty-six, because if you spend ten million pounds on a twenty-eight-year-old you're probably not getting that money back, and you certainly won't make any money out of them.

'Of course the academy is of fundamental importance to a club like ours. We sold Wayne Rooney for mega-bucks, which funded a lot of things. But the essential advantage has been in getting resale value. So you buy Joleon Lescott for about five million and you sell him for about twenty-five. Character is also extremely important, but the problem is that if you aren't paying much money for a player, there's sort of a trade-off. You can have the character or you can have the ability. You can't have both, because otherwise they're not available cheaply. They're big money'.

Smith paused, and laughed at the private mental image he had created: 'I can think of specific examples of players we've got here who have one or the other. We've got the guy who is a fantastic character, who wants to train every day and loves being here. He's desperate to prove himself in the Premier League but hasn't got the real top-level ability. We've also got the other end of the spectrum, the guy who has masses of natural ability, who for whatever reason can't quite sort his life out enough to get the best out of himself. But the bottom line is if his attitude isn't so good, he won't be here for long.

'The other variable is injury. You don't want people who are constantly missing games with funny little injuries. That's worse actually, than someone who's had a serious injury. That can happen to anyone. One of the things we do is keep a close record of stories in the media. Every player we're interested in has a file, so you can piece things together, but there isn't really any official way of knowing precise details. Theoretically, when they come to you for a medical, they've got all their medical notes with them. But very often they haven't, especially when there are things in there that they don't particularly want you to know about, and also by then it's too late. By the time you're doing the medical, you're signing them.'

To the right of that heavy door, beside an incongruous blown-up photograph of Johan Cruyff, the only non-Evertonian depicted in the building, is the office designated for chief scout Robbie Cooke and his principal ally, Tony Henry, the former Manchester City player. It is a place of clutter and transience; a half-eaten jumbo Kit Kat nestles among DVDs of Mexican and South American football. An underscored train timetable lies in an in-tray.

Cooke, who played with Moyes at Cambridge United and worked part time for him at Preston before following him to Everton in 2002, heads a two-strand scouting network. Henry helps supervise six part timers, who operate in the UK. Thomas Hengen, the former Borussia Dortmund player, operates, full time, from Germany. The structure is supported by 13 additional part-time scouts, based largely in Europe. Bryan King, the former Millwall goalkeeper, is responsible for a three-man team in Scandinavia. A series of internal scouting conferences analyse trends and standardise reporting mechanisms. Each scout must assess every player under the age of 24 at his match, and grade them on specific aspects of performance. Moyes has produced what he calls 'an MOT Test', where players are judged against a checklist of up to 12 criteria for each position. The optimal aim is to have up to 50 reports on a primary transfer target, written by between ten and twelve scouts.

Smith argued: 'What it's about is having the best system and the right people in the right places. It's about the flow of information getting to the right people, who make the right decisions. The whole business about someone's eye is so subjective it's untrue. It never ceases to amaze me. We've had well respected people go to the same game, to watch the same player, and come back with a different view of him. One guy will say "No, he didn't really contribute much – he had one good little bit of play where he beat a couple of players on the edge of the box but then shot wide, that's about all he did." And the other guy will say "Yeah, he was quite quiet, but you know what? He had this one moment on the edge of the box where he beat a couple and he nearly scored, and I saw enough there."

'We do a lot with video now. That's a big part of the job, because it gets around this business of the manager not being able to see as many games as you'd like him to see. So although he'd never sign a player without seeing him, and he goes to more matches than almost anyone, he can have a really good feel for the player before he's ever actually been and seen him. I'm almost talking about our own flaws here – but if you show the footage to a room full of people, they all go away with the same view of the player because they influence each other. So and so says "cor, that was good" and the others will go "oh yeah, it was"; or "I don't like that. . . . no, it was crap". But if you get them to watch it individually, they'll each go away with different views.'

Moyes occupies the corner office next door to Cooke.

It features a wooden desk with the dimensions of a full-sized snooker table, and a digital monitor that wouldn't be out of place in the local Multiplex. Visitors occupy three leather chairs, facing him. A picture window enables the manager to look out, across a balcony of wooden decking, on to the training pitches, which flow into one another on the 55-acre site, in the Liverpool suburb of Halewood. 'The master of all he surveys,' said Smith, reading my thoughts.

One of the definitive elements of the Moyes mythology is the nature of his job interview with Bill Kenwright, the chairman whose emotional commitment to Everton borders on the obsessive. Even he was surprised by the response when he contacted Moyes, and invited him to his home in London to discuss the position. The Scot refused to do so until he had done that night's work, scouting striker Nathan Ellington at Bristol Rovers for Preston. After the game, Moyes drove to the capital, leaving Kenwright at around 1.30 a.m. He completed his 550-mile round trip to Lancashire at 4.30 a.m., and took training five hours later.

His commitment inspires loyalty and, it must be said, a little awe. Steve Brown, who took Smith's role as principal performance analyst, hails Moyes' 'brilliance' in devising specific tactical strategies. The same qualities which make him a leading coach – according to Brown 'he's so detailed, thorough and methodical in his work' – make him a good judge of a player. The complementary disciplines coalesce in the preparation of a gameplan, which draws on detail contained in Everton's opposition scouting reports. Brown told *Sports Illustrated*: 'Now we tend to examine at least five games of the team we're facing, break them down, link them up with the scouting reports we have and the stats we get from Prozone. From that we build a detailed picture of how we think the opposition play and what we think their style, strengths and weaknesses are, what their intricacies are in terms of what they're doing positionally, and if their individual players have trends and tendencies in their play.'

In such a collegiate atmosphere, the pressure to develop professionally is subtle, but decisive. Smith admitted: 'I go to probably two games a week. That's quite important because of the credibility issue. How can you sit in a discussion and contribute to it by having an opinion if you don't know the players? So in that respect I'm just like any other scout, really. What I'm not doing necessarily, is disappearing off into Europe midweek because I need to be here. I go abroad at weekends to see games, to understand the realities of the job, the match tickets, airport and hotels and what's best for the guy on the road. If you never do it yourself, you can't understand it, and it also leaves you vulnerable to the guy to whom you're saying do this, this and this. He's saying, "Fuck off. Why don't you do it?" Well I do!'

Steve Round, Everton's assistant manager, works out of the office opposite Moyes. He was another early disciple of performance technology. Elements from a PowerPoint coaching presentation, entitled 'The Disciplines of Transition' are on a whiteboard, alongside the psychedelic graffiti of a child's self-portrait. The desk is dotted with reference books, fixture schedules and tomes on sports psychology. Round, too, is away, watching a player in Southern Europe. He has an integral role in the creation of a two-tiered gameplan with Moyes. The main strategy, which takes several hours to create, is distilled into a shorter, more accessible version for the players, featuring team shape, set piece analysis and opposition goals. Round enters the transfer process after first team coach Jimmy Lumsden has followed up leads sourced by the scouts, and sanctioned by Cooke. Again, the principle of collective responsibility applies.

Smith admitted: 'When I started at the club, I didn't know much about it all, so I've learned from the manager, from Steve, and the other staff. In the first job, I was doing all the pre- and post-match video work, so I spent a lot of time listening and showing them stuff, talking about stuff. Doing all the team meetings, travelling abroad, was a massive chance to learn from David. So I've got an idea of players from him. I kind of know what he's looking for, what he's thinking. I'm thinking out loud now, but my role is knitting it together, being a kind of a link between the manager and the scouts. He is the main man and the scouts aren't really here, for much of the time.

'Football is wracked with insecurity. Chief scouts are probably as good an example of that as any. For various reasons, their jobs haven't been secure over the years. The view is that they're the manager's man so if the manager goes then he goes with him. Robbie, our chief scout, wants to discuss things and be kept updated with what's going on. My role is to help him, make his life easier. Everything is fed back into the recruitment room. Anyone can just pop his head in at any time. It enables the manager to keep absolutely on top of what's going on. That's a lot of what I think David Moyes' success is probably about – keeping on top of everything and checking, making sure you're on it and it's not just drifting.'

The secret room is unprepossessing, long and thin. It has the feel of a teacher's study at a busy comprehensive. It is a mine of information, a tantalising glimpse of what might be, expressed in marker pens of different hues. The whiteboards on the walls have a logical sequence. To understand where Everton are in the recruitment process, they must be read from left to right. The first board features the most promising new foreign players, highlighted by the system. They are the pick of the 1,000 or so players under review, and are deemed realistic recruits. Annotated beneath individual positions, they span Europe and South America. Trends are highlighted: right backs, for instance, are in extremely short supply.

The next whiteboard contains live targets, who are monitored constantly. Their ages are written in red, on a yellow square. Those names in blue are potential free transfers, coming to the end of their contracts. Those in green are potential loanees. Those in red carry a price. There is an additional section, in the bottom left-hand corner, featuring three goalkeepers, who are seen as emergency loanees, if required. I had given my word not to be specific on names, but this list was deemed relatively insignificant. It included Brad Guzan of Aston Villa, Vito Mannone of Arsenal and Chris Kirkland, whose injury-plagued career had stalled at Wigan.

Some managers preach loyalty; Moyes practises it. The next whiteboard is a statement of faith in those closest to him. It features favoured Premier League players, personal choices who are not on any other list. They must be 26 or under, playing for a club outside the top six, and be regarded as realistic potential recruits. They have been voted for by Moyes, and his senior staff. Four players, out of the 20 or so featured, are unanimous selections. That gives everyone food for thought.

Time moves with terrifying speed in football: the next wall condenses the next three seasons into the five seconds or so it takes to scan a succession of teams, in Everton's favoured formation. This is why the secret room is off limits to players. It is, in essence, a Moyes mind map. The whiteboard contains a list of all first team squad players, with their ages, contract details, and appearance records. It starts with Moyes' idea of his best current starting 11, and what it will be, up until 2014. This offers an insight into which regulars he suspects will fade away, and who he hopes will emerge from the supporting cast. It is an imprecise science, because of the unpredictability of fate, but the gaps, when they appear, are ominous. This is a visual tool for the black art of management, moving a player on when his use has been exhausted, but his resale potential is still significant.

Moyes does not share the elitist view that the quality of players from the Football League has declined so markedly that it is negligible. His personality was shaped in the lower leagues, and he retains faith in their ability to nurture raw talent. The next whiteboard is smaller, and contains no player over the age of 23. The most promising Championship, League One and Two players are highlighted in blue, red and green respectively. One name stands out, and can be used because of its ubiquity. Everton, like the vast majority of Premier League teams, were casting covetous glances at Jack Butland, Birmingham's City's goalkeeping prodigy.

The last major whiteboard, the transfer window list, is, in many ways, the most important. This contains the names of players Everton are actively seeking to sign. On this day, it is in transition, from the January window, which has just closed, to the summer window, which awaits. This is the scruffiest section, because so many names have been scrubbed off, or re-entered, during the courtship rituals involving players, clubs, agents and assorted hangers-on. It is a movable feast – numbers range from 15 to 20. The process is so attritional only one of the names on the January 2012 list, striker Nikita Jelavic, was signed.

Smith has a smaller whiteboard, an *aide-mémoire*, to the right of his desk. It contains players from Japan and Korea, and features 'first contact' names, who require a file to be established. 'When I first got into this I had this idea that for each position you would have three players,' he said. 'You know: that's the one we really want, that's the next one, and that's the next one. Once one of those either signs for you or moves to another club you'd replace him with another one. In reality it's not that simple. If you're looking to fill a particular position, three isn't really enough. You almost need eight or nine. If you're Man City, or Man United maybe, you just need the one name, because you've got the money to go and get whoever you want. But if you're Everton you come up with a list of quite a few who you think could come in and do the job. You actually end up signing the one you can get.'

The human element will always be paramount. Peer recognition is pivotal. Moyes' brains trust uses individual contacts, including players, coaches and managers. Agents are regarded as most useful in South America where the web of third-party ownership can ensnare the unwise or the unwary. Work permits are a recurring issue in the UK, though unlike Chelsea, who use Vitesse Arnhem in Holland, and Manchester City, who have a Scandinavian network, Everton do not have a strategic association with a foreign club. The case of James Rodriguez highlights the dangers, frustrations and potential rewards. A young winger, regarded as the most naturally gifted Colombian player to emerge since Carlos Valderrama, he was on their radar, but dismissed because of the impossibility of securing a work permit due to his lack of international experience.

Porto, who operate in a more relaxed administrative environment, paid €5.1 million for a 70 per cent ownership package in July 2010. Rodriguez signed a four year contract with a €30 million release clause, and Porto quickly sold on 10 per cent of his economic rights. In November of that year Porto sold another 35 per cent to a Luxembourg-registered company, Gol Football Luxembourg SARL, for €2.5 million. They did something similar with the much-coveted Portuguese international João Moutinho. When Rodríguez scored a hat-trick in the 2012 Portuguese Cup final, Porto bought the original 30 per cent of the player they did not own from Convergence Capital Partners B.V. for €2,250,000. That meant they now controlled more than half his economic rights. He signed a new five year contract, with a €45 million release clause. Nice work, if you can get it. The scorpion dance was completed in January 2013, when Gol Football Luxembourg SARL sold their 35 per cent stake back to Porto for €8.5 million, a profit of €6 million. With such sums at stake it is unsurprising that Porto, like Udinese in Serie A and Villareal in La Liga, are pioneering video scouting.

Smith reflected: 'We're running into another era where the ability to stream games is incredible. You could come in here on any given Monday and have every game from, say, the French league ready to watch – bang, bang, bang. Maybe for a Premier League club, video scouting might be the next step. So instead of sending somebody out there, certainly in the initial phase, you just compile all the reports back here. Then, further down the line, someone goes out and follows up. You would never want to get away from first-hand insight but I would argue that you can get enough from video to make it worthwhile. Think of football in terms of being a normal business. You deal in footballers as a commodity, just like you would buy and sell anything else. You'd be more conscious of how you spent your money. You wouldn't have people travelling all over Europe, all over the world, speculatively looking at things, would you?'

He sees Borussia Dortmund as a more realistic role model: 'They nearly went bust about five or six years ago because they overstretched. They've rebuilt with a team full of young players, all with good resale values. They recruited really cleverly, from Poland, Japan, South America, and won the Bundesliga. The next step involved the Champions League, which gave them the money to invest in slightly more expensive players. It's like a virtuous circle as long as you can keep it going. It's a great example of how to run a football club. They also produce top, top players from their academy. That leads to self-sufficiency. You have to accept that every year you might have to sell one, and that will fund a process of evolution. So you sell a player for fifteen and you buy three for five million each. The hope is one of those will be sold for fifteen in a year or two, and so it goes on. Everton can operate a bit like that in the Premier League because it is acknowledged and accepted that we haven't got much money.

'The world is changing. In the old days, it seemed as if they did everything off the back of a fag packet. The old school scout would go to a game, and just have a general look, unless there was a specific player. He'd then speak to the chief scout on the phone and tell him what he thought, so basically everything was stored in people's heads. Well, they thought it was. It wasn't really, because you can't store it all in your head, can you? That's why reports have become so funda-mental. It's about intellectual property rights. That information belongs to Everton, because it was gained by people being paid by Everton, working for Everton.

The old school way, with the chief scout having it all in his head, gave no continuity. If he gets run over by a bus, he takes all the knowledge with him. I know I'm laughing at that thought, but we had a similar problem in the academy, several years ago. The head of recruitment left and there was nothing . We didn't even have the telephone numbers of the scouts! It was as if he'd never been here. An owner, or a CEO these days wouldn't tolerate that, if he's got anything about him.'

Some things never change. Great clubs are shaped in the image of their great managers. It is too simplistic to view Moyes as merely an autocrat, with the inflexibility that implies. Like his mentor Sir Alex Ferguson, he wields power decisively, but sensitively. He is comfortable with ultimate responsibility – indeed he demands it – but the democratic nature of Everton's recruitment policy informs us of the man, and the club he has created. They would not make Liverpool's mistake, of attempting to impose a sporting director in the mould of Damien Comolli. Kenwright is a fan; he understands the mentality of his club in the way an opportunistic owner from the United States never could.

When he arrived at Goodison, Moyes made a statement of intent. He hailed Everton as 'The People's Club'. The defiance of the gesture, and the horror with which it was greeted at Anfield, across Stanley Park, registered with his natural constituency. In wider terms, it begged a critical question: is football still a people's game? A League One club would assist in the search for the truth about England, and its national obsession, in the formative years of the twenty-first century.

4

Parklife

Wembley Stadium's signature arch, glistening in a weak sun, dominated the horizon. Viewed from the dereliction of the Warren Farm Sports Centre, across a valley mottled by the clutter of suburban housing, it had the splendour of a cathedral on a hill. Yet, like many things involving English football, its majesty was an illusion.

Miguel Rios understands the gulf between the presumptions of the apparatchiks, working in the Football Association's ruinously expensive headquarters, and the realities of the grassroots game. It cannot be measured by the three miles which separate the stadium and a symbol of sporting decay, where park footballers play beside abandoned cricket nets, in which saplings grow through ancient, shredded green matting.

He knows, one day, soon, the boys he watches, in

an attempt to detect and develop unrealised talent, will be evicted. Clubs are likely to fold. The travellers' ponies which graze, untended, on adjoining straw-coloured scrubland will, in all probability, be humanely destroyed. The bulldozers will move in, and, sometime in the 2014–15 season, Queens Park Rangers will have a new training ground. It is expected to win more awards for the men who designed and built the Olympic Stadium.

For the moment, Warren Farm is a regular port of call for Rios, a scout who is changing perceptions of Brentford, a homely football club with expansionist ambitions of its own. The men who write the FA coaching syllabus, and the politicians who encourage a conspiracy of silence about the sale of playing fields, and the betrayal of a generation, should meet him. It may be too much to expect them to be enlightened, but they would certainly be challenged.

His is a world where parents brawl, and referees cower in car parks, as the ignorant seek retribution. Lofty edicts about the technical development of young players are simply irrelevant. Coaches regurgitate second-rate TV punditry and tactical half-truths. This is England, our England. Children, as young as seven, have the first stoop-shouldered signs of physical illiteracy. They are active, by definition, but many are overweight, or burdened by social and cultural circumstance.

Rios is a football man with a conscience, who sees

the good in people, despite the dispiriting nature of his experiences. He is a refugee from the City of London, where he was a successful business analyst for banks such as UBS, Citigroup, BNP Paribas and Barclays Capital, until he could no longer accept the dehumanising effects of a lifestyle based on accumulation and consumption. He got out before he became someone he did not like.

'You kinda sell your soul to the money, but eventually you ask yourself why am I doing this?' he reflected. 'It is a pressurised lifestyle, but to be honest, I relished that. It was the other side which got to me. You see people who are financially secure, who decide they don't have to be nice to be anyone. They shed their humanity. There are everyday irritations – I don't miss the tube, that's for sure – but eventually I had enough of the egos. I just decided I didn't need to work there.'

He had played, semi-professionally, and was asked to coach, part time, at a sports school in Portobello in West London. There he met a teacher, who gave him an introduction to Barcelona's soccer school system. He spent three months there annually for four years, working as a translator and a coach, and refined his football philosophy. He was recruited by Arsenal's Academy, where he worked with Ose Aibangee, a coach with a similar perspective, and Shaun O'Connor, the scout who discovered Jack Wilshere. The three are now the pillars of Brentford's youth system.

Rios, a tall, mild, quietly spoken man, has responsibility for talent identification, and is head of recruitment for the Under 6–12 age groups. He has 15 scouts reporting to him and, on this particular Sunday, watched eight games, in Hounslow and Ealing. Against expectations, in an age in which the young are conditioned to believe you are the badge you wear, he was wearing a fawn hoodie, and a silver-grey gilet, rather than a club tracksuit.

'No uniform,' he said. 'The parents like you to have one, but most scouts wear it for their egos. I don't want to draw attention to myself. No one should know who you are. I prefer to be in the group. I listen for names, and try to fit players to parents. Essentially it is like looking for a needle in a haystack. At this level you need spotters, seeing as many games as they can. It is a cut-throat environment, where people try to undermine you. Why be a scout, then? I prefer it to coaching, because coaching is very binary. Its yes no yes no.

'The FA coaching courses seem driven by an economic imperative. They are not age specific. The system, at youth level, is too unstructured. A lot of coaches don't understand critical things like development cycles. The analogy I use is that most people see the car dashboard. They see the dials, indicators of what is going on under the bonnet. Scouts are the sat nav system, to see where we are going, and how to get there.'

We parked at Warren Farm, on what was once a series of shale tennis courts. Up to 20 games are staged here each weekend, on a 63-acre site, and the shortcomings were immediately obvious. An Under 11 game was being played on a full-size pitch: it was an absurd Lilliputian spectacle, closer to a cross-country race than a suitable contest in what coaches regard as the final meaningful year of a young footballer's technical development. The parents, mainly young mothers with double buggies, and fathers in a fog of cigarette smoke, loved it.

Rios was a familiar figure. He shook hands with several coaches, asked after the occasional boy. He was respectful, engaged and observant. As we wandered along the touchline of an Under 9s match on a mercifully truncated pitch, he pointed out a sullen youth, with his hands stuffed into the pockets of his baggy jeans: 'He tells me he's an academy coach. What do you reckon?' No answer was required. Had one been delivered, it would probably not have registered, because he had found what he was looking for.

An Under 15 game was in its final quarter. It was a frantic match, fuelled by unstructured effort and unintelligible instructions from the sidelines. 'Look at the ethnicity of the teams,' murmured Rios. 'Certain coaches can only handle certain types of boys from certain types of backgrounds. Their teams are a reflection of who they are.'

One of the coaches, in a white half-sleeved tee-shirt, looked like a middleweight boxer gone to seed. His harsh negativity – 'go on Smiffy, fuckin' have him' – matched his taut body language. His team was exclusively white and working class. The opposition was much more ethnically diverse. Their coach was white, but straight from central casting. He carried a clipboard, and wore a tracksuit top emblazoned with his initials. His three-quarter length cargo trousers and ankle socks did not give him the gravitas for which he so evidently yearned.

By the time I resumed following play – apologies to Mel Johnson, incidentally, for that schoolboy scouting error – Rios' demeanour had changed. He had his eyes locked on to Clipboard Man's number 9, in the way a gun dog follows the descent of a fatally wounded pheasant. The boy was tall, thin, and finely featured. At a guess, he was of Somali descent. His orange boots were out of keeping with the dowdiness of the day. 'Watch the speed of his feet,' said Rios. 'It's late in the game, but he's still chasing the ball. He's got desire, but he's not running willy-nilly. There's something there, allright.'

Once the match had ended, Rios approached one of the number nine's teammates, Michael, whom he had taken to train at Brentford after seeing him excel in a schools' match, several weeks before. The boy beamed at being recognised by the scout, and was eager to please.

It transpired the newcomer's name was Daniel. He came from an Angolan immigrant family. He had scored in the final minutes, converting a loose ball spilled by the goalkeeper, but had changed on the opposite touchline, and was already wandering away. Rios approached Clipboard Man, introduced himself courteously, and offered his business card. The response could not have been more guarded had it been a court summons.

'What do you want?'

'Can you tell me anything about Daniel?'

'Don't know anything about him. He just turns up on my doorstep every Sunday morning.'

'Do you know his family? I gather he goes to school with Michael.'

'See the Mum, once in a blue moon.'

'I wonder if you see her, you'd tell her that I'd like to speak to her. I'd be grateful if you'd give her my card.'

'Well, I'm not happy. He's with me this season . . .'

'Appreciate that. Thanks for your time.'

The resentment ran deeper than we realised. Bizarrely, the coach subsequently complained to the county FA about the nature of the approach. The innocence with which the day began, at Lampton School in Hounslow, was evidently an illusion. That was a different scene. Grandparents with ancient camcorders brought picnic seats and flasks. The boys, joined by a smattering of girls, were younger and more carefree.

The school, a product of 1960s functionality, was being updated. A patchwork quilt of starkly contoured pitches was folded around a site which combined Portakabin classrooms with new Alpine-style wooden chalets. The shrill sounds of childhood were intermittently drowned out by planes coming in low to land at Heathrow. United, BA, Singapore, Virgin. The world was evidently in unison.

This was QPR territory. The most interesting match, at Under 8 level, involved one of their feeder clubs, Old Isleworthians. Judged by his accent, the coach was South African. He had a prop forward's shape and character. A grey t-shirt was stretched across large, tense shoulders. He emitted a well-meaning stream of consciousness, barely pausing for breath as he told the boys where to run, and what to do.

'It's all so vocal,' said Rios, barely audible because he had positioned himself amongst parents, close to the halfway line. 'There are no technical details. He should be positive, let the game develop.' You didn't need to be a geneticist to realise that Isleworthians' number 6, Paolo, was the coach's son. He was like his dad, squat, earnest and shaven-headed. When he committed the cardinal sin of passing sideways, he was rewarded with a yelp of 'We are not playing for a draw we are playing for a win.'

Rios has worked for two years, identifying the most talented boys in the area, aged from six to eight. He has developed his own database, in which boys are classified by body shape and ethnicity. 'The game develops continually,' he explained. 'At a match like this we're trying to look fifteen years into the future. If you are a good footballer at this level, the kid who can score from the halfway line, it doesn't necessarily mean you are going to be an elite footballer.'

The Barcelona influence endures: 'I wanted to see inside their system. They judge by ability rather than age. They have A & B squads that can play up and down the age groups. Their physical literacy is much better than ours. Between the ages of six and eight, Barcelona do things that, if we tried them, we'd get laughed at. It is all about co-ordination. It involves balance, agility, a simple thing like hopping. They dribble the ball and rub their stomach at the same time. Then they change their hands. Can the boys cope with that? The coaches are usually teachers. They are looking for intelligence, the speed of execution of technique.'

He had spotted a boy, playing in an empty goalmouth on an adjoining pitch. 'Hi Derek' he shouted. The boy smiled, and waved, soundlessly. Rios had asked his coach, a Brentford fan, to try him in goal because of his agility and outstanding hand–eye co-ordination. 'Derek doesn't like it,' reported the coach, who had been half-volleying shots at him. 'He doesn't like to get dirty.'

Rios grinned. He believed in the rotation of

goalkeepers at such a young age, 'otherwise the biggest lad, or worst outfield player, goes in all the time'. His ideas met with resistance, because the coaches were wedded to winning, even when, officially, the result was not recorded. 'We've got one coach around here who calculates how his team gets on in non-competitive tournaments,' Rios revealed. 'He actually produces imaginary League tables on the club's website. The problem is the parents buy into that type of thing.'

A multi-cultural society produces multi-faceted problems. The stated ages of some young players, particularly those of African descent, are unreliable. Rios is acutely conscious of the danger of causing offence, but asks them, in a light-hearted manner, to smile, so he can check surreptitiously whether they have milk teeth. 'I had one player, a Nigerian with a German passport, whom they told me was 11. He was bigger than me!' he exclaimed.' Rios splits age groups in half, separating boys born between March and August from those born between September and February, because winter babies tend to dominate.

The value system, encouraged by the elitist nature of scouting, also needs to be addressed. Rios learned, at Barcelona, that getting the right boys into a club is only '20 to 25 per cent of the job'. Parents must be educated because 'the ones who chase the brand, the ones who talk and influence others, are a cancer'. Ose Aibangee, Brentford's head of youth development, has introduced a series of workshops for parents with boys in their academy, to give them an insight into their responsibilities. He explained: 'They basically explore how to work with their kids and how to work with us. The objective is to not make boys feel like they're under pressure every time they go on a football pitch. They are babies. Even we forget sometimes, because they're in their kit and you look at them like they're little mini footballers. We've had parents openly admit that they've over-pressurised their sons. That's good but I would imagine there is a bigger percentage that won't tell us. They probably won't even know that they're pressurising their kids because, in their minds, they are just supporting them and giving them feedback. They can do the wrong things for the right reasons, because they're all experts, aren't they? Everyone involved in football is an expert.'

Some have a more intuitive grasp of its demands than others. Shaun O'Connor, the club's head of youth recruitment, has been showered with stardust. He is one of the few scouts to have found 'The One'. His moment of clarity came in April 2001, in his last match as a coach at Barnet, who were closing their Centre of Excellence as a result of losing Football League status. Having already arranged to run a satellite centre for Arsenal's Academy, he had little motivation to fulfil an ill-timed fixture against Luton, but did so as a favour to their coaches, Dean Rastrick and Mark Ridgeway.

O'Connor was monitoring the Under 11s and Under 12s at the Furzefield Centre in Potters Bar, when he was informed the referee for the Under 9s hadn't turned up. He took charge of the match out of a sense of duty, and quickly had his attention seized by an eight-year-old, playing on the wing for Luton. 'Reffing was a complete pain, because it had been a really manic day, but this kid was quick. His close control, running with the ball, was the best I'd ever seen. He had fantastic balance, and didn't mind leaving his foot in. He had that nasty streak you need, had such a will to win. He tore us apart. As soon as the game had ended I asked one of their parents who he was.'

Jack Wilshere, a graduate of Knebworth Youth and Letchworth Garden City Eagles, was O'Connor's first recommendation to Arsenal. He went through proper channels, asking for permission to speak to his parents, and, helped by Steve Leonard, an Arsenal youth scout, lobbied Wilshere's father, Andy. 'I went over to a couple of tournaments during the summer just to make Jack feel that he was wanted by us,' he recalled. 'It was hard work to get him in because the old man was a bit sceptical about moving him out of Luton.'

Scouts are resilient sorts, who understand the value of the grand gesture. Arsenal staged a special Under 9s match for Wilshere against Leyton Orient, on the pitch at Highbury. Leonard recruited another Luton boy, Ryan

Smales, who played a year up. Jack waited until the last day of the registration window before agreeing to join Arsenal's Hale End Academy in Walthamstow. He thrived, but Smales regressed. The fresh-faced boy who sits alongside Leonard, in an Arsenal Under 12 team photograph for the 2002–03 season, faded, and returned to reality.

Just as the vagaries of life outside football are etched in the game's all-consuming spotlight, football fails to look after its own. It is widely believed Wilshere will be captain of England one day. He is worth conservatively £50 million on the open market. Arsenal paid O'Connor £50 when Wilshere joined the academy. He received another £250 when he signed a scholarship. The scout worked diligently for the club for a decade, at one point having 35 boys in the system, but had signalled his intention to leave just before Wilshere signed professional forms. Under a policy implemented by Liam Brady, Arsenal's head of youth development, this meant he did not receive the £750 usually due in such circumstances.

O'Connor is sanguine: 'That's Liam's policy. At the end of the day, if it wasn't for him I probably wouldn't have got a full-time job at Arsenal. He helped me get where I am today, and I'm very grateful to him. I wouldn't have had clubs asking about me. I could have joined Tottenham, and I sat down with Chelsea, although they weren't for me. There's a lot of politics in these clubs, and if I can't do it to my full potential, which is how I felt at Arsenal, I won't do the job.'

O'Connor had last seen Wilshere 18 months previously, when he visited his house to get a shirt signed. He follows his progress through Andy, his father, but feels no special affinity. 'I was there then, I'm not, now,' he said. Respect, of a more profound form, was paid by Aibangee, who pursued O'Connor relentlessly, because he had painful proof of his potential to play a pivotal role in the restructure of Brentford's youth system. There is, indeed, honour amongst thieves.

Aibangee is a watchful man, but the memory of O'Connor's larceny lightens his mood: 'Yeah! I mean, I hated him. That's why I brought him here, because he's the best at his job. I thought I was good at my job when I was at Watford. We had some good kids and Shaun took my best one to Arsenal. We had that boy for a good year, trained him, coached him, did all we had to do. Then two or three months before he was meant to sign, Shaun, my enemy, took him. I couldn't work out how he'd done it. It's the worst thing in the world, the absolute worst. But that's the job. Yeah, you take it personally, of course you do. I think if you don't, then the job ain't the right job for you.'

O'Connor agreed: 'It's emotional, exactly. I mean, when I was up at Arsenal I didn't like to lose at all. If I lost a player it would probably take me a month to get over it. That was a club I supported and grew up following round the world. I felt I had let them down, somehow. So I didn't like to lose anyone or anything, and it's the same here. I go home and I can't sleep. If I lose a player or I've lost out on a player, I can't let it go. It affects me.'

The pair are different personalities. Listen carefully, and you can hear the neurons colliding in O'Connor's skull like souped-up dodgem cars. He is a bundle of nervous energy. His eyes are bright, behind his glasses, and his greying, half-hearted goatee beard gives him the look of an ageing Labrador. Aibangee is an entirely different animal. Impeccably turned out, in tailored quilted coat, designer jeans and tan brogues, he has the stylishness and composure of a Golden Retriever. Together, they have prepared Brentford for the new Elite Player Performance Plan. They are a Category 2 Academy, which involves a £1.2 million investment. At a club whose record signing involved the outlay of £500,000, for Crystal Palace's Hermann Hreidarsson in September 1998, that is a huge statement of faith.

O'Connor has built a database of youth football throughout London and five surrounding counties, from scratch. He has employed fixture co-ordinators, who source contact details for club managers in upwards of 40 leagues; 70 new scouts, of whom only 25 receive expenses, are operative. All collect a £150 bonus if one of their recommendations is signed: 'We've put an academy in the shell of a centre of excellence. We've had two thousand triallists aged nine to sixteen in the past eighteen months. When we arrived we weren't at ground zero. We were twenty miles into the earth's core.'

His arms and knees are 'shot' from 20 years as a dry-line plasterer. He had a successful company, employing 30 men, but ran it down because he wanted to scout, full time. His only concession to conservatism was taking the Knowledge because 'in football you don't know what's around the corner'. He drove a cab for ten months, and drove himself and, one would imagine, a certain type of fare, absolutely nuts. It was just like the old days when he took me to training one Thursday evening. A six-mile journey from Griffin Park, across West London to an athletics centre just off the A40, took nearly an hour.

Streaks of salmon pink presaged a watercolour sunset. Temperatures dropped rapidly, and, as darkness fell, strangers became silhouettes, absorbed by personal ritual. Rugby players practised scrummaging in the shadows cast by lights directed at the artificial surface on which Brentford's boys were to train. Joggers eked out the last of the light on a circuit at the brow of the hill. Parents huddled in a doorway or retreated to their cars, where faces were framed by the eerie glow of instrument panels.

Everyone knew the rules. All the boys were obliged

to shake coaches and visitors by the hand. This was no chore: eyes were bright, eye contact was made. 'We do this to instil respect,' said O'Connor, before his mobile phone took him hostage. He walked as he spoke. The blue light on his headset became strangely hypnotic. His first words, on every call, were: 'What's happening?' A tremor of pride greeted my casual question about the England cap, which was the photograph on his iPhone: 'That's my lad's. Brett plays Futsal for England.'

Futsal, derived from Portuguese *futebol de salão*, which can be translated as 'hall football', is played once a week by every boy on Brentford's books. The game is played on a hard court surface with a smaller, heavier ball which, in consequence, has less bounce. There is an emphasis on improvisation, creativity and technique. The boys learn to flick and shape the ball with different parts of the foot, and develop an instinctive ability to see, and execute, sharp passes in a small space.

Its lingering influence was apparent in the Under 9 session, taken by Anthony Hayes, a young Irish coach. He had the boys on their toes caressing a ball – 'sole, laces sole, laces: just touch that ball slightly' – before introducing a series of passing drills. The air hummed with the percussive sound of footballs being struck against wooden side-boards. Coaches are rotated round the age groups each month. 'We don't want them getting favourites,' explained O'Connor, in a brief respite from his mobile. 'They are there to develop players individually, rather than create teams.'

Yet the Under 14s, coached by Danny Buck, another Arsenal refugee, had just beaten Celtic. The buzz was growing. Steve Watson was driving passes 'Stevie G style' at the Under 16s, to test their technique and composure. He typifies Brentford's strategic decision to give scouts a central role. Watson compiles opposition reports for the first team, and organises a group of non-league scouts. The accent is on the accumulation of information. Boys are measured monthly, and growth spurts inform selection decisions.

O'Connor's recipe for domestic harmony, turning his telephone to mute for an hour when he has his evening meal with his wife, is unorthodox, to say the least, but it appears to work: 'Every night, I have to give her an hour because the phone doesn't stop ringing. To give you an idea, I went out for dinner last night, and at the dinner table the phone rang about twenty-five times in an hour and a half. So that's why when I'm in the house I have to give my wife her hour. When I started this, I used to walk in the door and be on the phone, and she'd create.

'I mean, I'm a little bit cute, I have to say. Now I wait until she goes to bed, get back on the phone, and catch up with my emails. That's the bit people don't understand. This is a vocation. For the last two years there's been nothing else. My life has been put on hold until we get to a certain level. It's not healthy, I can tell you that now, because you're going to bed with a phone in your hand and you're waking up with a phone in your hand. But, to me, scouts are the most important people in the world. If I'm out anywhere and one of them rings, I have to answer the phone. It's very important they see I care, about them and this club.'

The emotional investment is huge, and the corrosion of innocence is an ever-present danger. Brentford's burgeoning reputation for previously unconsidered excellence in talent identification and development was double-edged. Praise was pernicious. Aibangee was used to scouts, literally lurking in the shadows: 'They sneak in and they'll just stand there, but when you've been in the game, you know the ones. They're not talking to any other parent, but the parent of the boy they want. You smell them. You know who they are.'

Some clubs were cutting out the middle man, and using agents as scouts. O'Connor's voice hardened, as his anger rose: 'We're trying to stop them, but they turn up everywhere. The bigger clubs think they're being cute, and it's worrying. We're going to have to increase our security. I tell you, I wish the people who came up with EP3 could come and see this. They are killing us. They have no idea how hard we work. Send them here. We're throwing the scouts out, but that won't help us, because from next season they can do what they want.

'We're getting boys to sign pre-scholarship agreements at fourteen, to give some measure of protection to the club, but agents are already whispering to them that other clubs are interested. All I can do is sit the parents down and explain they are going to get a knock on the door very shortly. My message is "Be ready, but your son doesn't need it yet." He's got to focus because he's not a football player at fourteen or fifteen. Brand names do not make them football players. Good coaching staff, good mentors, good advisors do that. You can be stuck at a big club until you're twenty years old but you won't get an opportunity. Here at Brentford, we're looking at putting them into a first team group at sixteen or seventeen.'

Aibangee maintained the argument, seamlessly: 'We've got to let everyone know it's not the category that makes the club, it's the people that make the club. I believe we've got people here of a better calibre than they have at Chelsea. We've got people here who are better at their jobs than those at Tottenham and Arsenal. We need to communicate that to the parents and the players. Forget about the category, forget about what people are telling you. Chelsea's first team will always be better than Brentford's, but isn't this the best academy for your child? We've got the people who can help him develop.'

Rios was on the radar. His group of Under 8s, assembled carefully over the previous two years, were already being stalked by scouts from Southampton, Aston Villa and Norwich. Mark Anderson was monitoring them on Liverpool's behalf. Rios was counting down the days to the third Saturday in April, when the boys had to confirm their intention to sign for the following season, their first as an official academy group. He knew the wolves were waiting.

What he didn't realise was that they had already been invited into his club, through the front door.

5

Hiding in Plain Sight

It was a moment to melt a mother's heart. Miguel's little men were innocence personified, bright-eyed and dressed identically in miniature black tracksuits which bore the Brentford crest. They filed into the main stand at Griffin Park behind their mentor, with the blind faith of ducklings following a parent across a lily pond. They were there to observe, listen and learn. Appropriately enough, promotional banners for the semi-final of the inaugural NextGen Series invited the audience to 'step into the future of football'.

The match, on March 21, 2012, captured the cosmopolitan nature of a rapidly evolving game. Brentford, formed in the autumn of 1889 as an offshoot from a local rowing club, played host to two of the most storied institutions in European football, Internazionale Milano and Olympique de Marseille. The competition, in essence a Champions League for Under 19 teams, met an incipient need to provide a platform for the young players who feed the star system.

The NextGen Series was modern football in microcosm: ambitious, entrepreneurial, opportunistic, international and commercially astute. It offered a better quality of competitive experience to emerging academy players, whose precocity promised to counteract UEFA's financial fair play rules. It provided an alternative recruitment opportunity, an insight into value disguised and distorted by a dysfunctional transfer market. It also allowed clubs subtly to position themselves for the ultimate fusion of money and meritocratic principle, a European Super League.

The setting was incompatible with the scope of the concept, and the identity of its creators was intriguing. The competition was the brain child of former currency dealer Mark Warburton, Brentford's sporting director, and TV producer Justin Andrews, who had studied European academies with Ose Aibangee, Brentford's head of youth development, for an online project. Their vision, driven by private funding and a belief in the latent benefits of elite competition, had taken four years to find its focus, but it was an idea whose time had come.

NextGen traded as football's finishing school. The best young footballers were taken out of their comfort zone, introduced to the rhythms and challenges of regular Continental contests. Could they cope with different climatic conditions, contrasting cultures? Were they sufficiently mature to deal with alien opposition, diverse tactical systems and coaches with a different mindset? For the scouts, attracted in ever-increasing numbers, it was a free rummage through a smorgasbord of talent.

It was an important occasion for Warburton. He established his credentials by setting up David Beckham's academy. He went on to develop Watford's ground-breaking academy, where he designed a holistic programme, which matched academic and sporting excellence. His role at Brentford was multi-faceted: he oversaw the scouting network, sourced potential players for first team manager Uwe Rösler, and liaised with owner Matthew Benham. His responsibilities with NextGen were another area of influence. In a world in which everyone has a price, the figures were alluring. Even those who had graduated to Barcelona's B team, the most coveted reserves in world football, were being paid a basic salary of only €1,200 a month. NextGen boys, outside the bloated economy of the Premier League, were earning even less.

Miguel Rios' Under 8 squad, like Warburton and the League One club itself, was hiding in plain sight. The boys sat just in front of Steve Gritt and a gaggle of lower division, or unemployed, managers, who were networking for their lives. They were five rows below the main body of scouts, who laughed self-consciously when Bobby Langford, who was representing Tottenham, joked 'we'd better keep our heads down.' Several scouts had been thrown out of Brentford's training ground the previous week, for being too overt in their interest in some of Shaun O'Connor's prize recruits.

'Trying to nick kids is the horrible side of the game,' acknowledged Mel Johnson, who led a four-man contingent from Liverpool. 'There is some fantastic work being done by some of the smaller clubs, and Brentford is a proper club. Blitz this area, and you will find talent. But as a scout, you have to do your job. If the kids are out there, and someone else gets them, you are asked why you haven't signed them.'

Liverpool had been beaten 6–0 by Ajax in the other semi-final at Langtree Park, St Helens' new rugby league ground. Raheem Sterling had excelled in previous rounds, but was as grateful as anyone that the Dutch effectively declared, with 20 minutes to go. Until they did so, I was convinced they were destined to reach double figures. Ajax stuck to their traditions, patterns of play established in the 1970s by Cruyff and co. They were fluid, inventive. Their movement was sinuous, intelligent. Liverpool's youngsters simply couldn't cope with their pace and athleticism, the accuracy of their finishing. Viktor Fischer swept inside, from an exaggerated position wide on the left, and scored a hat-trick of rare quality. He was being watched by a posse of scouts and coaches from Manchester United. Captain Davy Klaassen and central defender Stefano Denswil were also earmarked as ones to watch.

Slowly, a new teenaged aristocracy was emerging. Liverpool found compensation in the progress of Suso, a Spanish midfield player signed from Cadiz in 2010. They were so impressed by João Carlos Teixeira, when he played against them in the NextGen Series for Sporting Lisbon, they bought him for £850,000. Rosenberg also cashed in quickly, and sold Norwegian youth international striker Mushaga Bakenga to Club Brugge for €2.3 million. Tottenham were entranced by the potential of Alex Pritchard, a small, two-footed attacking midfield player who operated as a second striker as well. Barcelona, also beaten by Ajax, had two players of eye-watering potential. Sergi Samper was, according to Warburton, 'a superstar in the making'. Alex Grimaldo, a left back, was capable of turning hardened football men into fumbling, awestruck schoolboys.

'Oh, mate, magnificent,' said Warburton. 'I was sitting there at Hyde, watching Grimaldo play against Manchester City, with Stuart Pearce, Brian Marwood and Aidy Boothroyd. This kid would do a couple of things and you'd hear this collective gasp. He's sixteen, five foot six, but an outstanding professional both on and off the pitch. He just did things you struggled to comprehend, at such a tender age. Everyone in that team was just so comfortable on the ball. He shifts it so quickly he can play against man or beast. He simply doesn't get caught.

'The reality is, how many kids like him are going to

make Barça's first team? That's the key question for me. Let's say two, three, maybe four or even five. There are probably eighteen to twenty outstanding players who will not progress, in each group. What do they do from there? If we lack players of their quality in our game, we have to go and get them. That sets the standard. It's why we are all here. Look at the players who've already come through at the tournament. Lads like Suarez at Man City, Samper at Barcelona, Pritchard at Spurs, Gardner at Villa. They're all of a type, which can be difficult to judge objectively. Their stats might not leap out of the page at you, but how can you register something like speed of thought? At some stage, whatever your business, you have to rely on the expert eye.'

Warburton was cutting to the chase. There were lifetimes of untutored expertise in that stand. Mark Anderson pointed out Dave Goodwin, who discovered Rio Ferdinand, and still trawled through schools football in Blackheath and Lewisham in the hope of finding another star. At the other end of the age scale, Kevin Bidwell, a protégé of Arsenal chief scout Steve Rowley, was making copious notes. The fusion of instinct and experience had lost none of its effectiveness, according to Warburton:

'As a scout, there are things that grab your attention. We might be watching an under fourteen game, chatting about having had a drink in the pub the previous night, and a boy just does something. It might just be a first touch. It might be a little turn of pace, or an unusual type of pass. Now he's got your eye. You are watching that boy, looking for something that makes you turn your head. I'm not talking about beating nine men, or scoring from fifty yards. Far from it. I'm talking about comfort on the ball, the kid who always wants the ball. He might be physically smaller, but is he at ease? Can he evade the bigger boy who tries to clobber him? Now you are really starting to look. You are ticking off your mental boxes. Does he receive the ball well? Is he two-footed? Does he move quickly? Has he a low centre of gravity?

'I don't care if he is playing on a khazi of a pitch on a Friday afternoon in a local park with puddles everywhere. Those players just do something. It might be good delivery of a corner, the way he attacks the ball when he heads it. It might be the flight of a set piece. Those boys just do something which alerts your body and engages your mind. For the good scout, something triggers, both objectively and subjectively. The eureka moment isn't that bolt of lightning that everyone imagines, but the hairs do go up on the back of your neck because you know, just know, you are watching something special.

'I remember seeing Sterling for the first time. We played at QPR with Watford. I was with Andy, the academy manager, and we didn't need to say a word. We simply looked at each other. The pace, the sheer, frightening pace, combined with an end product. That was a fuck me moment, and Liverpool moved faster than anyone to get him. I had something similar with Marvin Sordell, who has just been sold by Watford for four million. I think he had been released by Fulham when he turned up. He'd be the first to tell you he was a raw, very angry boy at times. His mother was great in supporting him, but we once had to take him off the pitch at a tournament in Amsterdam, because he was on the edge. Then, when we were umming and ahing about keeping him, he'd suddenly have a turn of pace and bury a shot in the bottom corner. Everyone would simply go "wow".

'It sounds boring, but when you are assessing a player, you've got to go across the four key areas. Physically, what is he? If he's a centre half, he might be magnificent on the ball but if he's five foot seven he is binned straightaway. Has the full back got good energy levels – aerobic and anaerobic? Has he got a good turn of pace over five yards, is he good over sixty yards, can he do recovery runs? Technically, what is he? Has he got a good range of pass, a good first touch? Is he comfortable taking the ball from the keeper or is he going to hide? Does he attack the ball well, does he volley well? Mentally, how does he deal with things? When they go one–nil down with ten to go, what's his reaction? When they go one–nil up with ten to go, what's his reaction? Does he still want the ball? Does he hoof it? Does he respond to criticism well? Tactically how is his pitch geography? Does he squeeze at the right time? Does he drop at the right time? Is he aware of distance between units? Does he communicate well with his teammates? Does he look to act as a leader or is he more of an individual who has to focus on his own game to get the best out of his own abilities?

'All sorts of things go on with the kids. Seventy-five per cent of them come from fairly humble backgrounds. Football is a street game. Players come from inner city areas. They have a hunger and devilment about their play. There is a price to pay for that. The fact of the matter is that if their parents are offered a house or a job for the father, by one club, rather than another, what are they going to do? It's life changing. They will opt for the bigger offer. I look at banking, in the old days. If Goldman Sachs wanted the right people, they went and got them. There are so many comparisons between what I did, currency dealing, and football. High pressure. Short career spans. Team environment. Communication skills.

'But I know also that I am now dealing with some-one's son. At an academy level, you eventually have a horrible decision to make, about a lad who has been with you from the age of eight. How do you maintain the passion and compassion, and reach the right busi-ness decision? Never forget that football is a business. That, for me, is where the educational aspects of the system should kick in. If he doesn't make it, can you keep him in the game, either as a player at Conference level, or as a physiotherapist, sports scientist, scout or analyst? I'm trying to replicate the Watford model here, at Brentford, and I'm staggered bigger clubs don't go down that route. You have access to the boys ten, twelve hours a day and you get to know the families. It's great for the fact you can implement an ethos and philosophy in terms of discipline, and standards of behaviour, but it makes it all the harder when you have to say no.'

Football likes to think it has its own eco-system. It has turned introspection into a fine art. Yet scouts were increasingly obliged to factor social trends and attitudes into their decision-making process. The nature of players was changing, imperceptibly. Tottenham, who also had great hopes for striker Shaquille Coulthirst, used psychometric testing as part of their recruitment process. John McDermott, their academy director, stressed the importance of a boy's intellectual and social development, away from the training ground:

'I want everyone involved to understand our phi-losophy. Today's children are more curious and bolder than before. We have got to be able to be honest with our kids, have an empathy with them. We can do the scouting reports, examine the sports science, do the physiology, but we need also to look at the person. What is he like socially? Where, and how, does he fit into the group? It is a two-way process, in which trust can be built up over time. Remember, it could be fourteen years, from a boy being recruited, to him making his first team debut.'

McDermott expected his coaches to be 'igniters, inspirational people'. His scouts were encouraged to look beyond stereotypes: 'We do what I call Zidane work. Can our boys twist and turn, protect and use possession, when they have someone up their back? All our players have to have the attributes of a midfield player, that ability to play forward when they are under pressure. We have to be careful of being condescending, because the days of the thicko have gone. We have got to see beyond the now. The best players have football courage. Speed across the ground is not their single most important quality. Perception, and speed of thought, is as important.

'Only the mediocre are at their best all the time. We see if boys can cope, by playing up, beyond their natural level, and provide a safety net when they can't. Of course there will be a time when we have to decide whether the kid has hit the ceiling, and whether it is the end for him, with us at least. But until then, we won't drown talent, by accentuating fear. We live in a world where managers are three or four games away from the sack. Trying to get through to that culture is a major issue for all of us in English football.'

Recruitment was one of his five pillars of youth development. The others were coaching, offering the right environment, delivering holistic support, and providing proper career pathways and opportunities. In the single-tiered main stand at Griffin Park, attitudes were rather more prosaic. The prevailing view was summed up by one of those pressurised managers, Gary Waddock of Wycombe Wanderers. No one was inclined to offer much of an argument when he opined that the standard of the semi-final was 'shit'.

In a sense, Marseille's youngsters were too good for their own good. Five were withdrawn on the morning of the game, and returned home, to bolster the first team squad. This deprived Mel Johnson of the chance to evaluate one of his two main targets, Chris Gradi, a young striker who was sufficiently versatile to play wide, or as an attacking midfielder. Johnson's other intention, to assess Lukas Spendlhofer, Inter's Austrian centre half, was more straightforward.

Tall and athletic, like most of the Inter team, Spendlhofer had a nervous habit of sweeping his hand through his luxuriant hair at any opportunity. This offended old school sensibilities. It summoned images of Hugh Grant, never the most reassuring characteristic in a game of muck and nettles. He was callow in comparison to partner Marek Kysela, a Czech defender more in the mould of Arnold Schwarzenegger, but Johnson noticed his ability to read the game quickly and intelligently. He would be one to monitor, over the next year or so.

Since Liverpool would meet the losers in the third

place play-off, Johnson tossed a coin to decide which teams Anderson and Andy Stevens would use, as the basis for their opposition reports. Each compiled detailed notes, which matched individual assessments with the usual insights into set-piece patterns and team shape. In Anderson's case, the work was largely academic. Inter, his subjects, were 2–0 ahead by half-time, and in complete control of the game. Stevens, a postman attuned to early starts, had a late night ahead. The glowing report he had received that morning, from a periodic health check following a heart attack eight years earlier, was understandably reassuring.

A strange sense of torpor settled on proceedings. Johnson was occasionally engaged – 'why do they train every day of the week, and still come up with the same set piece nine times out of ten?' – but became increasingly distracted. He had been irked by the news that Kerim Frei, a throwback 18-year-old winger who played for Switzerland at Under 21 level before opting to represent Turkey, the land of his father, had signed a new contract with Fulham. He was on his shortlist of right-sided players, capable of addressing a worrying weakness in Liverpool's squad. Another, Jonathan Williams, of Crystal Palace, was being played out of position after making a rapid recovery from a badly broken right leg, sustained playing for Wales Under 21s.

Talk turned to other leading prospects. Angus Gunn, son of former Norwich goalkeeper Bryan, was following his father's lead at Manchester City. Jeremie Boga, an Under 16 midfield player who had already made his reserve team debut, was being quietly hailed as long-overdue justification for Chelsea's Academy. Arsenal were in the process of writing off a generation, and concentrating on their Under 16s, where Brandon Ormonde-Ottewill was regarded as the best left-sided prospect since Tom Walley converted Ashley Cole from a left winger to a left back. In a variation on a theme, Jack Harper, a prolific Scottish midfield player implanted in Real Madrid's youth system, was getting easyJet some business from the brethren.

The ritual of recommendation and rejection was ceaseless. Johnson brought up an email on his BlackBerry. It had been forwarded from Damien Comolli. Barry Silkman, one of the most media savvy agents, was touting James Sage, a raw Peterborough central defender, as a cross between Rio Ferdinand and Franz Beckenbauer. 'A little undercooked, don't you think?' said the scout, with an arched eyebrow. He had sourced Sage's biography and career statistics, which revealed he had played only four Under 18 games in three months. If Silkman was taking a punt – and he was – he had more chance of cashing in on a wager involving the moon being made of cheese.

Anderson had spent two years trailing Luke Shaw, a 16-year-old full back popularly assumed to be the next expensive product, prised from Southampton's Academy.

'Very relaxed on the ball,' he said. 'A bit splay-footed, but naturally left-footed. Gives you great width and gets his crosses in. When the opportunity is there to have a dig on goal he's not afraid to take it on. Arsenal could have had him for two million in the summer, but baulked at the price. Now it's three million and Southampton are not returning calls. I've a feeling he may stay.'

Paul Mitchell, a close friend of Mel's son Jamie, had just been head-hunted by Southampton from MK Dons, where he was head of recruitment. A former MK Dons captain, he was only 30, and had moved into scouting after being forced into retirement following an unsuccessful 18-month attempt to recover from a badly broken ankle and leg. Like many of the new breed, he had a strong sports science background. His brief was to inform all aspects of transfer strategy, and it left his friend on the horns of a moral dilemma. Jamie Johnson was extremely well regarded, and especially effective in developing a long term strategy in the loan market. He had to balance the central loyalties of his role, as Millwall's chief scout, with the economic realities of his trade:

'Scouts have no money, work all hours, and are always the first ones to be sacked. My only security is a three-month pay-off. I earned more outside the game, and that weighs heavily, when you've got two kids. We'd love to pay for their education, but we can't. To be honest, Mitch and I had a pact. Whoever got the big job would take the other with him. He's been on to me to join him at Southampton. The package would be better, but can I bring myself to let other people down? I just can't. We all have our ups and downs with managers, but Kenny Jackett has been very good to me. He gets out there, sees games, and understands what we do.'

Others would not have been so measured, because lack of professional respect encouraged a mercenary approach, and insecurity corroded the closest relationships. Yet there was a glimpse of humanity, as the match meandered to a close. Scouts are competitive, occasionally economical with the truth, but they have a strong sense of allegiance to their own. Mel Johnson suggested I shuffle along the back row of the stand, to meet one of the many men struggling in football's shadows. 'You're seeing a lot of people in the game, Mike,' said Johnson. 'I'll introduce you to Georges Santos. Do me a favour and see if you can get his name out there.'

At the age of 42, Santos, a former defender who picked up pin money playing Masters football for Tranmere Rovers, retained the muscular definition of a recently retired athlete. He was prone to the cold, however, and was swathed in a Puffa jacket and an elongated scarf. He proffered one of those revealingly thin, disconcertingly glossy, business cards, which can be produced for free on the internet. He explained, quietly, that he had been 'let go for financial reasons' by Blackburn Rovers. A former international for the Cape Verde Islands, he understood the demands of the English game, having played for nine League clubs in nine seasons, and was seeking to establish a niche for himself in the French market.

'These are hard days,' he admitted. 'I stayed in England for a long time because of the way you play the game, the passion of the football. I love it that the stadiums are full, and the fans have long memories. They like defenders who tackle. They are their warriors. In France it's difficult to be appreciated unless you're a goalscorer or Zinedine Zidane, but it is a place I know well. Many French players want to play here, and many French agents are looking to sell. They are cheap. I try to work in the middle.'

Football was a pan-European business. Frank McParland, the other member of Liverpool's contingent, was taking in the game before an early morning flight to Portugal from Heathrow. The director of the Anfield Academy, a small, open-faced man in a blue suit, was sufficiently at ease with his surroundings to have a man bag slung across his shoulder. He playfully pilloried Anderson for taking two miniature steak pies from the boardroom spread, and homed in on the Inter scouts, who had annexed the cheeseboard. McParland was attempting to get to the bottom of a rumour that Pablo Armero, Udinese's Colombian wing back, had been approached by Liverpool 'officials'.

'It's that time of year,' he acknowledged, with a world-weary smile. As a former chief scout, he was accustomed to the creative sales techniques of Udinese owner Giampaolo Pozzo and his son Gino, whose business plan was built on extensive scouting in underdeveloped markets and strategic husbandry of undervalued players: 'Old man Pozzo is obviously deciding who he wants to move on. The agents get busy, and no one knows or particularly cares, if the stories are true. It gets the name out there, doesn't it?'

McParland was friendly, without losing any of his political adroitness. As a former Kopite, he was known as a Dalglish loyalist, yet insisted he spent each Thursday with Comolli, 'talking through everything'. He was looking for younger players, aged between 15 and 19, who were capable of adapting quickly and efficiently to the high-tempo, high-pressing style Liverpool were attempting to develop. Financial considerations – 'at fifteen the boy will cost you five hundred grand, but by the time he is seventeen the price will have gone up to two million' – were unavoidable. McParland used Dalglish's stellar reputation as bait to attract Dan Smith, a schoolboy who was on the verge of a £300,000 transfer from Crewe to Manchester City until Liverpool's Academy director materialised with the offer of a meeting with the manager. Smith, duly anointed, posted a photograph of him, with his hero, on his Twitter feed. McParland was also preoccupied by the progress of Sterling. A series of unattributed stories suggested someone was briefing that the boy's mother was unhappy on Merseyside, and seeking to return to London. McParland was adamant he was content, loved and on the verge of a breakthrough: 'We really like him. He's nearly there. The first team next season? Maybe this.'

He was close friends with Warburton, who mindful of his wider responsibilities as Brentford's Sporting Director, was building a case for importing some of the NextGen players to the Football League. The thought of these youths being volleyed over the nearest stand by some of the Neanderthals who can be found in League One was disconcerting, to say the least. But Warburton was a true believer. He might have been speaking through his wallet, but his argument had genuine conviction:

'I've got massive respect for the guys who can go to a game like this and go "yeah, he'll do. He could adapt." They have fantastic eyes to be able to do it. I was watching the Sporting Lisbon kids recently, thinking, they're physically strong, they're quick, technically outstanding, tactically aware, and they've got real hunger. I turned round to someone and I said, "I'll tell you what, they would absolutely piss League One" and they laughed at me. "Don't be ridiculous," they said. But I'm thinking, hang on a sec. They're eighteen, nineteen. They've obviously got natural talent and they're well coached. I think you could take ten, fifteen, twenty players, who could slot comfortably into any Division One team, and probably most Championship clubs. They'd have the technical excellence to deal with the situation.

'I look at a player and ask: is he being challenged? You might see a full back up against a lousy winger. The scout would say he's rock solid, but if he's playing some crap winger, how can we be sure he is an outstanding defender? He obviously doesn't have to be on that particular day. That's where NextGen comes in. This is the best against the best. Times are changing. What seemed inconceivable yesterday is attainable, even normal, today. I always go back to the banking industry. When I joined it, there were teams of dealers, with branches in every major European city. Now, thirty years later, there's one European centre. Everything and everyone else has gone. But the old school guy is still making money, if he's good enough, and smart enough.

'So don't tell me that the scout who found Duncan Edwards wouldn't find a player today. Some scouts don't adapt with the times. I know so many football people who are uncomfortable with technology. I once worked with a manager, and promised to send him an email. He turned round and said, "none of that bollocks. You phone me. You write me a letter or you phone me." There are scouts out there, who have thirty years' experience of simply making a phone call to the manager: "You need to keep your eyes on this boy quick." Now they've got to log into a database, do a match report, and animate three key session plays. You know, and I know, there's a number of good people lost to the game because of that. But it doesn't mean they've lost their ability to see a player – I just think you've got to be savvy enough about it to combine both. You've got to adapt to the modern game but at the same time retain some of the old attributes.'

Warburton was offended by the institutionalised insecurity he saw around him that night. He was a proud host, and proof that preconceptions in football are perilous. Brentford were out there swinging, punching above their weight.

'People talk about the big clubs, with their fantastic databases, and almost belittle the smaller ones. The fact of the matter is, there are some outstanding people at smaller clubs. They just don't have the financial muscle or the budgets to implement what they'd like to do. These guys have to work with budgetary restraints, but if you buy a player for ten grand, or for fifty million, it's a financial investment for your company, relative to the size. If Man United buy a player for a hundred and fifty grand, that's irrelevant. If Brentford buy a player for a hundred and fifty grand, it's very relevant.

'I'm looking for the very best people to make sure the foundations are strong and I can take the club forward because I've no doubt the laws governing home-grown players will get more stringent. Competition for players will get ever tougher. We've got an outstanding recruitment team in our academy. We've invested a lot of money in it. I want a player to be impressed with those around him. I want his parents to look at the consistency of discipline, the appearance of our boys, the respect they have for their coaches. I want Brentford to have the highest standards. It drives me nuts when we have got a twelve-year-old player on a three- or four-year contract, and the staff member who is the most important person in his football life is on a three-month or one-month notice period. How does that work? What other business would do that?'

It was a rhetorical question. He knew few industries devalue their workforce with such craven disregard for their welfare as football. The servitude of coaches and scouts confronted by short-notice terminations was taken for granted, because of one awful truth: they were the lucky ones.

6

Mileage Men

The silver C class Mercedes saloon, a deceptive symbol of affluence, had covered 232,000 miles in the four years since it had been purchased, in a discount deal offered to members of the Professional Footballers' Association. On this cold, clear spring night, it was required for the shortest journey of Steve Jones' working life, a ten-mile round trip to the Valley from his home in the South-east London suburb of Welling.

In the glory days, the PC World car park, three minutes' walk from the ground, would have been officially off limits. But the security guards who once supposedly protected spaces for shoppers were gone, their scams collateral damage in Charlton Athletic's plunge from the Premier League to League One. They used to accept a cheeky fiver for looking the other way, and Jones wasn't complaining at their absence. Had he been unable to park for free, he would have been operating at a loss.

This was subsistence scouting at its most stark; Jones was a specialist whose professionalism and experience were belittled by systemic lack of respect. His opposition report on Colchester United would be thorough, concise, and an important managerial aid for his latest boss, Danny Wilson at Sheffield United. It would cover 13 pages, and be informed by more than two decades spent in the backwaters of the Football League. Jones was working so far below minimum wage levels it would have made a sweatshop owner blush, yet in football no one batted an eyelid. It was how it was, how it will be until the laws of supply and demand cease to exist.

'I'm on mileage only at Sheffield United, and I can't get back in full time until something changes,' Jones reasoned. 'This keeps me ticking over. I promised my wife I wouldn't come back, but I am waiting until the summer, to see who is in and who is out. Until then I'll take it as it comes. So tonight it's ten miles at forty pence. I'll be out, at and around the match, for about three, three and a half hours. Once I get home, I'll do my match report. That'll take another two and a half hours or so. Now you tell me, in what other business would you go and do six hours work, for four quid? I'm not ashamed to say that because you know what the game is. What gets me, though, is you see people who don't do the hours, who don't do the mileage, who don't do the stats, who have not played, coached and managed at every level, suddenly come in and get eighty-grand-a-year jobs.'

There is something supremely ironic in football's feudalism and its unthinking misogyny; without the support of his wife Julie, who ran Ultimate Beauty, a hairdressers' and beauty salon in Sidcup, Jones would have been denied access to the game which had absorbed him since adolescence. His had been a constant, tellingly typical struggle to survive, in which self-pity was pointless. The blow of being released by Southampton as a teenaged trainee had been eased by Harry Redknapp's decision to sign him for Bournemouth, but within a fortnight he had ruptured his cruciate ligaments. The mundane nature of the incident – he landed awkwardly after competing for a header in pre-season training – belied its significance. His playing career at the highest level was effectively over.

Jones persisted in non-league football, worked on a succession of building sites, and 'ducked and dived' to eke out a living in the professional game. He coached Gillingham's Under 10s, and created a niche for himself running the club's Centre of Excellence, a role which involved cleaning the dressing room, polishing first team players' boots and driving the minibus. He scouted in his spare time, even coached and managed the reserves. Gary Penrice recognised his hunger, and offered him the chance to become Plymouth's European scout. He subsequently recommended him to Millwall. Jones was responsible for opposition reports before he accepted an approach to join Sven-Goran Eriksson's staff at Leicester. The Swede was as natural a fit in the Championship as a camel in Antarctica. He needed Jones' street wisdom and working knowledge of the division. It was a quixotic episode, expensive, and destined to end messily.

Eriksson lasted 13 games of the 2011–12 season, and ambled away from the wreckage with the insouciance of a serial opportunist. Leicester's Thai owners, conscious of the marketing strategy for their duty free shopping empire, paid him off with as much grace as they could muster. They were not the first to be seduced by the civility of a coach who was now a caricature, a Cuban-heeled lothario. Others, like Jones and Bill Green, the chief scout to whom he answered, could not afford to be so sanguine. They were vulnerable, understandably fearful. Green advised Jones to work normally, and not to overreact.

A football club in the process of upheaval is a place of disconcerting light and shade. Good people are suddenly disposable chattels. They are wraiths, invisible and uncomfortable. According to Jones, the chief scout was 'completely blanked' by the new regime when he reported for duty, the day Nigel Pearson began his second spell as manager at what, in these subservient times, has been rebranded as the King Power Stadium. Green and six other members of the scouting staff soon received cursory emails, thanking them for their services, but confirming they were no longer required. Jones remained in limbo over the following weekend, when he covered the last of his 101 games for Leicester in a four-month spell.

Jones reasoned he had the limited security of a contract lasting until May 2012, the end of the season, but still dreaded checking his laptop and mobile for messages. The good news, when the inescapable email arrived, was that he was still wanted. The bad news was contained in a proposal that he be paid £50 a week to remain at the club. It was, according to Steve Walsh, the newly installed head of recruitment, 'a take it or leave it offer'. When Jones demurred, he, too, was airbrushed from history.

Walsh was no cartoon ogre; he had combined football with a full-time teaching job for 30 years until José Mourinho asked him to become a senior scout at Chelsea. The holistic approach he developed, as head of physical education for three comprehensive schools, was tested by the transition to a world of fleeting fortune and sudden, seismic change. Walsh had profited from the patronage of Sam Allardyce, who took him to Newcastle. It was there that he formed an allegiance to Pearson, whom he subsequently followed to Leicester. They signed 32 players in two seasons as the Foxes won League One and reached the Championship play-offs, but were culled on a whim, by the then-chairman Milan Mandaric. What goes around, comes around.

Jones understood: 'When you get sacked, moved on,

call it what you will, you get on the phone. You soon find out who your friends are. The first response, when you're looking about, is usually "I'll get back to you." You hear nothing, and when you check again it is all "sorry mate, been frantic, leave it with me". You still hear nothing, and after a while they don't even reply to your texts. I don't want to sound all bitter and twisted, because I know how things work, but I'd much prefer it if people were straight and said they had nothing for me. I believe if you do the right things, present yourself well, you will get what you deserve. I'm only forty-four, and young enough to get what I want.'

A brief spell at Hull ended when scouts were suddenly informed they would no longer be paid. In such circumstances, Sheffield United's willingness to pay 40p a mile was instantly attractive. Hull, emboldened by their economy drive, subsequently announced they were joining Crawley Town and Southampton in insisting that scouts pay for their match tickets. Charlton, thankfully, only asked for Jones' ID, following a series of incidents in which visitors, masquerading as scouts, took pre-assigned tickets, before melting away into the main stand.

A single circular table, to the right of the entrance to the Valley's Millennium Suite, featured a laminated sign which proclaimed 'Football Scouts Only'. It contained two plastic platters of unedifying sandwiches – the choice was between cardboard white, with crystallised crusts, and suspiciously musty brown – and a flask of lukewarm tea, which appeared to have been brewed in a previous century. Needless to say, the mileage men fell upon the repast with the glee of Dickensian scavengers. Some had come straight from a reserve team match between Spurs and Southampton, and were sharing anecdotes of former England winger Mark Chamberlain, a combustible presence on the touchline. Jones, who had wisely had a snack before leaving home, surveyed the scene and mused, 'Charlton must be more skint than I imagine.'

He introduced London cabbie Brian Owen, cheerily informing me: 'He's got one of those little black money boxes.' Hibernian's scout in the South of England was a thick-set man, with the ruddy cheeks and friendly demeanour of a rural publican. He walked hesitantly, favouring his right leg, and was in obvious discomfort. 'My legs are giving me gyp,' he confirmed. 'This game is no good for someone like me. The seats are too small, see. They do your back in, as well.' Jones was respectful, attentive. When the older man had switched the focus of his attention to the night's team sheet, he confided: 'Brian's a lovely man, who turns up everywhere, but I do worry about him. There's regime change at Hibs. He's only on a pittance.' Owen admitted later: 'It'd be good to pick up a fare on the way home.'

Most scouts followed the progress of St Johnstone manager Steve Lomas across the room – Owen murmured, 'He's a long way from home; he'll be looking for free agents' – but two were oblivious to his presence. Retired teacher Les Padfield, a regular member of Gary Megson's retinue, was talking quietly to another senior citizen, who wore fingerless mittens and had a digital stopwatch, bizarrely frozen at 0.23 seconds, slung around his neck. It was a strange conversation, triggered by Padfield's search for a suitable portable television, with a Freeview package, for his bedroom. To complete the counter-cultural collage, he was dressed in hiking chic. His green waterproof jacket was unzipped, and revealed a Windsor-knotted tie, beneath a round-necked chain-store sweater with an angular pattern. He wore thick woollen trousers, and stout walking shoes.

Padfield was respected for his insight, but had a detached, slightly sour manner, and surprisingly hard eyes, behind full-framed glasses. He was representing Sheffield Wednesday, 'for today at least. Not that sure about tomorrow.' A familiar story, of intermittent crisis, unfolded. Told Terry Burton was on his way to assist new manager Dave Jones, he blurted: 'Well, Chris Evans is still there. He's my man: assistant manager, chief scout, chocolate teapot.' Padfield was hardly enamoured of his immediate task, monitoring Colchester. 'Why now?' he asked no one in particular. 'We're not playing them for six weeks.'

Job satisfaction seemed at a premium. Jason Halsey, son of referee Mark, was there on behalf of Bolton, who, to universal envy, compensated him with a small retainer. He wasted no time in complaining that 'The train was bleedin' packed. I couldn't move and I cricked my neck.' He consulted his iPhone to plan his getaway and announced, a little too brashly for some, that he would be aiming to get to Liverpool Street by 10 p.m. Like Jones, he had been at Chelsea reserves' 2–0 defeat by Arsenal the previous day. 'Poxy,' he concluded. 'I've spent seven hours today, doing my match report. Try telling the analyst at the club that.'

Halsey was expected to be a human time-code machine. He was obliged to record the precise time of every significant incident, to facilitate editing of the match video. Each set play had to be annotated, and five factors about each player, both good and bad, had to be tabulated. Unlike Jones and I, who had been randomly allocated seats at the back of the directors' box, Halsey was forced to deal with the added distraction of being amongst the crowd. He was knowledgeable, and incisive, but it was understandably difficult to take a measured view of a typically functional League One match.

Jones did the basics, and attempted to be a little more intuitive. Detecting collective strengths and weaknesses required tactical nous and unexpected emotional intelligence. He was looking for unconsidered nuggets of information; the psychological profile revealed by a player's reaction to being substituted or the group's response to things they could not control, such as a referee's flawed decision. He understood his subject matter, the lower-division footballer. Most find their level; League One features a favoured few, on the way up, and a lumpen majority, whose careers have flat-lined because of limitations in talent or defects in temperament.

Charlton, 13 points clear of second-placed Sheffield United, fell behind after five minutes to the sort of goal which deserved a better stage. Anthony Wordsworth, a tall, languid left-sided player, cut in from the touchline before fashioning a 20-yard shot which dipped and swerved on its way into the top right-hand corner of the net. Impressive, but deceptive, according to Jones: 'The boy is cheating himself. He's quite happy picking up his two grand a week, being the best player in an average side. People have been looking at him for two or three years. It tells you something that he is still there.'

As Jones turned, to compare notes with Steve Lomas, who was sitting next to him, a season ticket holder, separated from the directors' box by a wooden partition, indulged his curiosity. 'What do you think of Wordsworth, then?' he asked, mistaking me for a scout. 'Rumour has it we're looking at him. Do a job I'd say.' I parroted received wisdom, which seemed to satisfy him. Presumably, it was sufficient to enable him to peddle 'inside information' in the pub. He sagely advised me to keep an eye on Chris Solly, Charlton's full back: 'Bit small, but he's got skill on the ball, loves a tackle and gets forward well. You probably know that, though.'

Jones, meanwhile, was sketching set pieces into his notebook. These would later be converted into animated computer images, on the Scout7 network. He abbreviated a series of functions: AS meant Attacking Shape, DS Defensive Shape. BH defined Colchester's best headers of the ball, and MM their main markers. PP depicted pattern of play which, in their case, was a bog standard 4–4–2. It was insight, in shorthand.

'This is a shape I'm used to,' Jones said. 'When England play 4–4–2, they play. When a League One team play 4–4–2 they smash it down the park. The goalkeeper works off Odejayi, the big striker. He also dives to complete the save, when it is not strictly necessary. It buys him ten seconds' thinking time. At this level it is all about working knowledge. I know who does what, their roles and responsibilities. I rarely write a lot in the second half.'

Full backs were on the agenda at half-time. Halsey recognised the potential of Chelsea's Todd Kane, whom we had both seen at that Youth Cup tie at Staines Town: 'Always liked him. Decent. Pace. Discipline. Gets forward well. What about you?' Jones permitted himself a knowing smile, as Halsey circulated, asking a similar question about Solly, his obvious target for the evening. 'There you go,' he confided. 'He's looking for answers and reassurance. We're not short of people who try to pick your brain in this game.'

Gary Smith, the Stevenage manager, was on the

fringes of the conversation, monitoring the progress of the night's matches on a television with his assistant Steve Guppy. He understood the environment; he scouted for Arsenal before making his name in the United States, where he won the MLS Cup with Colorado Rapids. His father, Roger, was recruited by Charlton after leaving Cardiff, where he was chief scout, following the sacking of Dave Jones. Father and son respected the bonds which tied the brotherhood tight.

Each had strong links with Arsenal, where Roger coached at youth level, and scouted in Europe: 'In truth Steve Rowley [Arsenal's chief scout] did say there would always be a job for me but there's a slight problem. It isn't just about money for me now, but more about involvement. If you are not full time, particularly at big clubs, you can almost be on the outside looking in, you know? I had a conversation with Phil Chappell, Charlton's chief scout. He is a thoroughly decent guy, very well organised. That might sound odd because you'd think all of them are well organised, but I can assure you they're not.

'I'd given in my notice at Cardiff, and they'd been somewhat difficult about arranging for me to go to games. It was bizarre. It was almost because Dave had got the sack, and I was associated with something nasty, that they didn't want to be tainted. Phil, as somebody I knew well, was getting me tickets so that I could circulate and let people know my situation. I've done the same thing myself for other scouts who are out of work. I try to send them to a game. They might do you a little favour with a report but basically you know they're looking to get back in.

'After about three months, Phil asked me what I wanted to do. He was honest, that a full-time job might be difficult, but was really keen to do something. I told him I didn't just want to put one report in a week and then sit there waiting for the following Saturday for a game. It would be nice to be centrally involved. Thankfully, Phil has been as good as his word. Unless they do something radically wrong Charlton are going up, so we're already looking at players who not only might serve us well in the Championship but at a push, could even play in the Premier League. They've obviously had their problems at this club in the last ten years but as somebody put it to me, they've bottomed out. They're coming back the other way, not only on the pitch, but off it as well. These things go together, don't they?'

His son was doing the managerial equivalent of the Knowledge. He was working 18-hour days, watching as many games as possible. He had inherited a muscular, instinctively conservative side from Graham Westley. His predecessor was a distinctive character in a game more accustomed to laddish orthodoxy. He was a successful businessman, a new age service provider who turned up for training in a Bentley and sweated alongside his players in a self-funded weights room. Change would, by necessity, be gradual, but Gary needed help to find players with pace and potential in the loan market. The obvious option, employing his father, was understandably forbidding.

Roger admitted: 'It's obviously crossed my mind, and his. I'm not sure, because I think that could put him under undue pressure. Listen, let's put it another way round. Blood's thicker than water and if he wanted me to join him, I wouldn't be able to turn him down. But I'm still not sure that is the best route. It wouldn't be a nice day when both of us got the sack, would it? No matter how well it goes, you know at some stage it's going to happen. Clearly Gary knows he can lean on me for what knowledge I have of the leagues. I'd certainly give him advice because he's been in America for four years. He'll remember players who spring to mind easily, but there will be others who have developed while he has been away. He'll go "I don't know him, Dad, I'd like to get to see him," but therein lies his dilemma. He needs to make one or two decisions, and in the short term, it's highly unlikely he's going to be able to get to see as many players as he needs. At least if I don't know a particular player, I'll probably know someone who does.'

They were collaborating on a search for a striker. Jordan Slew, the star of the Sheffield United side which reached the Youth Cup final in 2011, had disappeared without trace after being sold to Blackburn Rovers for £3 million. Roger used his contacts to ascertain a basic profile: Slew was quick, measured in front of goal, and a 'decent lad' who needed to distance himself from the chaos of a club which was redefining the concept of mismanagement. Gary called England Under 20 coach Brian Eastick, who had visited him in Colorado the previous year. He passed him on to Noel Blake, who had coached Slew at Under 19 level.

'People help one another, because they know what the game is like. Noel has given Slew a really good mention. Somewhere along that route, Gary may have to take a punt, because otherwise he ain't going to get anyone in. I'm not telling secrets out of school, but from what I've seen of Stevenage, they are short of quality. Gary says they're a fantastic group in terms of their togetherness, but, particularly up front, they have no pace. I mean, you could probably run as quickly as one or two of them, you know what I mean? It is a strange one. Westley has just gone to Preston and sacked all the scouts. OK I suppose, if he wanted a change because he knew better people, but he actually didn't want any scouts. I can't get my head round that.'

My garrulous neighbour in the main stand attempted to engage his son in conversation as the second half meandered, losing any shape or sense of purpose. 'You're with that rugby club, aren't you,' he said, delighted with what he self-evidently considered a flash of original humour, rather than a tiresome recycling of a cliché, created by Stevenage's reputation for physicality. Gary Smith smiled thinly, and offered several pained platitudes. He was as surprised as anyone in the vicinity when the fan suddenly began yelling 'fish', as if an unseen hand had sprinkled a hallucinogenic drug in his half-time tea.

The mystery was solved by a glance at the big screen, at the left-hand corner of the stand. This depicted a goldfish being chased by a giant net. The home supporters cheered as it evaded capture. It was a surreal image and ritual, which emphasised the marginalisation of the match. Charlton were abject. Their fate was confirmed by a late goal from Steven Gillespie, who closed down goalkeeper Ben Williams, and blocked an attempted clearance. 'He's been doing that all game, fair do's,' said Jones, as we headed down an unmarked staircase which led to the main reception.

It had been a profitable evening, in one sense at least. Jones revealed Lomas, the St Johnstone manager, had offered him £50 a week to monitor English players. It transpired he was in London visiting his children, and building a business case to broaden the Perth club's recruitment base. He called Jones the following day, asking him to travel to Scotland, to meet his chairman. The scout's luck just might have changed: 'It's all sweet. With Rangers going sideways, a Europa League place opens up. Steve wants me to talk about setting up a scouting network for them. All this has come about by me sitting next to him at a match. That's how this game works. It is about being in the right place at the right time.'

His enthusiasm was infectious, yet there was still a sense of transience; Padfield and Halsey would be looking for new clubs in the summer. The financial cataclysm in Scottish football would claim Owen, too. Fate had not finished with Jones. The mileage men were increasingly expendable. Good judges such as David Pleat, who acted as a mentor to aspiring managers like Dean Austin in addition to operating as a recruitment consultant to Tottenham, understood the strictures of a new breed of manager and chief executive:

'A scout has got to be loyal, conscientious, and he's got to feel he's being listened to. Otherwise he gets very irritated and anxious, and he starts telling people, "Eh. Saw a fucking player last week. Told the manager, he wasn't interested. You want to go and have a look at him." What happens then is they all start talking to each other. I know they do. I've been in the room with them over the years and they are nice people, who love the game. They're either not wealthy enough to let it go, or they've not got another hobby to distract them. Their life revolves around meeting people and going to football matches. But I have to say, the forty pence-a-milers aren't listened to probably as much as they should be. They're disregarded. Therefore, when you start adding up the money, which we did at Tottenham, you start asking "What are we getting back for this?"

Some of them don't write proper reports, you see. They're not emailing, and I remember Alan Sugar saying to me, "I don't want names on the back of envelopes, you've got to learn technology boy." They won't survive.

'You need a chief scout. You need things properly organised. But I see a lot of, for want of a better word, random scouts. Without purpose, you know? You should ask the questions – who are you going to watch, why are you going to watch them, there has to be a reason. A lot of them just watch games, and they'll put their report in, without adding anything of note to the pool of knowledge. We all know who the better players are in any given team. I'll give you an example. Watford played Blackpool last week. I was going to go, but my back hurt and I decided not to. After the game, Dave Bassett called me. He said it was very poor and that I'd missed nothing. I asked about Matt Phillips because I knew he'd be a bit better than the others. Sure enough, Dave said he was the only one worth bothering about. He's moving upwards, but I don't know whether he will be quite good enough. I know the players off by heart, and I'm not unique, lots of people do. Harsh as it sounds you don't need to pay people mileage to confirm what you already know.'

So, what did Sheffield United get for their £4, the going rate for another night on the road? Jones devoted the first six pages of his report to a dissection of

Colchester's shape at defensive and attacking corners. He also annotated the roles and movement of each player at set pieces. This led into a general comments section. For all you budding English teachers out there, he couldn't quite get the hang of the word 'their':

> Colchester were hardworking, disciplined, organised, and competitive. They came with a game plan, scored an early goal and then defended with there [sic] lives. At times, they rode there [sic] luck. They looked to hit CAFC on the counter, or directly long. When attacking from GK they would push 15-9 onto the centre halves, and 22-16 onto full backs. GK would target 15 with 9-16-22 gambling off. If first phase isn't won, Rowlands and Izzet work hard to win ball back and regain possession. They move the ball wide for 16 or 22, who then play inside with Gillespie and Odejayi. If possession isn't kept, they get bodies in quickly behind the ball. They make themselves compact and defend deep to allow opposition to come onto them. When it breaks down, they go again.

Jones considered Colchester's most viable strengths to be their physicality, discipline and work ethic. He warned of their threat at set plays, the potency of their long throws, and of the potential of Wordsworth 'if he is in the mood'. He felt they were too rigid in their game plan, and lacked pace, especially at the back. He advised targeting centre half Tom Eastman, whose positioning

earmarked him as their weakest defender. And he
warned:

Playing 4–4–2 against these will give them an edge as they
can match us up. They are big and strong, and that might
frustrate us. There [sic] not really playing for anything as they
seem to be safe and will finish mid table. Playing 4–3–3 will
move them about, especially in wide areas at full back. Target
the right back Wilson, who stands off the winger. The two
CH will head it and compete in the air all day. With the GK
coming for everything from wide areas, there may be chances
with crosses into the box. In central areas there are only two
of them. They may be experienced, but there [sic] legs have
gone a bit and we can pass around them.

Each player, in order of team shape, was ranked as
follows:

1   Ben Williams   Age: 29   Height: 183cm / 6' 0"
     Position: GK   Rating: C   Foot: Right
Not the biggest. Kicks well hands and floor. Comes for
crosses. Wasn't tested enough.

20   Brian Wilson   Age: 28   Height: 178cm / 5' 10"
     Position: RB   Rating: D   Foot: Right
Didn't want to join in. Stood off marker. Over-covered, and
allowed play to get in behind him. Lacked pace. Weakest full
back.

4   Magnus Okuonghae   Age: 26   Height: 189cm / 6' 2"
       Position: CH Right Side   Rating: C   Foot: Right
Big, strong, athletic. Competes well in the air. Good upper
body strength. Strongest CH. Threat both boxes.

18   Tom Eastman   Age: 20   Height: 191cm / 6' 3"
       Position: CH Left side   Rating: D   Foot: Right
Weakest CH. Competes well in the air. Got pinned, rolled and
moved about too easily. Lacks recovery pace. Threat both boxes.

25   John White   Age: 25   Height: 182cm / 6' 0"
       Position: LB   Rating: C   Foot: Left
Sat in rarely got on. Long throw final third. Got caught with
pace down the side of him. Experienced at this level.

16   Ian Henderson   Age: 27   Height: 179cm / 5' 10"
       Position: RM   Rating: D   Foot: Right
Poor game. Didn't get around marker. Played out/in. Can
play better.

10   Kemal Izzet   Age: 31   Height: 173cm / 5' 8"
       Position: Holding Mid   Rating: C   Foot: Right
Busy. Tenacious. Holder. Lacks presence. Moves the ball
sideways.

17   Martin Rowlands   Age: 33   Height: 175cm / 5' 9"
       Position: CM attacking   Rating: C   Foot: Right

Experienced. Tenacious. Sees a pass. Patient. Disciplined in role.

22   Anthony Wordsworth   Age: 23   Height: 185cm / 6' 1"
      Position: LM   Rating: C   Foot: Left
Good size. Good range. Can be a threat if in the mood. Lacks pace. Plays out/in. Quite happy to play at this level. Good left foot.

9   Steven Gillespie   Age: 26   Height: 175cm / 5' 9"
      Position: CF   Rating: B   Foot: Right
Good work ethic. Chased lost causes. Worked there [sic] back four. Gambles off well. Decent in the channels.

15   Kayode Odejayi   Age: 30   Height: 190cm / 6' 3"
      Position: CF   Rating: D   Foot: Right
Target. Nothing sticks. Poor technically. Poor when back to goal. Strong, athletic. Lacks mobility.

All that remained was to answer 15 key questions. The 16th, about Colchester's penalty drills and personnel, was not applicable.

How many players in midfield? 10–17 act as a shield in front of the back four. They are both experienced in this role. The two wide men tuck in to overload centrally.

How many back players, and do they push either of the full backs into midfield to mark flank players? The back four stayed as a four and got in 22–16 to cover CAFC wide players when defending. From opposition GK, they get two banks of four and make it tight and compact.

How deep do the flank players play? Both wide men drop in to support. 22 is reluctant at times and is laboured getting back in.

Do they ever push out quickly from the back either in free play or from free kicks? No they were quite happy to defend there [*sic*] 18yd line and allow CAFC to have the ball in front. Then they just clear there [*sic*] lines and defend again.

Do they have one or two big central defenders? Both centre halves are big and strong and compete well in the air.

Do they have one or two big front players? 15 is there [*sic*] target and outlet.

Do they play with a winger, if so, which side? Both wingers played out/in rather than squaring up FB and getting around him. Henderson is the quicker one but he lacks quality. 22 has quality and is a threat.

Is the goalkeeper big? Is he good on crosses? GK isn't the biggest and struggled making the right decisions when coming for the ball. At times was left in no-man's land.

Does the keeper throw the ball out? Which full back is the most willing to accept it? GK kicks every time, targeting Odejayi up top.

Do they build up from the back, through midfield, or do they play balls early to the front players? No they are very direct in there [sic] play. The back four will look for 15 early either diagonally or directly.

Do they pressure the ball well? Early? Gillespie will work the line well if opposition are playing out from the back. Once he goes, the others shut down space to force long ball.

Do they have any outstanding players? Wordsworth, Rowlands are not outstanding but will both be a threat.

Do they have any particularly aggressive players? Izzet, Rowlands, Gillespie will put there [sic] foot in and get around the park.

Do they have anybody who is frightened of a fierce challenge? Wilson the right FB dropped off and didn't want to engage wide player.

Do they have anyone who can throw the ball long? White in the last third can hit 6yd line with a long throw.

The report was 1,677 words in length. Jones was on Dickensian, penny a line, rates. Yet those around him, his peers, respected his unconsidered professionalism, and empathised with his ambitions. Barry Lloyd, Brighton's former manager, who was involved in the club's burgeoning youth recruitment programme, spoke for the men who rarely speak for themselves:

'Steve's in dire straits. I don't know how he does it. I hope he bleedin' gets out of it quick, touch wood, but it's only the love of the game that keeps him going, and a good missus. That's another thing you need. You have to have an understanding family, because her indoors wants to see a few quid. She wants a holiday, wants something nice and you're chasing shadows to get that kind of dough in. People don't understand that pressure. It's another thing about the game that does your head in.'

7

Chat Show

'*I've been doing this for six years, and these three people
have influenced me more than anyone. They have my
respect. That's why I asked them to come along. We've
spent many an hour in the car, or on the tube, talking
about the general state of football. We talk every day on
the phone. We go out every day. I've known them through
the system, and I trust them, and that's why they're around
this table. I'm learning from these guys because they do
what I want to do. Listen to them. . . . .*'

Steve Jones was so insistent, so secure in expressing
his admiration, it seemed churlish to refuse. At a time
when the tribal structure was being undermined, these
were elders, who spoke of, and for, their generation.
Each was in, or approaching, their 60s, and had spent
a lifetime in the game. Barry Lloyd, Allan Gemmell and
Pat Holland represented different clubs – Brighton,

Nottingham Forest and Arsenal respectively – but a distinctive, unifying culture.

Lloyd, the former Fulham defender who spent nearly seven years as Brighton manager, had the air of the Commodore of a South coast yacht club. His grey hair was impeccably cut, and lapped gently on to the collar of a crisp blue, shiny-buttoned blazer. Gemmell, a key aide for his brother-in-law Peter Taylor, over three decades, wore an open-necked shirt and could have been mistaken for a university lecturer. Holland walked with the rolling gait of a former footballer whose body was protesting about ancient exertions.

Holland played 245 times for West Ham between 1969 and 1981, and apart from a brief loan period at Bournemouth, was a one-club man. He coached the youth team at Tottenham, and managed Leyton Orient. He had two principal spells as a chief scout, at Millwall and MK Dons, where he underpinned the work of Roberto Di Matteo. Arsenal, through chief scout Steve Rowley, recognised the value of his analytical expertise in the critical 16–21 age group.

The three are sitting around a circular table, crammed with the obligatory sandwiches. The vegetarian platter lacks the appeal of the tray featuring coronation chicken and rare roast beef. These men are employed to have the courage of their convictions. Their verdicts can appear harsh, even insensitive, but strident opinions are their stock in trade. Holland has the floor. Let's eavesdrop, as the trio do what scouts do best. Talk.

PAT So it's the night before we're playing Liverpool. Jimmy Greaves' home debut for West Ham, 1970, I'm nineteen. I'm out in the council estate. There's a knock at the door. 'Message from the club. Would you come down and play, Pat?' I said, 'I can't. I've turned my ankle over.' So I phoned the physio: 'You soppy fucking bastard, get down here now.' I've driven down to his clinic opposite the ground. He put a pressure bandage on. 'Don't say anything. We'll see what it's like in the morning.' Now in those days you had twelve players – a team and one sub. No margin for error. So I go in the next day, he looks at it and says, 'I think you'll be allright.' Out we go. We win one–nil, and I get the goal. I'm telling the story because of what you said, Allan, about Arsène Wenger saying there's no technical development in a boy after the age of twelve. Well, against Liverpool that day, I take a corner. I get it to just where the six-yard line is on the first post, the near post. It's cleared. Geoff Hurst jogs back and says, 'Son – get it to the far post,' and I say, 'I can't reach that far.' Allright. Now you're telling me I ain't still developing? You know what I mean? I had a chicken's legs. Now as I got older, twenty-three, twenty-four, I could curl it, fade it. I had length and strength. I know what Arsène is saying but you ain't half got to be careful with that kind of statement.

BARRY Look at the stats. In England, the vast majority of players make their debut at or around seventeen or eighteen. You go to France, Germany, Spain, Europe. The average age is twenty-one, twenty-two. So what I'm saying is they actually work harder at developing them before they expose them to the first team. We have kids who drop out when they're eighteen for various reasons, but if the desire is there, they'll get picked up two years later through non-league clubs. That's where sometimes we're stronger in this country.

PAT Listen. We let Warren Barton go from Leyton. He was a lovely, lovely little boy. Eighteen and he was tiny. I then get a phone call from Leytonstone saying, 'Would you take him?' I said, 'I'd take him tomorrow.' Then he goes to Maidstone, then to Wimbledon, and then he plays for Newcastle and England. And I know they're one-offs, but you can't just go boom and say players aren't going to develop – it will kick you up the backside.

BARRY There is a ninety-five per cent drop-out in the academy at the end of the season. That's hard to deal with. But the worst thing is what those ninety-five per cent do. Eighty-three per cent never play the game again. Now, you're not telling me that in that eighty-three per cent of that ninety-five per cent there isn't real talent. If they've got the desire, real desire and the love and enjoyment of the game, they do come through. There are probably three a season who probably come through the non-league route.

PAT If you look at the process, they are bringing kids in at six years of age. They should be playing Cowboys and Indians. Six years of age. You've got that kid for ten years. You see the cycle repeating itself; the disappointment, the failure, the parents. They don't see the glory of football. They don't see it at all. They're not proud. I've got to be careful here, because this is a broad statement, but I think at the end of it, they see only a few quid. That's the worrying thing.

ALLAN There are no guarantees. Johnny Bostock went from Palace to Tottenham. They took him off us for seven hundred and fifty grand. His career has just dived, from going to Barcelona and Tottenham and all these lovely places. Really he's struggling like mad. So sad, because he was a real talent at one time.

PAT I've been coaching kids since I was a boy of seventeen. John Lyall got me coaching at West Ham on a Tuesday and Thursday night and I went right through to a man of twenty-eight. But, in all that time, did I really know what the parents said to the kid when he left me? I have to be honest and say no. None of us really know what goes on in the car, or when the boy is at home. All I can do is talk to the parents about how my father dealt with me. My dad was steady. It was either 'I've seen you play better' when I didn't do well, or 'that's the way you can play' when I had a good one. That was it. But if he said 'I've seen you play better' I may as well have run into the broom cupboard, and hid. He never said 'you were useless', he never said 'you should have done this or that'. It was 'I've seen you play better'. And it killed me. I don't want to sound cynical, but the development of young players is a real issue. We know, because we are out there, that they are not coming through in abundance. If you look at Tottenham – and not only because they sacked me – the last one to come through, over the last five years, is Jake Livermore, who's a squad player.

BARRY We went to Spurs Lodge yesterday with our development squad. Beat them four–one. And it didn't surprise me.

PAT Yeah. And they say they're putting youngsters in. There's always an excuse. I understand it's a different ball game now. If there's nothing there you can buy a three-, four-, five-million-pound player. Clubs ain't going to hang around for the likes of Jake Livermore to develop. You wonder about the quality of player coming through. That's the worrying thing for me. We've watched Ajax bash Liverpool with all the money that's gone into it, millions. Look at Chelsea, and the money they've spent.

ALLAN Chelsea are buying in all the time. They have just bought Patrick Bamford from us for two million quid. He's eighteen. They've just spent one point seven on an Italian under sixteen goalkeeper. Bamford played Wigan and scored five. The following week he played Southampton in the Youth Cup and scored four. He's done well, but he ain't that. He ain't ever going to play in their first team. Not a chance in hell. But, by buying him, Chelsea are stopping other clubs getting the boy. Pat's hit the nail right on the head.

PAT I watched Bamford pre-season at Burton Albion. I thought, right, you're not bad up front Blondie, not bad. Don't want to head it, not quick, but you're a good footballer. We try to keep tabs on him. He's supposed to be from a nice family. I speak to Allan. He then has this surge where he gets about a hundred goals in four games. So now, our boys go and watch him. And I'm not talking about the scouts, it's the coaches. They're saying: 'Well, he's only one point five.' And I'm thinking, it's as if it's a drop in the ocean, as if it's a hundred quid. You have got to be liable for that money; you've got to put your stamp on that. Now that might frighten a lot of people. If you said to me, would you pay out that sort of cash, I'd say no.

ALLAN But is that where we're wrong now? I think it is. To us, one and a half million for a kid is a lot of money. We know it is a huge gamble. For Abramovich, or someone like him, one and a half million for a sixteen- or eighteen-year-old isn't a lot of money. I think we'd say we're not paying that. Are we out of step?

BARRY My chairman's got fucking loads of money. We're the luckiest club alive. We can spend ninety million pounds on a new stadium. If Gus wants something he gets it. We've built the EP3 thing, the training ground. Another thirty million quid. We had a meeting with him and the board. We've got a five-year plan. We've got to have at least five home-grown players in the first team. We've got to do this and that. This went on for about an hour and a half. And the chairman said, 'Barry, you haven't said anything.' I said, 'I'll tell you what Tone, why don't you go down the pier, and throw all your fucking money in the sea.' And everyone fucking looked at me. And they laughed, and Tony said 'Bal, what do you mean by that?' I said, 'Arsenal, Chelsea, Fulham. How many players in the last ten years have they actually brought through?' Straight away he said, 'John Terry.' No. They got him from West Ham. 'Did they?' Next one? He couldn't name one. It's really hard. I'm not being difficult, but you have to be realistic.

PAT So who is accountable? Does Daniel Levy go to the academy at Tottenham and say, 'You've spent ten million on players, and not one of them has made it. You're all out'? That's a lot of dough, ten million. And I know what they'll come back to him with. It'll be: 'Wait until three years' time. We've got a plan' and all that crap.

BARRY I think if you're paying one and a half, two or three million pounds for a player in their mid-twenties, you can put together a case. That is a sellable asset. I went out to the under seventeen World Cup in Mexico last summer and the best team by a mile was the Ivory Coast. I flagged five players. I've come back with all the reports, read the paper, and saw that Harry Redknapp had signed one of the players I'd flagged up. One and a half million. Souleymane Coulibaly was his name. Nine goals in four games. He'd come from an Italian club. You see him now, and I'm not saying he's not worth the money, but he looks a stone overweight.

ALLAN Patsy asked me about Jamaal Lascelles at our place. I wouldn't hesitate. That's the best value any Premier League club would get for their one and a half million. You see, you've got half a chance with that lad because he's gone to Stevenage on loan. So I can now go as a scout, coach, manager, and I can analyse that boy in his football. I'm telling you, he's got everything. Every little thing. Every little bit needs a bit of development, but he's got everything. He's a Rio Ferdinand type. I remember working with the England under twenty-ones and watching Ferdinand, and saying to Pete 'I'm not sure about him on the old defending.' West Ham weren't at the time, to be fair, but he's gone on to be a top player. Top players have an aura about them. It's the way they turn up for training. Lascelles is the bollocks. He won't come in in a pair of jeans. You know how we were talking about discipline? You look at him around people, and you look at him on the football pitch, and it is all ticks. I swear to you.

PAT And I bet if you look at his school record that would be the same as well.

ALLAN What do we think of Shelvey at Liverpool, as a player?

BARRY He's allright, not bad.

ALLAN Is he going to be a top player for Liverpool?

PAT He might train on. I'd say he needs experience.

ALLAN What I'm trying to say is, he's got a five-year contract and that boy has never, ever got to work again. I know that for a fact because Phil Chappell told me exactly what the deal was when he left Charlton. So, why should he want to go on and be a top player at Liverpool? He hasn't *got* to play football. That to me is where a lot of desire and hunger has gone.

PAT But how do we know that feeling? We can't know that feeling. So how can we say he doesn't't?

ALLAN I've heard of a young boy, who pays a woman fourteen grand, upfront, to look after his dog. And a month after he gets it, the dog dies. The woman wants to give his money back and he says, 'Oh, don't worry about that.' I'm not sure how much Premier League football he's going to play, that kid, but he's loaded. That's why it's a big, big thing to find out what a player is like as a lad. If you get a good response when you ask about, you think, 'Right, he can handle the other stuff.'

BARRY There's certain things that they do which draw you towards them. The way they apply themselves to the task is a big one.

ALLAN And how do we know that, Bal? Because we've got experience. I tell you what, there are some young lads about now who I see scouting, and I'm sorry, are you telling me they know what we're talking about here?

PAT I think it's the same in coaching. I know I'm digressing from scouting, but you think, you haven't got the knowledge. It's all about personality. I think I'm not bad at spotting the way a boy's going to be, as a person. I look for triggers. When I had the Tottenham youth side, they had to come to work smart casual. No jeans. The academy director was an academic, a lovely fella, and he went 'Pat, do you think we should lessen the load a little with them? Can't they wear tracksuits?' I said no because I believe you are privileged to be a footballer, I really do. It's a great career. Anyway, I relented on away days. They could have a tracksuit. But it was shirt in, collar down, boring old Pat. I think they take that discipline on to the pitch. Life's about discipline. I was on the train today and as I got on, there was a geezer sprawled out. His girlfriend's got her foot on the seat. So I sit down, and I knock his foot. He's entitled to say 'you just knocked my foot' and I'm entitled to say 'yeah, you're in my space, mate'. He never said a dickie bird. And I thought, sit there nicely, behave yourself. Now where is football any different to that? You tell me, because I don't know. It's the old farts like us – the new ones want to be with the players – who realise there's a line. I mean, we come from people like Shankly, Cullis, Greenwood, Busby, Nicholson. They're the ones who rode over the top of us. I mean, they frightened the life out of us.

ALLAN As you know, Peter Taylor is my brother-in-law. I've worked with him for thirty years, until recently really. Peter, Colin Murphy, who was his assistant at Hull, and Mick Jones, Warnock's assistant, are almost father figures to me. They are genuine people, where others would do you big time. Everybody in here knows Peter. He's got loads of promotions but he'd also go and manage Dover, because he loves football. He'll manage Stevenage, Wigan, Dartford, Enfield.

He'll manage England under twenty-ones, because he loves football. If another one comes along, like Leicester or Gillingham or Brighton, he'll do it. There are still a lot of people like Peter, Mick, Colin, us lot, who love football. Unfortunately, there's a lot of people in the game who don't. They just want the money. That's sad.

BARRY Young people don't love their football. We talk about the old games Pat, we have done this morning. There is a lot to be learned, but if we tried to tell youngsters about Bobby Moore, they wouldn't want to know. They'd say, so what? When I was a kid I lived in West London, near Heathrow. I don't know why; my father was involved with a league round there. I used to watch Hayes quite regularly. Then I started going to Arsenal, and there was a bloke on the pitch called George Eastham. I used to go every week, and I'd get home and my dad would ask 'what was the score?' and I didn't know. All I did for ninety minutes was watch him . . .

PAT He was my idol.

BARRY Was he? Unbelievable. Here's a lovely story. Many, many years later I met him in the boardroom up at Stoke. I told him how I'd try and do things like he did, in my school matches and stuff like that. I thanked him for helping me build up a decent understanding of the game. How embarrassing! But I think it quite pleased him.

ALLAN Bet it did. Well, we all had our idols, didn't we? Mine was Bobby Moncur.

PAT Who influences you when it comes to finding players? My greatest influence as a scout is me. I always had a thirst for knowledge. As a kid I'd be up in the offices of the manager. Out I'd come, cup of tea. 'Why are you doing that? What are you going to talk to them about?' You know? We were hungry, and I'm still hungry. I watch a match and go, I like that, that'll do me. I'm sixty-one years of age but even as a little boy I would study the game. I mean the '66 World Cup, one of my favourite players was Florien Albert, the Hungarian. Now, people wouldn't have a clue about him. But he was one of the greatest players. 'The Emperor', they called him. Died last year. As a little boy, I'm watching the telly and I'm thinking, what a player! So you're analysing even in those days, aren't you? So I think you can't teach a scout.

ALLAN There are some very good managers who wouldn't know how to select a player, or recruit a player, because they leave it to other people. Neil Warnock's a classic – he leaves it all to Mick to make the final decisions on players, because Mick is very in-depth with it. It is 'yes or no, Mick?' and if he says 'yes, we'll have him' he signs him. He wouldn't have a clue, Neil. He honestly would not have a clue. At the club they won't see Warnock till Thursday, because he's taken his wife out for lovely lunches, but the impact he has on the Thursday for an hour, is frightening. And when he's in the dressing room . . .

PAT As a manager you've got to know what you're good at. It is no different to managing a company. Ask yourself: what are my strengths? Delegation is the greatest thing. The difficulty with the managers is they don't go to games.

BARRY If you don't go to games, how do you know if you want to sign players? This is a fucking classic, unbelievable. Russell Slade was manager, when I was chief scout, and he asked, 'Have you seen Liam Dickinson at Derby?' I said, 'Funnily enough, I only saw him play when he was at Stockport. He got twenty-odd goals. He waddles around the pitch, he can't fucking jump, his first touch is crap, can't head the ball. Anything else you want to know?' He said to me, 'He's playing for Leeds at the moment.' I said, 'Fine. I'll tell you what I'll do. I'll have a word with the lads up North, and I'll have a look on my laptop.' One of the lads had seen him, and said the only thing he didn't do was put his hands in his pockets. So anyway, it gets serious. Three days later the chairman rings me up, says we've agreed a fee with Derby. The story was, Paul Jewell bought him from Stockport for three-quarters of a million quid. He played a reserve game for Derby, which Jewell attended. A week later he goes to Huddersfield on loan. Then he goes to Blackpool and Leeds, on loan. So the chairman rings up and says, 'We've negotiated four hundred and fifty thousand for Dickinson.' I said, 'You're having a fucking laugh, aren't you? Have you seen the reports?' The only reason I'm still in the job is that if I put in a report to the manager, I copy in the chairman. I tell him I'll give Gwyn Williams a ring up at Leeds, just to get a flavour of the boy. Russell said, 'Look Bal, I want him and that's the end of the story.' We signed him. Within a month, we're trying to get him out on loan, because he was so bad. And of course Russell didn't last longer than another couple of months.

PAT I went for an interview with Barry Hearn for Leyton Orient. I go round to his house, and he says, 'Tell me about yourself.' So I said, 'Well, I enjoy coaching. I like to develop young players.' I'm saying all the wrong things. I don't know the League, Division Three. I haven't gone to reserve games. I wouldn't know how to negotiate a contract. Anyway, I get the job. Steve Shorey was there. Lovely fella, went on to be chief scout at Reading. No videos, no reports, nothing. I lost my job because the majority of the players weren't good enough. I was chasing my arse. One day Steve asked for a word. He went 'I heard the apprentices talk about two of the lads we brought in. They do drugs.' I went 'You're fucking joking.' One was banned for a year, Roger Stanislaus. Forty thousand he cost me, from Bury. I phone up three people I respect about him. 'It's OK' they tell me. 'He's a great lad.' He got done by the FA for taking cocaine. Now I look at myself and think, you should have known better. But I didn't.

ALLAN As scouts we put people up and they are signed. Most are good players who go on to do well. We only get targeted with the ones that don't happen, the ones who don't do it for whatever reason. Then we get grief from above. It is disheartening at times, because of the work you put in.

BARRY I used to get like that but I don't any more. I just push it to one side. When I've seen a player that I've flagged up sign for another club and do well, I have a little smile. That's all, nothing else. I have a little smile and go, 'OK, next one.'

PAT Steve Rowley. He's one of the best in our game, correct? He's been fantastic for me, from day one. He's not what I'd call a mate, but he's a friend in many respects. He's a West Ham supporter, but he's a lovely man. Sometimes I can see on his face that he's under pressure. We take everything so personally.

ALLAN You do. It's your living.

PAT When I was out of work, after the sack at Leyton Orient, Arsenal sent me to an age group international at Auxerre. I was fucking dreading it. I'd never been abroad. So, now I'm watching the game. Vieira's in centre-midfield. France had a fucking good side. Silvestre also played. Anyway, I get back. Steve asks, 'How did the left winger do?' I said, 'Erratic; nearly killed a fucking pigeon with one shot.' You know who it was, don't you?

BARRY Henry?

PAT Thierry Henry. I told the story to Frank Arnesen. He said, 'Pat, I watched Henry six times. Did he play outside left?' I said yeah. He said, 'For me also, it was no, no, no every time.' For some reason, Arsenal sent me to another game in France. Before I go Steve says, 'Anelka mustn't play.' So what am I supposed to do about it? 'Just tell the interpreter to tell the team manager that he mustn't play.' So we get there, I send the poor little bastard down. He comes back, said the manager was very upset. I watch the match, nothing special. Again, when I get back Steve says, 'How did Anelka play?' I said, 'He didn't. You told me he mustn't play.' Steve said, 'We were fucking winding you up.'

BARRY Classic. The average lifespan for a manager is anything up to eighteen months. The reason for that is poor team selection and poor recruitment. End of story. Most managers fail because of poor recruitment but clubs underrate it.

ALLAN It's a fundamental part of a football club. If you don't get that right, you've no chance. Yet we have no professional guidance on what we can do. Some clubs treat you like ponces, as if you're only there for a free ticket. They don't think about the two hundred mile drive to get there, or the one hundred and thirty odd games you've done in a few months. Some places you don't get a cup of tea. They give you a seat by the corner flag, or put you in one they can't sell, because a pole is in the way.

BARRY One of the analyst lads is always asking me to do a bit of scouting. He lives down in Eastbourne so I've been sending him locally. We've got a goal-keeper, Mitch Walker, on loan there. When the kid comes back with his report, he's written a fucking book. It's *War and Peace*, without the content. There's nothing really relevant. He asked me what I think of Mitch, and I said, 'He doesn't fill the goal.' He said, 'What do you mean? He's six foot two.' He didn't really understand presence, things like that.

ALLAN Our fella, the analyst, is a lovely lad. Good boy, knows his stuff. He also wanted to come out with me. Well, the moment the first corner comes in, he's asking, 'How do you do it?' It's the striped shirts, with the numbers you can't see. He doesn't know what's going on. I tell him in scouting you've got to see the big picture. That's why we wouldn't watch a game on the telly . . .

PAT Unless you've got a telly that's sixty yards long.

BARRY You haven't got the buzz, you haven't got the

noise. The fucking camera angle's always wrong. They came to me six weeks ago and said 'Bal, think we're going to sign this centre half from Scotland. A lad called Wallace. Would you have a look at him?' They didn't want me to go up there. They wanted me to watch on the desk. They didn't tell me what his number was, but I picked up who he was. Left-footed centre half. 'What do you think?' they ask. 'Well,' I said, 'I can't tell you off the DVD because when the ball is on the left wing and the opposition have got it, I haven't got a clue where he is because of the camera angle. I've seen him put his hand up a couple of times and been lucky to get an offside decision, but . . .' We didn't take him.

PAT Can I say something? Someone asked me whether I'd miss scouting. But even if I didn't have a job, I'd still want to do what I've always done, go and watch games. I love watching football. The feeling of seeing a player, knowing he is a player, is difficult to describe. I mean, I've got one at Southampton, a boy called Callum Chambers. He's going to be a fucking player. Shaw is the one they're all beating the bush about, but I like Chambers. They play him everywhere, bless him. He's going to be an outside right. You wait and see. That's the beauty of watching football, isn't it?

ALLAN Absolutely. José Fonte was definitely the one for me. I went out to Portugal, to Setúbal. It's a pretty dire place to be honest with you. José was centre half and we knew about him. I was chief scout at Palace, and I had to say yes or no. Well, we signed him, for about three hundred and fifty grand. He went to Southampton for about one point two, so we made some good money on him. He was somebody who wasn't tried and tested in English football, but instinct told me he'd do well. It was the same when I was a player at Tottenham. There was a kid who took my eye. Everyone went, 'I don't think he'll make it here.' I actually spoke to Jack Charlton about him. I went, 'Fucking hell, he's going to be a player, isn't he?' It was Graeme Souness. Jack bought him for thirty grand for Middlesbrough.

BARRY It is all about using the information at your disposal. Most of the phone calls I get will be about players at my club that other people fancy. They will ring me to say, 'What's he like, Bal, as a person?' You wouldn't ring certain people because you know you'd get a load of bullshit. There are those you trust, and those you don't. But the majority of us get on great together. We're all at the same places . . .

ALLAN We've got our own little domain. Very friendly people, get on great, the majority of us. I would never pull a stroke. If Barry phoned me up and said, 'What do you think about so and so at Forest?' I'd give him an answer. And, of course, every year there's a lad who appears on the non-league scene. There's a mad rush. I think the classic was the boy Chambers at Dulwich Hamlet.

BARRY Oh yeah, unbelievable. Michael Chambers. There was a little clip in the newspapers about this kid who had gone on trial at Manchester United. I'd seen him play for the youth team the year before, and thought nothing of it. Suddenly everyone's there. There's sixty-three scouts at a game, watching this one kid. It was the third time me and Pat had seen him. I'm sitting there thinking: what am I doing here? Simply, it was because somebody at the club read about him. They said, 'Bal, will you check up again?' It didn't alter my opinion, but Palace have taken him. We could all be wrong.

ALLAN People like to know about the one that got away or the one you spotted, but I don't think it's ever as black and white as that. If you go to Barry's office, he will have a list of six goalkeepers, six different outfield teams in 4–4–2, 4–3–3. There will be sixty or seventy names on his desk. Unless you are not doing your job properly, it's pretty much impossible to miss someone. We all speak to each other; we all identify the same talent. The people in this room work twenty-four days a week, but I also know a lot of scouts who don't. I know a chief scout who has put seven thousand miles on his car, in a year. Now he ain't out there doing his job. Whether it is watching a park game on a Sunday morning, or Bromley, or Dartford, or Manchester United or Liverpool, you've got to be there. You've got to put the miles in. You've got to be there, because if you ain't wearing those tyres out, you ain't going to find that one.

Suddenly, the spell was broken. The elders drained their tea, and dispersed. Everton Reserves were in town. Aston Villa's development squad needed to be checked out. There were things to do, players to see. I, too, got my coat. It was time for a fateful trip to the seaside.

8

Big Boys Lost

The Fish House, situated in a parade of shops 150 yards from Roots Hall, home of Southend United since 1955, is a place of pilgrimage for football scouts. The portions are generous, the plaice is exceptional, and the batter is light, crispy and golden. The chips have the thickness of a labourer's fingers and the mushy peas prove that the dish is not exclusively a Northern delicacy. Mel Johnson found a corner table, close to the door, and ordered a large cod, to be washed down by his customary black tea.

The place was packed with supporters, and a florid man in a cheap grey suit offset by a chain-store shirt-and-tie set asked to share. He was friendly, forthcoming. A veteran journalist on a local news agency, evidently with good contacts in the Southend boardroom, he regaled us with tales of lower-league ducking and diving. Freddy Eastwood, a Welsh international striker from

Romany stock who had just returned to the club which once sold him for £1.5 million, was a potential source of regular freelance income. 'Piled on the weight a bit,' he said. 'Still decent at this level, but he can't really run.'

Johnson, Liverpool's senior scout in the South, shot me a glance. He knew I was obeying the first law of football scouting: reveal only what is convenient to you. The journalist's news editor would not have been amused. He left without asking what either of us, who admitted to having no allegiance to Southend or their opponents Cheltenham Town, were doing at a League Two game on a Friday night. The 'Liverpool swoop' story that was one pertinent question away from realisation remained unwritten. 'Information, information, information,' said the scout, with a chuckle.

Johnson and I had met at a hotel just off the M25, and travelled down the arterial road into Southend in his Audi saloon. Gossip was punctuated by a call from his son, Jamie, who, crestfallen, reported that Kenny Jackett, his manager at Millwall, had 'the right hump' with him. Jackett had been impressed by Karim Rekik, a young Dutch defender of Tunisian descent, who was on loan at Portsmouth from Manchester City. He wanted to know why he hadn't been alerted to his potential at left back; Jamie had monitored his progress with City's youth and development teams, who played him as a right-sided, left-footed centre half, and argued that it was impossible to make a telling judgement when he was being played out of position.

'That's scouting,' consoled his father, who retained close links to Jackett, with whom he worked at Watford and QPR. 'You feel like dogshit and there's nothing you can do about it. If you had offered him up, after seeing him as a centre half, Ken would have had none of it. It just so happens he saw him have a worldie. I was there, and I could see him thinking: why haven't I been told about this kid? When that happens, and a manager sees something he loves, you are powerless.'

Mel, my mentor, was pursuing a pet project, Jack Butland. The teenaged goalkeeper had been sent out on loan to Cheltenham by Birmingham City, who cherished him as an indigent would treasure a winning lottery ticket. The received wisdom, that Butland was destined to emerge as the most viable competitor to Joe Hart at international level, needed the reality check of constant assessment. Southend was an entirely different environment from Switzerland and Colombia, where Johnson's interest in the goalkeeper had been piqued. This would be the ninth time he had personally monitored his progress.

'I first saw him play in Nyon, with the England under nineteens, against Switzerland. When I got back I called Chris Hughton at Birmingham, who I know well. "You've got a goalkeeper on your hands," I told him. "His shirt is out, his socks are down. He doesn't look the part, but he's got it allright." He must have had a word because the next time I saw Jack, at the world under twenties in Colombia, I was really impressed by how he'd changed. He'd got taller. He held himself better. The shirt was in and the socks were up. He looked professional, an England player. I watched him four times out there, and he was outstanding.

'That was a good side. I got excited, put a report in the system straight away and got a message to Damien. I did some groundwork, and arranged to meet Jack's agent. We had a coffee before one of the Cheltenham games, and I got to know his deal. John Achterberg, our goalkeeping coach, and Alan Harper went to watch him. There are lots of rumours going around. Chelsea are interested, Man City, Arsenal, the usual suspects. Everybody's been to watch him. I don't know about other clubs, but we're still on the fence. To us, he doesn't come and catch the ball with conviction. He doesn't come off his line and smash it away. He doesn't come between the bodies and claim it. At the moment he looks hesitant. The one thing we hope is that this is a passing phase. The worry is that it is a real problem.

'It is so difficult with young players. I was with Stuart Pearce at Wycombe the other night. Stuart told me he loved Jack to bits. That's reassuring because of the respect I have for him. I had a great conversation with him about the development of the young ones. I threw names at him. I asked what he thought of Lewis Dunk at Brighton, the centre back who is interesting quite a few. Stuart's had him in his under twenty-one squad but I don't fancy him at all. I will still keep watching him, just because he's young and a left-sided centre half, but he only ever kicks with his right foot. He's not for me, but it was interesting to gauge Stuart's reaction. In England, for Liverpool at the moment, it's all about the recruitment of young players.'

Excellence in scouting, as in any other profession, involves the accumulation and application of knowledge. Johnson had acquired experience, over three decades, at clubs as diverse as Cambridge United, Crystal Palace, Fulham, Tottenham, Huddersfield and Newcastle. He was not a goalkeeping specialist, but had a rare insight into the complexities of the trade. He almost earned himself a niche, as the man who discovered Joe Hart:

'You see a Gareth Bale and things work out well. There are other boys you don't sign, like Joe Hart. Kenny Jackett was managing Swansea in League Two when I went to Tottenham; Frank Arnesen took me there in February 2005 from QPR, where I was chief scout. One day Ken called me and said, "Mel, there's a boy at Shrewsbury in goal called Hart. You've got to go and see him, he's fantastic." So I went and really liked him. Frank had brought me in to get the best young players to Spurs and I told him Joe was one worth having. He liked the idea. Hans Sagers, Tottenham's first team goalkeeping coach, went to watch him play at Barnet. He liked him, too, and we decided to go for it. Frank spoke to the chairman, and then spoke to Gary Peters, who was Shrewsbury manager. They wanted a million pounds for him. Frank said no.'

His instinctive laughter at the nature of the misjudgement provided an exclamation point to the tale: 'Man City were always very, very interested. They got him for six hundred grand. It didn't work in our favour, but that deal is a good example of how we get players. We build up a network of contacts, managers, other scouts, agents and coaches. I'm constantly scanning the internet. I know this is old school, but I also love a newspaper. I'm continually looking for information on players. You also need to be a talker to be in the game. You need to network. If you don't, you'll struggle to get back in when you are on the outside, looking in. When my manager friends lose their jobs I always tell them to get to games. A lot of directors ask us about coaches and managers. They want to know who is being seen on the scene. They ask who we would recommend for a job. The flip side is we also get a lot of managers calling us, regarding players. It is the usual stuff – "do you know so and so, what do you think about him, anything I should know" – but it makes the world go round.'

The read on Butland's character was promising, despite his adolescent slovenliness. He was self-sufficient from the age of 14, insisting on making a two-and-a-half-hour train journey from Bristol to Birmingham alone, three times a week. He refused to burden his parents with the chore of driving him there, though it would have taken half the time. He spent all day Tuesdays and Thursdays training with goalkeeping coach Dave Watson, but still passed all his GCSEs, earning two A grades, six Bs and a C. His most difficult decision came at 16, when he gave up rugby, much to the disappointment of his father, whose own rugby career was ended by a car accident.

For the first half, at least, Butland would be a distant figure. Southend herded the scouts into two executive boxes in the left-hand corner of the main stand, between the by-line and the edge of the penalty area. They had the feel of monastic cells, and were obviously difficult to market. Two rows of chairs were set out before a grimy picture window, but only those seated at the front had an uninterrupted view of the far end of the pitch. Even then, those on the right-hand side of the box had to squint through a forest of supportive posts.

Ewan Chester, Birmingham's chief scout, popped in to pinch a team sheet and assess the level of interest. A dapper man in a dark raincoat, he had spent more than 20 years in two spells at Rangers, where he was trusted implicitly by contrasting managers, Graeme Souness and Walter Smith. In this context, he was a cross between an auctioneer and a foster parent. His presence re-assured Butland that he had not been abandoned. He would also provide immediate feedback to Hughton and Watson on the value of Birmingham's investment. 'We watch Jack every game,' he said. 'We know he has got a big chance. He's the best young goalkeeper I have ever seen. He's unbelievably mature, as near a certainty as you can have.'

The first box was full. Ours, for some reason, contained only one other scout, Paul Dyer from Queens Park Rangers. A voluble character, in a full-length black leather coat, he had the bearing of a former military man; his gaze was firm, his posture was positive and though he smiled readily there was latent aggression in his eyes. At 58, he was making a living as a cabbie, and trying to deal with an enduring sense of betrayal. Colchester United, the club to which he had devoted the majority of his working life, had not only cast him aside. In his eyes, they had also defiled his dedication, by using it against him, at an employment tribunal:

'I did everything for that club. I was there twenty three years and Paul Lambert blew me out. That meant nothing to him, and everything to me. Colchester is my club. I played there. I painted the roof of the stand during that long, hot summer, seventy-five, seventy-six wasn't it? Imagine the heat that roof radiated. It was unbearable at times. I drove the minibus. I managed the reserves. I swept the dressing rooms. I put up the hoardings on the side of the pitch. I made them nine million on players when I was chief scout. What did that get me?'

The searing experience of having a claim for unfair dismissal rejected. The tribunal decided his employment began when he signed a contract in 2006 and not in 1991, as he argued, when he became part of the back-room team. He disputed the club's insistence he was merely a volunteer for those 15 years. Colchester's redundancy procedures were criticised as being 'flawed' but this was deemed insufficient to allow the claim. Dyer had rejected £5,800, and then a further £2,000, from the club during the arbitration process. The price of service had a physical dimension; like many former footballers of his generation, he suffered badly from arthritis:

'I was a bite and scratch midfield player. They used to say Kevin Beattie at Ipswich was hard. I used to have him in my pocket. Alan Hunter always used to say I was the biggest pain in the arse he played against. I put it in every day, every game. I kept fucking going. When I was injured they put morphine directly into the joint to stop the pain. My knee was like a building site. I told them to clear out all the shit and still went back for more. I was in more pain than I had ever been in my life.'

There was a telling wistfulness to his reminiscence, which ended as the teams filed out to a welcome which failed to match the hysteria of the public address announcer. An athlete's career is like a phantom limb, which can still be sensed by an amputee. It leaves a spiritual void. Dyer, jolted back into the present by proximity of the kick-off, didn't need to ask about the nature of Johnson's mission. It was of marginal significance since he was concentrating on full back Lee Hills, who had been loaned to Southend by Crystal Palace for the last two months of the season. The word was that he would be released in the summer. 'He's worth a look,' the scout rationalised. 'The Premier League might have gone for him but Mick Jones, who knew him at Palace, reckons he's not bad.'

Johnson leaned forward slightly in his seat as he focused on the far end of the pitch, where Butland was a light blue speck. 'I'm waiting for him to come off his line and catch it,' he muttered as the home side, emboldened by the early dismissal of Cheltenham full back Sido Tombati for a lunge on Michael Timlin, put the goalkeeper under pressure from a series of set pieces. Though let down by his defenders, who allowed Kane Ferdinand to score with an unchallenged shot, five yards out, in the 28th minute, he was failing to command his penalty area. A night which had begun badly was destined to get much, much worse.

Butland's first major error extended Southend's lead before half-time. He made the elementary mistake of failing to get his body behind a swerving shot by Ryan Hall. The ball nestled in the centre of the goal in tacit admonition of the blunder. Unnerved by the calamity, the goalkeeper became increasingly static. 'This is why you go to games,' Johnson said, to Dyer's murmured approval. 'Jack needs to be getting plenty of games, playing for a team with something to play for instead of a meaningless development squad. Cheltenham want to go up, and he's with old pros who'll tell him: "Sort it. We want to win this for the fucking bonus."'

Butland, last off at the break and first to return, was now in our eyeline. His features were suddenly distinct. It was disarmingly simple to read his body language. Bizarrely, he released his nervous energy by bouncing up and down in the team huddle which presaged the second half. It was an arresting sight, almost as if he was trying to trigger a hokey-cokey, but the levity of the moment was soon lost. Southend should have been 3–0 up almost immediately; Butland was rooted to his line as Eastwood, in his first game at Roots Hall for five years, missed a simple header from a Hills cross.

The agony of self-doubt deepened in the 51st minute when Eastwood controlled Hall's long ball, cut inside, and attempted a speculative shot, which went in off Butland's right arm. 'Oh Jack,' Johnson exclaimed, as the magnitude of the misjudgement sank in. 'What a nightmare.' The mental degradation was almost complete. Butland's inner turmoil began to affect his kicking. Usually it was one of the better elements of his game; he was comfortable on the ball, which he struck with a languid grace that evoked comparisons with a finely honed golf swing. Now he began to unravel technically. He was slicing his clearances and goal kicks with the undisguised desperation of a weekend hacker. It was no real surprise when, midway through the second half, Butland dived over a straightforward 20-yard shot by Bilel Mohsni.

'This is the real world,' said Dyer, breaking an uncomfortable silence.

'If I didn't know him I would have crossed him off, but I know he is better than this,' replied Johnson.

'He's eighteen. He's only a baby. He's got twenty more years ahead of him as a goalkeeper, at least.'

'I know, but what worries me is his heart. He looks right – he has great size, all the attributes – but does he have that inner strength?'

For me, it was a moment of epiphany. The scout's trick, of concentrating on an individual with a lover's intensity, was becoming instinctive. The colours of the crowd began to coalesce. Eventually they were as monochromatic as the floodlights, set against the inky darkness of the night sky. The chants were muffled to the point of inaudibility. Senses were subjugated, yet heightened. My field of vision was filled by a big boy, lost. Butland exuded a touching vulnerability. His unconscious act of chewing the neckband of his shirt was a child-like gesture, which radiated fearfulness and isolation. He would periodically exhale so violently that his chest heaved, and his breath condensed in the cold air. He attempted to maintain appearances by barking orders at his defenders, but they, too, were being consumed by the quicksand of self-doubt.

Dyer was impressed by Hills, who would eventually sign for another interested witness, Stevenage manager Gary Smith. Like Johnson, Dyer prepared to leave with ten minutes still to play. He had a late-night fare to pick up at Stanstead airport. 'Regular punter,' he reported. 'He comes in from Gibraltar, with plenty of readies. Always pays in euros. Ask no questions, eh?' Johnson smiled, and said his goodbyes. His report would be in the Anfield system by 2 a.m. He felt the night had to be put into the context of Butland's previous excellence. His view, together with video clips of the goals, stimulated immediate debate about the nature of Liverpool's interest. Achterberg, in particular, was unimpressed. But first, Johnson had to deal with a text message from Mark Cartwright, Butland's representative. 'Not a good scoreline. How was Jack?' it read. The reply was brief, but heartfelt: 'Don't ask.'

Destiny beckoned, with a wink and seductive grin. Anyone who suggested, at that moment, in the early hours of March 31, 2012, that within five months Butland would become England's youngest goalkeeper, after playing for Team GB in the Olympic Games, would have been humoured, pitied or sent to lie down with a soothing mug of cocoa. Yet football has an infinite capacity to amaze and appal. Providence had its eye, also, on Liverpool.

The following Friday, Good Friday, Johnson picked up Damien Comolli at Gatwick airport. The Frenchman had been summoned to the United States to see Liverpool owner John W. Henry, where he presented an overview of the club's redevelopment. He and the scout to whom he was most closely aligned ran a final check on Crewe's Nick Powell in a 1–1 draw at Crawley Town. They left when he was substituted eight minutes from time, discouraged by well-sourced intelligence that Manchester United intended to activate their option to sign him, for a fee of £4 million.

The weekly conference call between the main players in the recruitment department took place, as usual, on the Tuesday, after the extended holiday weekend. On Wednesday Comolli was called into another emergency meeting, in Liverpool city centre. On Thursday Liverpool's official website was leading with a preview of the weekend's FA Cup semi-final against Everton, featuring Steven Gerrard. It was entitled 'Make yourself a hero.' Then, in early afternoon, it carried a fateful four-paragraph statement:

> Fenway Sports Group and Liverpool FC confirmed today that Director of Football Damien Comolli has left the Club by mutual consent.
>
> Principal Owner John Henry said: 'We are grateful for all of Damien's efforts on behalf of Liverpool and wish him all the best for the future.'

Liverpool Chairman Tom Werner added: 'The Club needs to move forward and we now have a huge game on Saturday. It is important that everyone joins us in supporting the manager and gets behind Kenny and the team and focuses on a strong finish to the season.'

Damien Comolli commented: 'I am grateful to have been given the opportunity to work at Liverpool and am happy to move on from the Club and back to France for family reasons. I wish the Club all the best for the future.'

Johnson was at home, setting up a DVD, when he received a call from Andy Stevens, one of Liverpool's part-time scouts. 'Have you seen *Sky Sports News*?' he asked, breathlessly. 'If not, get it on.' As Johnson did so, with a mounting sense of dread, he instinctively flicked on to his emails. There, in his inbox, was an unread message from Comolli: 'Thank you for all your hard work. I will contact you soon.' The rest of the day sped by in a blur. Shock quickly mutated into alarm:

'Bloody hell. Where do I start? The phone, text and email has gone mad. I'm ploughing through the messages, getting back to people. It's a massive shock. Everything looked OK. After Damien's meeting with the owners in the States we were talking about our plans, players and money. We carried on as normal. He sent me an email about targets yesterday and then, bang. I know this is football and you shouldn't be shocked but . . .'

Insecurity has an avalanche's speed and destructive power. It swallows people, whole. Steve Hitchen was immediately besieged by his network of international scouts. All were anxious, yet aware their contacts were transferable. If they were surplus to requirements, they had arrangements to make. Hitchen sought an early meeting with the Liverpool hierarchy to stress the scouting staff's need for reassurance. Airy public statements, reiterating support for Kenny Dalglish, were of limited relevance. Lines of communication were fractured, and Chinese Whispers multiplied. The sacking of Peter Brukner, the club's head of sports medicine and science, and suggestions that Achterberg would be moved on at the end of the season, were ominous. 'We just don't know who is going to be our boss,' said Johnson. 'We will be seen as Damien's men, but all of us want to stay at Liverpool Football Club, if they want us.'

Concern scoured his vocal chords, but professional pride dictated his priorities. On Friday he took a brief break from preparing a profile of Paulo Gazzaniga, an imposing young Argentine goalkeeper who had materialised at Gillingham, to take Jan, his partner, for lunch. Even during that respite, 17 messages stockpiled on his mobile phone. Callers were split into two distinct groups. The first, professional acquaintances, were seeking inside information on events at Anfield. They could be fobbed off with generalities. The second were friends from within the game, whose concerns were more personal. They ranged from managers, such as Jackett and Gary Waddock, to fellow scouts, like the venerable John Griffin, a man of huge knowledge and instinctive kindness, who was working in impoverished circumstances alongside Waddock at Wycombe Wanderers.

Saturday was surreal, a fusion of the past and an uncertain future. Johnson was in the car park at the Kassam Stadium, listening on the radio as Andy Carroll, a central character in Comolli's downfall, scored the 87th minute headed goal which took Liverpool into the FA Cup final. He was accompanied by Dean Austin, whose professional duty, assessing Gazzaniga's potential for Bolton, gave him the opportunity to offer moral support. When Johnson entered the press room, which doubled as a watering hole for the scouts, he was approached by a string of colleagues. Most offered sympathy as bait. At least one, Bob Shaw, seemed authentic in his compassion.

Shaw was a month from his 65th birthday, but looked 15 years younger. His shoulders were broad, and though his torso was encased in a leather bomber jacket, zipped to the chin, there was no sign of excess fat around his waist. His eyes were clear, and his silver hair was short and neat. His opinions, incisive and robust, reflected a schizophrenic working life. He had combined 34 years underground, as a coal miner, with spells as chief scout at Hull, Derby, Bolton and Sunderland, where he was a victim of a purge instigated by Roy Keane. He was compiling opposition reports for Plymouth Argyle, as a favour to Peter Reid.

'I'm glad I didn't need football to bring up my family,' he told Johnson, as they sipped tea from polystyrene cups. 'We've all taken the wrong jobs for the money, and we all know that if there are problems, people are managed out of football clubs. When I get this season out of the way I'll take a long hard look at things. I'll only take the job I want, for the right reasons.'

A contemplative mood settled on the conversation. Shaw recalled his father, who worked in the coalfields of the East Midlands from the age of 14 to merciful retirement, at 65. He contracted pneumoconiosis, a lung disease caused by breathing in dust from coal, graphite or man made carbon over a sustained period. The legacy of his employment was a hacking cough and shortness of breath, caused by dust which had drastically reduced his lung capacity. The family fought for years to gain appropriate compensation; he died soon after the legal battle was won.

Oxford summoned memories of Johnson's father, who worked for 25 years on the Morris production line in nearby Cowley. The scout scanned the city, shimmering in the spring sunshine beyond the opposite stand in the three-sided ground, and pointed out the factory. 'This is my club, really,' he said, in a tone which suggested he longed for lost innocence. 'This isn't a proper ground, like the Manor. I was brought up on Oxford United. Those were the days of Ron Atkinson and his brother Graham. They won us the Southern League in sixty-two. Happy days . . .'

He was roused from his reverie by the appearance of Gazzaniga, who had also attracted the attention of Jim Barron, from Everton, and Perry Suckling, goalkeeping coach at the Tottenham Academy. Tall, 6ft 5in, and athletic, he was from good goalkeeping stock. Born in Murphy, on the outskirts of Santa Fe, he moved to Spain at the age of 15 with his divorced father David, who held the appearance record for a goalkeeper at River Plate. His move to Gillingham, after his release by Valencia, was facilitated by Gary Penrice, Wigan's European scout.

Johnson's journey was worthwhile within minutes. Oxford's Asa Hall was allowed to turn, on the edge of the six-yard box. His shot was instant, firm and destined for the bottom corner. Gazzaniga showed remarkable elasticity, throwing himself down, to his right, to make one of the best one-handed saves I have seen. Johnson made eye contact, and paused for dramatic effect. 'That,' he said, 'was a truly great save. We're on to something here.' Meanwhile, below us, Gillingham captain Andy Frampton broke professional protocol and applauded the youngster with big hands and a big future.

Austin was making notes on his BlackBerry, which

would be transferred on to his online database. He still yearned to coach or manage, and there was a rigour to his analysis with which many of the part-time scouts around him could not compete. His portrayals of players could be cutting, but they were concise and unerringly accurate. One glance at Gillingham's corpulent striker Danny Kedwell prompted him to type the dismissive words 'will always be non-league'. It also led to the creation of the sort of nickname which tends to stick.

'They got him from AFC Wimbledon, didn't they?' asked Johnson, with mock innocence. 'KFC Wimbledon, more like.' Austin, attuned to the caustic humour of the dressing room, beamed. He, too, recognised the potential enshrined in The Save, but noticed room for improvement. 'You can see he's a kid who has not played many games,' he confided. 'Look how he is trying to drill his goal kicks into the wind, on to KFC's head. This is a strange ground, because of the open end, and he's trying to be too precise. That's why he's kicking them out of the park. There's an awful lot there to work with though. He'll soon be able to do the lot.'

The game deteriorated rapidly into a dour goalless draw, which benefited neither team, whose hopes of a place in the League Two play-offs were receding. It also invited more acidic comment. Liam Davis, a rangy centre half, saved Oxford with two last-ditch interceptions. Austin was unequivocal: 'He's got everything you need to be a top player except the one thing you cannot be without – a heart.' He was especially irked by the response of Gavin Tomlin to his early substitution. 'Doesn't look like he's got an attitude, does it?' he remarked, as the Gillingham striker trudged off with the sullenness of an adolescent making the walk of shame out of the pub after being refused a pint following the presenting of a fake ID.

Rather than joining Austin in an early exit, Johnson waited for the traffic to clear. He was in reflective vein, and dwelled on the frustration radiated by the younger man: 'Deano would make an exceptional scout, because of his tactical and technical appreciation of the game, but he wants to coach. I really feel for him. He gets upset when he sees people without his talent and drive getting jobs, while he is on the outside, looking in. I can understand that, because he is a fantastic judge of a player.'

Footballers know their own kind. Immediately after he had showered, Frampton sat in the away dressing room and sent a text to a friend. It read: 'Paulo's just put another nought on his fee.' The defender, a model professional with managerial potential, explained: 'Word moves fast at our level. He knows the interest he's generating. He shares a car with Danny Kedwell. He doesn't know much English, but today, driving in to catch the bus, he just said "Sunderland?" Yup, we told him, that's a big club.

'I know I'll get stick but I just had to applaud him for that save. That shot was right in the bottom corner, and he swooped down with such a strong hand. His kicking was a problem today, but that is usually a strong point. As centre backs, we split and pull off to give him an angle if he needs it. But he drives the ball, about two metres off the ground, with fantastic accuracy and power. He's getting better at communicating, and is learning all the time. Obviously, the higher he goes, the better the tuition he will receive. He's a lovely lad but he's not going to be with us for long.'

In football, it is every man for himself.

9

Moneyball, RIP

Damien Comolli landed in Nice just before Mel Johnson joined the queue to leave the Kassam Stadium, which had shrunk sufficiently to require only a 200-yard crawl from Frankie and Benny's, purveyors of overcooked pasta to time-poor football scouts. It was a humbling retreat for the Frenchman, who considered himself *Général de brigade* in the Sabermetric Revolution, which was spreading from baseball with increasing speed. He took to exile with Napoleonic restlessness, and vowed to return.

In truth, he was not widely mourned. Johnson valued his faith and friendship, but Comolli was a classic victim of the conservatism of English football. The prevailing view of many within the game was crystallised by the frigid lucidity of Tom Werner, Liverpool's chairman: 'We have a strategy we need implemented and we felt Damien was probably not the right person to implement that strategy.' The wider implications were summarised by a two-word tweet, posted by Henry Winter, the *Daily Telegraph*'s football correspondent: '*Moneyball*, RIP.'

That succinct appraisal of an ill-starred initiative, which involved 26 separate transfer deals and the ultimate belittlement of a legend, Kenny Dalglish, resonated with those who resented the achingly fashionable application of science. The original intention of *Moneyball*, in essence the strategic use of statistical analysis to identify undervalued players, was in danger of being lost in the fog of a 60-year war between arithmetical scrutiny and gut instinct. The ghost of Wing Commander Charles Reep, hailed as 'the first professional performance analyst of football' by the *Journal of Sports Sciences* after his death aged 98 in 2002, stalked the ruins of the Anfield project.

Reep pared football to its essentials. He used rudimentary statistics, together with the tactical philosophies of Herbert Chapman's Arsenal from the 1930s, to develop a quasi-academic theory supporting the use of 'direct passing', or Hoofball, to give it a 21st-century twist. His passion gave him plausibility; Stan Cullis, the pre-eminent manager of the era, was convinced by Reep's achievement as an 'advisor', in helping Brentford avoid relegation in the spring of 1952.

They collaborated in the aftermath of Hungary's devastating victory over England at Wembley the following year, devising a pattern of play that purported to blend the artistry of the Magic Magyars with the artisan, 'wholly English' principles espoused by Reep. Wolves, under Cullis, won the League three times in the 1950s and, as Reep's portfolio expanded to analysis of 2,500 games including a number of World Cup finals, his influence extended.

He was a regular contributor to academic journals, recounting his partnership with Cullis in a tome entitled *Are We Getting Too Clever?* His theories were implanted at the highest level of the game, through the Football Association's arch-fundamentalist Charles Hughes and emerging managers such as Graham Taylor. The former England manager took issue with simplistic suggestions that his philosophy was flawed, but his trademark lament − 'can we not knock it?' − was an unwitting echo of another of Reep's agonised treatises, *This Pattern-Weaving Talk Is All Bunk!*

Football, like any major undertaking in sport or in life, cannot be dictated by absolutes. The Nowhere Men were an increasingly endangered species, but no one had found the magic bullet, the ultimate statistic which proved, beyond doubt, a player's worth from a spreadsheet rather than a stream of consciousness, scrawled on the back of an envelope by a scout who felt football in his bones. That wasn't going to stop their detractors trying, however.

Bill James, the founding father of *Moneyball*, regarded the 2012 MIT Sloan Sports Analytics Conference, which drew 2200 delegates to the Hynes Convention Center in Boston, as 'the culmination of my life's work'. His baseball theories, honed during night shifts as a security guard at a pork and beans cannery, and enshrined in Hollywood mythology by the film featuring Brad Pitt, had spawned an industry. The convention featured only one research paper and a single break-out session on football, but technical scouts from Premier League clubs were eager to learn at the feet of the master.

James, an august figure with a bushy beard, was evidently at home in a world in which earnest young men in pinstriped Oxford shirts and chinos spoke of 'franchise value' and 'the metrics of physicality, strength and flexibility'. Apart from one pertinent intervention in the major set-piece debate – 'Usually the public desperately wants you to do one thing, at a time when the coaching staff wants you to do something entirely different' – James allowed others to speak for him.

Scott Boras, who controls 175 Major Leaguers as baseball's so-called 'super agent', exuded the astuteness, detachment and candour of his trade. He mocked perceptions of the analytic movement as the province of 'geeks, nerds, and cheerleaders from Harvard' and envisaged a future in which the financial and intellectual rewards of professional sport would attract the best and brightest, regardless of their affinity with athletic endeavour:

'Everyone is looking for an edge. Internal metrics are already being kept as state secrets. There's a trend for hiring NASA engineers to write programs. Where can we progress from there? We should be training psychologists to understand the game and the players, because we know talent can be a state of mind. How can players be so hot and cold? How can they be so sound for ten days, and lost for five?'

Rocco Baldelli represented the other source of fresh talent, refugees from the locker room. A former Major League outfielder, forced to retire at the age of 29 by a mysterious metabolic disorder, he was kept on by the Tampa Bay Rays to work in scouting and player development. 'I don't want to use the word secrecy, but there is a time-sensitive nature to the stuff we do,' he explained. 'We are only limited by our ideas. We sit around for hours, looking for unique ways to look at the game. The information is there, and more is coming. The cycle of trying to define value never ends.'

Jeff Luhnow, general manager of the Houston Astros, highlighted the moral ambiguities football would face, as it spread its net, ever wider, in search of raw material. 'Baseball is now buying in the Dominican Republic and Latin America,' he said. 'We are spending millions of dollars on fifteen-year-old kids. That brings with it a whole range of issues. We're dealing with false ages, coaches operating as agents, and problems with performance-enhancing drugs.'

Mark Shapiro, president of the Cleveland Indians, advised his audience: 'You are going to be second guessed, no matter what. There is a swirl of emotions around decision-making in recruitment. You can't explain decisions for multiple reasons, and you get more free advice than you can cope with. These are not the jobs where you want short-term approval ratings. The full valuation of a recruitment decision can take four or five years to emerge. Only then can you factor in the human element, and determine whether you are wrong, or right. Players are not assets, they are human beings.

'When we first started out, in 1992, technology was an Excel spreadsheet. We worked with stat books on our laps. Now there are so many technological elements involved. But we still apply language, honed over fifty years of watching the game. No machine is ever going to spill out the answer for which we are all searching. There is still an art to it.'

The human element struck a chord with Scott McLachlan, who, as Chelsea's head of international scouts, was a pioneer of performance profiling in football. He oversaw the collation of intelligence, such as transfer tendencies. He was responsible for database design and management of recruitment statistics, such as player migration trends. Like Everton's James Smith, he was a graduate of South Bank University, where he earned a Masters degree in sports coaching science. Unlike Smith, he reported to Technical Director Michael Emenalo, rather than the first team manager.

Each club has its own culture; Chelsea's was intensely

political, and driven by the autocratic certainties of owner Roman Abramovich. McLachlan drew strength from the diversity of the clubs for which he had worked. Mentored by Roger Smith at Wimbledon, he spent three years in a youth development role at Northampton before working under Sir Clive Woodward at Southampton. He specialised in technical scouting at Fulham, where he flourished under chief scout Barry Simmonds and chief executive Alistair Mackintosh:

'The Fulham CEO could see the future, before the whole *Moneyball* thing became a parody of itself. He believed we could combine analysis and metrics with scouting. It was frustrating, because in football getting something new across is like uphill skiing. I am going to four or five matches a week, because I don't want to lose touch with the essence of the game, but at Chelsea my role has changed. It is more managerial. I have about twenty scouts working to me. It is my job to educate them scientifically, to tailor their observation and analysis to data presentation. I've got to stop them using silly clichés, like the boy does this and that, and get them to focus on trends and averages.

'What is crazy is that, to pick a moment in time, two hundred and sixty-nine million was spent in the transfer window in January 2011. How much of that was down to quantitative analysis of the facts? How much objectivity was used in the signing decision? How much involved real scrutiny of the data? If you are going to make a capital investment of fifty million in one player, how are you going to discover what you are getting for your money?

'Let's make a comparison: say I need to buy an office printer. I know I need to buy one that will produce fifty thousand colour copies each year, for an average of five years. I can research the purchase and monitor the risk. In football that doesn't apply. That's why we at Chelsea are looking at how we measure and quantify talent. That's why we are seeking links with performance scientists from all over the world.

'In football we make big decisions on peer group testimonials. We try and interpret their potential without really knowing them. Who is our player? Does he play for the money, his family, or the glory? What is his mindset? Even the army has a twelve-week training period, during which they can weed people out. We don't find out about our people until the money is down. That's an issue when you've paid millions for someone you don't really know. You need to try to protect yourself.'

A simple aim, but complicated given the atmosphere created by the random collection of alpha males who inhabit the average Premier League club. These are inherently unstable platforms on which to test theories often formed in the vacuum of academia. The miscellany of opinion, developed across the generations in football, makes innovation appear irregular to an influential minority. All teams have elements of social engineering; any formula, designed to designate value or potential, must factor in the nature of the modern player.

According to Bill Beswick, the sports psychologist who came to prominence by working with Steve McClaren for Middlesbrough, Manchester United and England, 'We have to change the culture from human doings to human beings.' His analysis is inevitably emotive. It is the polar opposite of the clinical certainties of the analytic movement. It challenges anaemic algorithms and the rituals of scholarly disengagement:

'The eight-year-old boy runs from his dad's car to play because it is fun. Then he gets to be quite good. He's with a club, and people start to treat him differently. Everyone gives him the ball, because he's the best player. His under ten coach says, "I know I should be developing him, but I want to win." Gradually, he's seen, not as a kid, but as a five-bedroom detached house. There might be three other kids in the family, but now they traipse behind their mum and dad, to watch the Golden Boy train.

'Two things can happen. The kid doesn't make it. He's fifteen or sixteen, and has been left desolate, emotionally damaged. Or the kid makes it. He's one of those who breathes in, and crosses that white line. He's one of those who have made a decision what to do with their lives. He becomes an eighteen-year-old millionaire by signing his first major contract. All those kids he left behind are waiting for him, in the car park, after the match. He loves the game, but there are all these people around him. They all want a piece of him.

'What chance has he got? It is all about coping with pressure. The anxiety of the coach might be killing the players. If our kid is lucky, he might not be the biggest or the quickest, but he will have the best attitude. Performance follows attitude. He won't dwell on setbacks. All great athletes fight themselves, fight the loss of belief, but they prevail. That's why I say that calling any kid talented is a very dangerous thing to do.'

Each to his own. Ben Knapper, Arsenal's principal performance analyst, returned from Boston with a preacher's ardour. His role, in what he terms 'the chaos of a season' is to inform, and discreetly educate, Arsène Wenger, his senior coaches and scouts. It is a delicate, diplomatic process which involves thinking on his feet. His background – two seasons at Scunthorpe United, followed by a stint working for analysis providers Prozone – did not allow much scope to develop the street wisdom required in a dressing-room environment:

'We are data rich, in terms of GPS, medical and performance data, but we are in our infancy in interpreting it, so the coaches can get something meaningful from the process. We are miles behind the guys in the States, in terms of how data impacts on decision-making. It is a huge cultural issue, because it is a new field, and it is not for everyone. You can have the best information in the world, but unless you can engage with the people who matter it is worthless.

'I have to ask myself: can I measure my input? I have to relate to executives, coaches, scouts and the manager. Analysts have to be multi-lingual, in performance terms. It is essential to be flexible, and to be aware of who you are addressing. To get these guys onside, to be able to share your message, you have to appreciate the importance of their expert eye and their intuition. Any work you do has to reflect the club's fundamental philosophy, and contribute to the overbearing aim, of performing on the pitch.

'I am fortunate because the boss is used to my type of stuff. He has an economics degree. He is comfortable around numbers. He believes everything is measurable. He challenges me, pushes me, forces me to move forward. The key thing is never to be happy with what you are doing. The game is so fast paced, and it is my job to say, "can we do this?" You have to continually push on. That takes a lot of energy, and you have to be passionate about what you do.

'The coaches are so emotionally attached to their jobs. The boss expects emotionally driven debate, but wants to combine it with something tangible, like an objective analytical framework. I sometimes watch matches back with him. It is an unbelievable experience. He will occasionally spot something, and admit, "I didn't see it like that at the time." It is so interesting to see how perceptions can change.

'Recruitment is a big area of influence. If clubs are spending vast sums, they have to be able to objectively support their investment decisions. Guys like me are the iPad, laptop generation. Those in their sixties, like many of the flat cap scouts, do not find it normal to use technology. It is easy to scare people if you are not careful. When you get to that stage it is a tough battle.'

The technology is impressive, and best studied in Knapper's more natural environment, a Football & Science conference in London's Docklands, organised by Jon Goodman, the former Wimbledon striker whose performance consultancy, Think Fitness, is used by leading clubs and players. I was there to moderate the keynote debate, but was intrigued by the breadth and simplicity of the Arsenal analyst's work.

Knapper split the screen, to illustrate an extract from Arsenal's 2–1 defeat of Barcelona in February 2011, so that match footage could be compared to an animated view. Basic information, such as the distance between central defenders, and player movement at set pieces, acquired an additional dimension. Intriguingly, young players, emerging in the academy, can be benchmarked against stellar players, such as Theo Walcott and Jack Wilshere. Walcott, in particular, seeks to study his numbers; others are more comfortable being assessed in traditional peer groups, like a back four. Such feedback, overlaid with video from the performance itself, is increasingly being downloaded on to a player's iPad or phone.

Much of the data is deemed too sensitive to be in the public domain. Wenger, for instance, is extremely protective of physical data, used to determine levels of fitness and effectiveness. A player in the red zone, for example, is deemed to be suffering from cumulative fatigue. His 'high intensity output', his ability to reach a speed threshold of seven metres per second, is regarded with the reverence afforded holy writ. There are around 3,000 so-called 'match events', which can be distilled into movements, collated every tenth of a second. It can never be an exact science, because of the human element, and the major issue in recruitment, according to James Smith, Head of Technical Scouting at Everton, is the quality of the data:

'We're at the point where we're teetering on the brink. At the moment, the stats are not quite insightful enough. Leon Britton at Swansea and his one hundred per cent pass completion rate is a great example. It doesn't tell you anything. Nine or ten years ago, when I first saw Prozone, I thought: wow, that's incredible. You can tell me how many headers he's won? Tell me how many tackles he won? Wow. But now, that doesn't really mean anything. What I need to know is how many headers he won in the opposition penalty area, how many headers he won in the attacking third. How many does he win from set pieces? How many does he win from set pieces in his own box? How many of them were contested? How many of them lead to a goal attempt? We need depth of data.

'The data is sold on its objectivity. It's fact. But how is it interpreted? An example: you play the ball back to your full back and he's been told that we're going to clip it into the channel, whenever possible. So he does that, and the opposition full back comes across and heads it out for a throw-in. Now in data world, that's an incomplete pass, because the opposition won it. In the real world, the real football world, we've just won a throw-in in the opposition's final third. So the full back has done exactly what we wanted him to do. Well done, son. That's where the people using the information have got to be intelligent enough to understand what they're looking at, and understand its limitations. The crux of the role in many ways is about information. How you get information, how you manage it and how you use it.'

There's gold in them there geeks. Some clubs buy raw data and attempt to develop their own mathematical models. Others use external analysts to initiate the recruitment process. This gives a suspicious, oversensitive or simply lazy manager the comfort blanket of a list of suggested targets, tailored to his needs. Companies such as Prozone and OptaPro seek to assist the process of comparison and cross-checking, which precedes the stampede of a transfer window. They drill down into the quality of passing and possession; plot goals against probability and record a player's touch and stamina.

Prozone's Recruiter programme offers clubs access to detailed biographical and technical information on more than 80,000 players worldwide. Scout7, the English company which bills itself as 'professional football's global leader in the provision of scouting, recruitment, player administration and management solutions', works with 150 major clubs, and has a database of 130,000 players, in 130 nations. It also provides a video scouting package, containing 1600 matches a month, drawn from 126 Leagues across 60 countries. Suddenly, an old school scout's contacts book looks dog-eared, and as relevant as a quill.

Jack Dodd, a Scout7 analyst who specialises in youth recruitment, has seen the weaknesses of the system at first hand: 'Scientific principle can make a difference, even on quite a basic level, but some clubs still judge a twelve-year-old right back by the same criteria by which they judge an eighteen-year-old striker. For want of a better word, it is the lazy part of the football industry. There's something similar in the way some miss the point about *Moneyball*. That was not just about the use of statistics. It was about the use of statistics no one had previously looked at properly. It was about finding value in things people didn't value.'

The profit motive fuels change, and invites extremes of jargon. Prozone's business development director Blake Wooster, whose clients include Manchester United and Real Madrid, espouses the concept of Player

Archaeology. This involves retrospective longitudinal research, which attempts to place pivotal moments in a footballer's development into perspective. Manchester City's James Milner, whose transient career has involved five clubs since his emergence at Leeds as a 16-year-old winger, is deemed to be the perfect specimen.

Wooster's analysts distilled Milner's natural characteristics, such as showing for the ball, crossing, passing and shooting, into a single statistic, Offensive Efficiency. This, in short, was calculated on the number of successful passes, crosses and shots for every pass he received. Two patterns of behaviour stood out. It took time for him to adapt to a new team's playing style, and he often flourished after a loan spell, most pertinently when he spent a season at Aston Villa, from Newcastle, in 2005–06.

Wooster admits: 'Of course, the key is not necessarily what happened, but why it happened. We can all speculate on why Milner's performances improved, and data doesn't provide all the answers, but it's fascinating to use the Player Archaeology as a platform to go back in time and attempt to understand the underlying factors behind performance development. More importantly, if we can consistently identify success patterns, then we can endeavour to replicate the things that worked and avoid the things that didn't.'

True Believers recoil, and bemoan the commercialisation of their community. The sports analytics movement has been largely driven by bloggers and statisticians who have the principled defiance of struggling poets entombed in an attic. Money means more to them in an equation than in a bank account. They disseminate knowledge through cyberspace, on online forums and in research papers. They argue that the reticence of Premier League clubs to offer more than generalities in their sphere of interest ignores the benefits of the 'wisdom of crowds' approach, which has enabled baseball and basketball to develop advanced analytical frameworks.

Ironically, Manchester City, the club backed by unfathomable wealth, best understands the nuances of the process. Gavin Fleig, their head of performance analysis, became the new hero of the Sabermetric Revolution when he persuaded Opta to allow him to share data from the 2011–2012 season, which was coming to a close.

He oversees a team of ten analysts. Four are employed to dissect the performances of the first team. The rest monitor age group squads, from the Under 21 elite development group down to the under 9s. They all operate from what was once a small interview room on the first floor of City's Carrington training complex. The place where such managers as Kevin Keegan, Stuart Pearce and Sven-Goran Eriksson would be within armpit-sniffing reach of sweaty scribblers has been extended to include docking stations, for players to assess the minutiae of their performance. Those undergoing rehabilitation programmes can watch motivational personal highlight packages.

Fleig's manifesto, best expressed in an interview in the *Guardian* in August 2012, was heartfelt, unexpected and a potential game changer: 'Bill James kick-started the analytics revolution in baseball. That made a real difference and has become integrated in that sport. Somewhere in the world there is football's Bill James, who has all the skills and wants to use them but hasn't got the data. We want to help find that Bill James, not necessarily for Manchester City but for the benefit of analytics in football. I don't want to be at another analytics conference in five years' time talking to people who would love to analyse the data but cannot develop their own concepts because all the data is not publicly available.

'The responsibility for developing analytics has always tended to fall on the clubs and that hasn't really changed, even as the community of statisticians, bloggers and students who are focusing on performances and analytics has grown dramatically. Bill James didn't work for a club. He was a statistician with a normal job outside of the sport but he was able to get hold of the data because it was made publicly available by the broadcasters and the league itself. There is a data culture in America. There isn't a data culture in the UK, although we are getting there.

'The whole reason for putting this data out there is to open the doors. The data has value, previously it has been kept in-house and behind guarded doors, but there is now a recognition that clubs need to help this space develop. There are a lot of people out there blogging and doing their own research and they can do a lot more with this data. I hope it will have a big impact on those who want to do research. It might just be the armchair enthusiast. If the worst it does is show a few people that there are different ways of looking at a player's performance, then great. If it helps universities and gets the blogging world talking and coming up with fantastic ways of modelling performance, that is what we want. We want to engage with them.'

Reports of *Moneyball*'s demise in English football had apparently been exaggerated. But, elsewhere, on the dog days of another season, those players beyond the influence and imagination of keyboard dreamers were playing for their lives.

10

Ghost Games

It was just another day in purgatory. The Shrewsbury Town team arrived at Prenton Park in a rust-streaked transit van, borrowed from the Centre of Excellence. The remnants of breakfast, sandwich cartons, cereal bar wrappers and plastic juice bottles, littered the footwells. The collection of strangers, strugglers and condemned men, obliged to represent Tranmere Rovers in a game that officially did not exist, were left to their own devices.

Such matches, played behind closed doors and off limits even to scouts, are football's equivalent of a visit to the Tidy Tip. Professional footballers, items which were once shiny, new and cherished, were being recycled. Of the 13 players used by Tranmere in a 2–0 defeat watched only by manager Ronnie Moore, his coaching staff, chief scout Dave Philpotts and myself, only defender Michael Kay would be around for the 2012–13 season.

Six would be released immediately. The lucky ones would be scattered like seeds on the wind, and find clubs as disparate as Inverness Caledonian Thistle, Wrexham and 1461 Trabzon Karadenizspor, a feeder club in the Turkish First Division. The unlucky ones were left in limbo. Martin Devaney, a typical victim of football's recession, would play a single Irish League game for Bohemians, endure an unsuccessful trial at Portsmouth, and would still be searching for employment in the January 2013 transfer window.

Perhaps the veteran winger, and those around him, should have paid more attention to an abandoned banner which fluttered at the back of a deserted terrace. It read: 'Where there is faith, there is light and strength.' On this mid-May morning in 2012, on a hard pitch scarred by a long season, all three were in short supply. Philpotts, a kindly man despite the harshness of his trade, had seen it all before, in the 16 years he had been searching for bargains on behalf of Merseyside's traditional second club.

We met in the club shop, and paused in an alcove used by groundsman Andy Quayle, close to the dressing rooms. They count the tea bags at Tranmere; these were jumbo-sized, triangular and had to be stretched to infuse four cups. We took the brew, milky and surprisingly strong, upstairs and along a narrow carpeted corridor. Philpotts fumbled with his keys in the darkness before unlocking and furling a metal grille which blocked the entrance to the directors' box. He was at ease, at home.

Born on the Wirral Peninsula, in Bromborough, Philpotts played 221 games for Tranmere in two spells between 1974 and 1985, punctuated by two seasons with the Carolina Lightnin' in the short-lived American Soccer League. He was a rugged central defender in an era in which few prisoners were taken, but the highlight of his career was a headed goal in a 2–0 win over Stockport at Edgeley Park, which secured Tranmere promotion from the old Fourth Division in 1976. The other goal was one of 37 scored that season by Moore, who had returned to the club for a second spell as manager in March, 2012.

The two men resembled a pair of old slippers: they were comfortable, well-worn and perfectly matched. Moore joined us, silently, midway through the first half and took a seat, two places down, to the right of Philpotts. He had worked without guarantees before being given a year's contract as a reward for saving the club from relegation. There was an unconscious chore-ography to their movements, which were marginal yet reflected the ebb and flow of what was a desultory, one-paced game. Their eyes flicked quickly, constantly across the pitch. Their facial expressions were weathervanes, which predicted turbulence. Words were secondary, occasional chimes of doom.

Devaney was the most conspicuous of those going

through the motions. 'He doesn't want to be here,' muttered Moore. As epitaphs go, it was concise, intuitive and damning. Philpotts, whose duty was to focus on the future, nodded without averting his gaze. He was paying particular attention to the triallists, whose performances were shaped by difference in character, as much as variance in natural talent. Midfield player Luke Dobie, in particular, appeared recklessly self-possessed.

'Another day, another dollar,' he had announced to his 1,904 followers on Twitter that morning. 'The cream always rises to the top.' He had obvious technical ability, but a telling fondness for the unproductive Hollywood ball. For a teenager who had been nurtured by Crewe, released by Everton, rejected by Middlesbrough, and had four games on loan at Accrington Stanley, he was remarkably sanguine about the uncertainty shrouding his future. He did himself few favours by conceding possession and allowing Marvin Morgan, Shrewsbury's leggy striker, to score the opening goal.

The second goal highlighted the inner turmoil of goalkeeper Ben Woodhead, who had been released by Burnley at the end of his second year as a scholar. He had travelled from Grimsby, where he had just completed an unsuccessful week's trial. Tall and slender, he was a young 19, conspicuous by his cropped ginger hair and his audible nervousness. He peppered unfamiliar defenders with a stream of consciousness which failed to register, and was a skittish, unconvincing presence.

The staff at Turf Moor had given him a persuasive character reference; he was diligent, intelligent, and regarded as coaching material. Yet the pressure of the occasion had clearly got to him. It was no surprise when he, too, was caught in possession on the right-hand edge of his area. He panicked, and conceded a penalty which Morgan despatched with the minimum of fuss. This prompted Woodhead to emit an unintelligible howl of self-reproach, and volley the base of his left hand upright. 'Fucking hell,' said Philpotts, under his breath. He had seen enough.

Bizarrely, the sounds of children playing in a nearby schoolyard invaded the consciousness. Their joy was an ironic counterpoint to the simultaneous struggle of Ryan Brunt and Jack Law, forwards from Stoke City and Oldham Athletic respectively, to impose themselves. Long before the match ended, Moore had decided to look elsewhere for the two strikers, two wide men and three midfield players he sought to supplement a squad that would be reduced to 18 or 20, for financial reasons.

Philpotts, who had a brief spell as Wigan manager after joining Stockport as a youth coach and scout at the end of his playing career, understands the cadence of life in the lower leagues. He accepts the consequences of the club's frugality. His role had been downgraded to a part-time post for the previous two years, yet he still routinely worked a 70-hour week, in addition to making pin money scouting for Fulham in the North of England.

The game sustained him, but did not dominate him, despite the ferocity of his commitment. He took two weeks off a year, each June. He thought nothing of covering a night game at Exeter, although unnecessary lane restrictions on the M6 and M53 in the early hours, towards the end of a 520-mile round trip, drove him to distraction. On this morning, like so many others, he had let himself in to the ground at eight o'clock.

Tranmere's budget, one of the lowest in League One, precluded the payment of transfer fees. The indignity of unearthing players, who promptly signed for better-paying non-league clubs, came with the territory. Philpotts redressed the balance by delving into local football in Wales; his principal summer loan target would be Jake Cassidy, a richly promising Wolves striker he logged scoring 28 goals in 32 games for Llandudno Junction in the Welsh Alliance. The numbers don't lie:

'At our level, the going rate for a good striker is about fifteen hundred a week. That's way too top heavy for us. Can we get to a grand? We won't mess a lad around, and stretch out negotiations knowing we can only afford a couple of hundred quid, but there's not more than three or four hundred around for most young players. We tell them we will put them in the shop window. You can get frustrated, though, when you see them going into non-league football simply for financial reasons.

'Even if you find someone in non-league you have to be quick. Leave it for a month or six weeks and another league club will have moved in. If three or four get interested there's an auction and a transfer fee. That's us out. I understand the economics of the situation. I understand where the chairman is coming from. He has put six million into the club. He would sell it tomorrow, if he could get his money out. He'd never take this club under, though, because he realises what a friendly, family club it is.

'We all know there are a lot of people in this area suffering, economically. We try to make football as accessible as possible to the public. The club matters to people. We try to attract the younger generation, parents and kids. They identify with our players. I think everyone, fans and directors alike, is realistic about what we are capable of achieving. Logically, with a budget this tight, that means surviving in the division. But that shouldn't stop us from striving to be better, to push for the highest level possible.'

The balance had shifted, to a degree. The days when players would consider a trial as being beneath them were over. Contracts were short term, and trials open ended. Sometimes they stretched up to a month. Decisions were complex, and occasionally dictated by a player's compatibility with the group. This could only be judged over time, when guards would be dropped and true personalities would emerge.

'Trials are useful, but my satisfaction comes in the loan that works out well for everyone. We had Marvin Sordell here, and put him up in rooms above an Italian restaurant close to the ground. It wasn't the Hilton. It was a little test for him. His mum brought him up here; he was a quiet lad, whose confidence only became apparent at game time. He's gone on to do ever so well since, and I feel we played a small part in that.

'The one thing we can offer young players, who might otherwise be lost in the system at a Premier League club, is a good chance of a first team place. We promise never to stand in their way, if they excel. We will also do anything we can for them, as footballers and as young men. I love to sit down with them, and hear what they want to achieve. They are conditioned to keeping a lot of things to themselves. I always tell them that all they have to do is knock on my door, if they have any problems. I hate to think of them as being isolated, with no one to turn to.'

It is that humanity which defines a certain type of scout, and a certain type of club. At the age of 58, Philpotts had acquired the wisdom required to play a pastoral role, suited to Tranmere's social status. He saw the human cost of progress in his profession, and rejected the cost–benefit analysis of a new generation of cyberscouts, who lacked experience, empathy and understanding.

'The Prozone stuff is putting a few good men out of work. We can't afford it, and I've been fortunate to work with managers who like to sit opposite me and get answers about players face to face, instead of on a computer screen. The industry changes so much, so quickly, and I've been at this club for such a long time. We've had our ups and downs but the honesty of the place attracts me. People ask me why I'm still here. I've had my opportunities to move on, but family is more important.'

The disappointments of the day would be put into perspective, soon enough. Philpotts was a registered carer, not just for his aged mother, but for his younger brother. He was 51, and suffering from the same unexplained disease which claimed the life of another brother, at the age of 51. The prognosis was not good. Prenton Park provided a release. It was not a place to waste time, dreaming about what might, could and should have been.

Neither was the Griffin Park boardroom, which had been opened up for a boot sale, a behind-closed-doors match against Reading's development squad. The scenario was similar; players on both sides had the vulnerability of abandoned kittens. In this case, 18 scouts were in on the deal. Each, without exception, paid their respects to John Griffin, a man who exuded the quiet dignity of an old soldier at a regimental reunion. There was a reassuring generosity of spirit in the gesture of

John Ward, Colchester's manager, who put an arm on his shoulder and chuckled: 'We'd turn up for an opening of an envelope at this time of year, wouldn't we?'

Griffin is the scout's scout. He has spent 40 years operating in and around London, largely for Crystal Palace, Fulham and Brentford. Hundreds of players owe their careers to his perception and sensitivity. Some, like Alan Pardew and Sean O'Driscoll, have developed into accomplished managers and coaches. They still call for discreet advice. Others, such as Stan Collymore and Ian Wright, were complex, compulsive characters, reinvented as media seers. All revere a man of Gandalfian sagacity, whose serene disposition disguises sharp street wisdom.

At 72, retirement was not an option. Griffin was working in straitened circumstances at Wycombe, where his loyalty to embattled manager Gary Waddock had a paternal intensity. The club was in meltdown. Griffin responded by helping to raise £1 million. He liaised with Waddock to alert Mel Johnson to the availability of Jordon Ibe, and engineered a £350,000 move to Cardiff for teenaged winger Kadeem Harris. Relegation to League Two was of minimal significance, compared to the arrest, on February 24 2012, of club owner Steve Hayes as part of Operation Tuleta, the Metropolitan Police's investigation into allegations of computer hacking.

Hayes, a former double glazing salesman who once

sold secondary mortgages for his father-in-law, was said to be worth £50 million, following the sale of an internet loans company he established in 1997, and promoted through tenuous links to such gaudy celebrities as Jordan. But Wycombe, together with Wasps, the Premiership rugby club which Hayes also owned, were in limbo. Griffin's determination to prepare for the 2012–13 season would be irrelevant if negotiations to cede control to a Supporters' Trust broke down.

'Some of these players we're watching today will be available for loan next year,' he rationalised as he sipped tea at one of six tables, arranged beside the bar in the Brentford boardroom. 'That's all I can look for, and that's if we have got a club at all. The way things are going with the owner there has to be a doubt. He says the club is losing a million pounds a year. I find that difficult to believe. We are the worst-paid team in League One by a distance, and we've sold the two kids for a million. Yet when we wanted to buy a lad from non-league for seven and a half grand we were told there's no money. How can that be?'

A sardonic smile signalled the irony of the moment. He had survived similar strife during two spells at Brentford. 'They named this place after me, you know,' he said, with a self-deprecating laugh. Experience and necessity dictated that he develop a Micawberish mentality that something would turn up. He was made redundant after his first period as Brentford's chief scout, in the mid-1980s, but was the pivotal figure at the club during his second spell, between 1997 and 2008:

'Twice, when we thought we were going into administration, I sold somebody I brought here for nothing out of non-league. The first was Paul Smith, the goalkeeper. I'll be honest, I stuck some stories into newspapers to try and liven it up. I got him sold to Southampton for three hundred thousand. That kept us going. A few years later I took DJ Campbell from Yeading. I was sitting in this very room, doing the deal, when Martin Allen, who was manager, walked in and said: "Just tell them to fuck off." I told him the kid was going to score a lot of goals, so he took him for twenty-five grand. We were in trouble again within six months, and we sold him to Birmingham for half a million. I don't look for credit, but I've seen some things. I know I saved this club from going to the wall, twice. That's a fact.'

The circumstances which led to Griffin's initial association with Brentford were revealing. He had made his name by helping Terry Venables assemble the so-called 'Team of the Eighties' at Crystal Palace. That was destined to disintegrate after Kenny Sansom, its marquee player, was sold to Arsenal, and he was in the process of developing another youth programme at Fulham when he left on a point of principle:

'Ted Buxton was chief scout at Fulham when I was at Palace. To this day, I still think he's the nicest man

I've met in my life. They wanted to make Ted a paid director, and he must have told them about me. Bobby Campbell, who was manager at the time, took me aside after a game and had a long chat. He said they wanted me to come over as chief scout and youth development officer, but that I could never have the title. Ted would keep that so he could be paid as a director. That was how it was done in those days. People got a little extra by a tweak in the system. Matt Busby tried to keep it quiet, but everyone knew he had the club shop at Man United.

'I loved it there, and brought a team through. I signed Jim Stannard, who played about five hundred games in goal, and Paul Parker, who did major things with England and Manchester United. John Marshall, who played about four hundred games, later became chief scout and now works for England. Dean Coney played for England under twenty-ones. I'm as proud of that group as anything I have done, but one day Bobby Campbell wouldn't take a schoolboy player I'd recommended.

'The boy stuttered, badly. When I put the lad up, Bobby said to me, "he will really struggle to have a career" and never signed him. I left for that reason. Brentford had been chasing me for ages and my best friend at the time, Fred Callaghan, had just become manager. I rang him up, and said, "If you let me start a youth policy, I'll come over." I was determined to start that lad off, and give him a career.'

Terry Rowe signed youth forms for Brentford, where he made 105 first team appearances before leaving for the United States. He justified the faith of his mentor by having a 17-year professional career, playing in four separate leagues for such iconic American clubs as the Tampa Bay Rowdies.

'It's strange,' said Griffin. 'People still ask me what I see when I spot talent. I see a player but I also try to see the person. I've signed hundreds of players, and I can't remember all their names because the old memory is going to be honest, but each one is special to me. Over the years I've found them all different ways. I've taken players from the Wessex League, the Conference, the Southern League, everywhere, anywhere and anyhow. I took Sean O'Driscoll from Alvechurch to Fulham, simply because I used to have the *Birmingham Evening Mail*, the one that came out on a Saturday evening with all the games in. It would arrive at Craven Cottage on a Monday and I just kept seeing the name, well two to be precise, Sean O'Driscoll and Richard O'Kelly. It's funny how they've remained together, in management.

'I just had to go up there to see for myself. They were both good players but within ten minutes I knew Sean was exactly what I was looking for. Scouting is about following up that hunch. It's about your nose for a player. With Stan Collymore, I was having a goalkeeper at Stafford Rangers watched. People had gone two or three times and said, "good keeper, got a chance, but a major mistake in every game". One Saturday I couldn't find a game to go to. I saw Barnet were playing Stafford in the Conference, so went to see the keeper. He did allright. In fact, he went on and played for Birmingham – can't remember his name, but he was big, six foot five, six foot six, and had a little bit of a career.

'But I'm standing there, when the teams run out. As they did so, I went, "Why has nobody told me about this fella?" It was Stan. You just knew by his movement, by his athleticism, by the way he walked, even, that he was a player. Within five minutes I knew I was going to sign him, just knew it. I really believe if you're a good scout you can honestly walk out after half an hour, and know what player you could take. It was the same with Ian Wright. I knew instantly we had to have him. It had nothing to do with his ability. His attitude just marked him out. I've never seen a player with such visible hunger to prove everyone wrong.

'I always say to my scouts, once you've seen it, your job's over, go. It doesn't matter if it takes ten, fifteen, twenty minutes. You're not there to enjoy the game – it's a job, very much a job. I've walked out many times at half-time. It's nothing to me, a game between two sides I have nothing to do with. You either see the player in time, or you don't, and you go home. No one is infallible. There have been times I haven't spotted a player, when I should have done. I once saw Leyton Orient play Newport County with Maurice Evans, who was then manager at Reading. I knew he was scouting someone, but couldn't work out who it was. The following week he signed John Aldridge. He's still one of my favourite players ever, and I never noticed him. Everybody laughs at me when I say Joe Public can judge a player. The fan who knows the game could name, within twenty minutes, the best player on the pitch. I don't think you have to be the football brain of Britain. The trick is to lose concentration on the game, and concentrate on the individual. I do get annoyed with managers and coaches. You send them to see a player, and you will be amazed the amount of times they come back and start talking through the game and the systems. I've no interest whether a team started off playing 4–4–2 and then changed to a 4–3–3.

'You're there to look at the player. It's not in their psyche to do that. They look at it in a completely different way, with a coach's eye. Even if you specify what you want him to see, he will come back and tell you about every player, everything. You might not say it, but you'll think, no, that's not what you're there for. They can't concentrate on an individual, in the way a scout is brought up to do.'

Outside, raindrops, shed from the roof of the main stand, were refracting in soft sunlight after a sharp shower. The match had just kicked off when we parked ourselves at the back of the directors' box. Seven of the Reading side, including striker Jacob Walcott, a distant cousin of Arsenal's Theo, would be released. Griffin did not reveal his intentions to those around him, but had confided his interest in Gozie Ugwu. The long-limbed striker had been brought to his attention by Liam Daish, one of his former players, who had managed him during a two-month loan at Ebbsfleet United in the Conference. 'A foal,' he murmured. 'Got to grow into himself a bit, but would do us for a season.'

It was another eerie, ritualistic exercise. Players' studs clattered across the deserted terraces as they retrieved the ball. It was a harsh, percussive sound, lacking the soothing rhythms of well-shoed horses, cantering along a country road. Urgent entreaties – 'c'mon, winners' – seemed utterly out of place. Everyone winced at the rifle's retort of a clash of heads between Brentford defender Leon Legge and Reading defender Angus MacDonald, who carried on, bloody and groggy.

Brentford's goalkeeping coaches were watching discreetly from the upper tier of the Wendy House stand, behind the left-hand goal. Antoine Gounet, signed from Tours, conformed to every Gallic stereotype. He attempted step-overs while under pressure in his own penalty area, punched the ball when he should have caught it, and generally behaved with a manic lack of care and consideration. 'He'll be on the way back at half-time,' said Griffin. 'You'd never guess he's French, would you? No, no, no. Taxi for Calais.'

Gounet was, indeed, replaced at the interval, when

Griffin was approached by Luton manager Paul Buckle and his technical director Lil Fuccillo, who returned just as the second half started to ask for a number for Steve Shorey, Reading's chief scout. 'They're interested in my player,' Griffin whispered. 'I'll get the gaffer to call on the way home. We'd be good for the kid for a year. We'll see what he can become, rather than what he is now.'

Football works in mysterious ways. It transpired that Reading wanted Ugwu to go on loan in League One. Yeovil manager Gary Johnson, who happens to be Griffin's nephew, was the beneficiary of Wycombe's rejection. The veteran scout didn't share Waddock's enthusiasm for Reading's Jordan Obita, which would also remain unrequited. Griffin did not see enough to trust the young winger's intermittent flashes of instinctive talent in a game which was won by Brentford, courtesy of an Antonio German penalty.

Memories provided respite from the tedium of a match which staggered over the line like a dehydrated marathon runner. Griffin recalled the unforeseen benefits of sending Dennis Bailey, whom he had signed for Palace from Farnborough, on loan to Bristol Rovers. 'There was always a goal in Dennis, and Steve Coppell asked me to keep tabs on him,' he explained. 'I watched him four times, but my eye kept getting drawn to the Rovers keeper. I told Steve we just had to sign him. It was Nigel Martyn. We bought him for a million, and sold him for five. He played for England. I saw him recently. He has a caravan in the New Forest. I went to a site down the road and there he was, larger than life. A real nice Cornish man. His wife was a strong one. Not like today's players, eh?

'I remember Gal, my nephew, signing John Akinde for Bristol City from Ebbsfleet. It was a strange one. It was the first transfer ever decided by a poll of the fans. I first saw him when he was eighteen and working in a cinema in Gravesend. He helped Ebbsfleet win the FA Trophy. Akinde had it all, pace, strength and power, but he had no idea what he was going to do when he came anywhere near the ball. He was a million miles away from being a player, but there was something there. Gal took a chance on him, but when I heard the details I rang him and said, "What have you done?" He'd given him fifteen hundred quid a week, a car and a flat for six months. Where was his incentive? He was ruined. With a player like that you give him three hundred quid, and tell him to earn it if he asks for more. I love Gal like a son, but. . . .'

If blood is thicker than water, Griffin also understood Dave Philpotts' concerns about the culture shift which was accelerating, and subtly changing the dynamics of his job. He identified with the insecurity of Mel Johnson, who was in limbo at Liverpool, following the sacking of Kenny Dalglish. Johnson attempted to retain a semblance of normality, submitting cautionary reports on such young players as Blackpool's Matt Phillips, but received no feedback. The silence was unnerving, unyielding.

It was impossible not to relate to his quiet dignity and sense of impotence. 'I've had a great run,' he said, as the rumours swirled. 'I've been very, very lucky. I've always worked hard. I've always gone to as many games as possible. I love watching players. I've only ever been moved out once in twenty-seven years. It can happen straight away or it can take time, or you can get to know the people that take over and you can be OK with them.'

In extremis, the Nowhere Men look after their own. Despite the distractions, Johnson joined Griffin in attempting to promote scouts for whom he had respect, on a personal and a professional basis. Each continued to encourage Dean Austin to pursue a role as chief scout for a club of appropriate stature. Griffin also recommended Steve Jones, who had been released by Sheffield United following their loss on penalties in the League One play-off final at Wembley, for a newly created post at AFC Wimbledon.

'If you're a chief exec, scouting is the first thing you'll cut back on if things go wrong,' Griffin rationalised. 'They've always looked for petty savings from us. I did hear a story from Terry Venables about Alan Sugar. He reckoned one of the first decisions he made when he got into Tottenham was to cut the two pints of milk in the scouts' area to one, to save money, because he was always trying to save money.

'You still need the old-fashioned scout who goes out and stands on the grass. The analytical scout can go and make a further judgement if necessary. They do their jobs well, but are a different breed of people. They would never dream of standing behind a goal and watching. I don't disrespect them for that. We are totally different animals. What they do is also expensive. I don't think it can filter down into League One or Two.

'At my level, it is difficult to employ more than one or two scouts. At Wycombe I've just got the one guy, who is on expenses only. That's all I can have. Financially we just can't do any more. I can understand why people talk about the benefits of technical scouting, but it would cost so much to set up and run, it couldn't possibly be done below the level of the Premier League, or a really top-quality Championship club.'

It was not shaping up to be a Summer of Love.

11

Yellow Ten and the Custard Cream Kid

The chosen few lounged on beaches lapped by the Caribbean, or partied in seven-star ghettoes beside the Arabian Gulf. The wannabes, who envied the lifestyle of football's rich and famous, and had convinced themselves of the legitimacy of their ambitions, sought to emulate Sakho Bakare. As career strategies go, that had its limitations. Bakare was unemployed, separated from his family and sleeping on the sofa in a succession of friends' houses.

The French forward was deemed a success by those unversed in the ways of the football world, simply because of his rarity value; he got something for the £50 he paid to participate in the lottery of a mass off-season trial. It had earned him a year in the Evo-Stik Southern League with St Albans City, where he was given £100 a week and as many free chips as he could eat from Andy's Gourmet Burger van, situated in the corner of the tree-lined Clarence Park ground.

I had seen him play there just before he was released, at the end of the 2011-12 season. Clarence Park was a place of suburban gentility, reached by a wooden walkway from a bridge. Anxious parents fussed over children, amusing themselves noisily on swings and climbing frames in a rubber-crumbed playground. A sheepdog, with a blue and yellow Saints scarf wrapped around its neck, dozed in the shadow cast by another van, which dispensed coffee. Bakare had justified his pedigree as a one-season wonder in the Swiss League with Neuchatel Xamax by scoring 15 goals, yet was utterly dysfunctional.

He was tall, and the thinness of his legs was emphasised by the fashionable habit of stretching his socks over his knees. He loped, rather than ran, and his lack of co-ordination suggested he was not in full control of his limbs. He struggled to do the simple things automatically, and had the peripheral vision of a mole. His awareness of his teammates was minimal, and a source of collective frustration. But he had a physical presence. Occasionally, in a fusion of fortunate timing and sheer instinct, he took the breath away.

He provided the highlight of a dour 1–1 draw with Banbury United just before half-time, when he met a headed clearance on the right-hand edge of the penalty area. He fashioned a scissor kick as he fell with the grace of a flamingo in a high wind. The ball swerved and dipped, but cannoned to safety off the crossbar, with opposing goalkeeper Andy Kemp as astonished a spectator as the rest of us, in a crowd of 482. The Official Sakho Bakare Appreciation Society had 173 likes on Facebook, but the fans' forum which summed him up as 'egg beater or world beater' represented a more measured judgement.

Bakare was 27, too old, too unreliable and too high maintenance. Scouts representing Morecambe, Dagenham & Redbridge and Luton were unimpressed. St Albans manager David Howell was sanguine about their disinterest. A protégé of Barry Fry, he understood the limitations of the type of open audition staged by Barnet, one of a number of small clubs who used them to address cash flow problems. He liked the man, a devout Muslim whose love of biscuits had led to him being given the soubriquet 'The Custard Cream Kid' in the local press, but knew the shortcomings of the footballer:

'Sakho definitely has ability, but has to learn to work within a team. At this level you have to put the work in. A lot of the lads are part time. There's really nowhere for us to train. We can only use certain parts of the pitch in midweek. That in itself is challenging. People have been looking at him, but not enough boxes are being ticked. Is he mentally strong enough? Is he a one-trick pony? He needs to listen, to follow instructions better. It is as simple as that. His mindset is telling him to do something different. Our biggest enemies, as coaches, are deeply ingrained bad habits.

'The trial at Barnet was awful, to be honest. There were players with their agents, their parents, their partners and their mates. It was a free for all. I asked for numbers for three or four players, to disguise my interest in Sakho. We were light up front and needed someone to fit into a pattern. It is strange, but I remember the exact sequence of play when I noticed him. He took the ball on his chest around about the halfway line, went to go right and shimmied back on to his left. He got the ball out to the right wing, and immediately headed into the box with a real sense of urgency. That stuck.

'He's a lovely lad, but he speaks no English. He fell out with his agent and I kept getting texts from his landlord, who wasn't getting paid. It turns out he was going from house to house, relying on friends and sleeping where he could. He was on the streets for one or two nights. His family is still in France, and he is seeing where football will take him. He has his dreams and aspirations. This is his way out. But, at this level, a lot of people are deluded.'

The truth behind such a bleak statement was written in cyberspace. Scouts of any substance tended to shy away from the open days, unless they needed a little pocket money to see them through to the pre-season friendlies. A whole range of initiatives, some as well intentioned as others were brazenly exploitative, gave the impression that fame was just a click, and a series of 20-minute trial matches, away. It was here, on the internet, that football's flotsam and jetsam found a disembodied, confused voice:

Hello Scouts, Agents and Managers, I have a Ghanaian footballer who plays just like Ashley Cole of Chelsea fc, anybody interested to have him try out how good strong, talented left footed young boy.

I HAVE TOP STRIKER 1994 FROM EGYPT PLAY IN THE BEST TEAM IN AFRICA AND NT OF EGYPT. WANT TO PLAY IN ENGLAND OR SPAIN OR TOP TEAM IN EUROPE. FOR CV AND VIDEO PLEASE CONTACT ME.

PLAYERS. SPANISH INTERNACIONAL U16 LOOKING NEW CLUB TOP IN EUROPE. Contact Sergio.

Scout, Manager and Agent interested in coming to Nigeria to Scout for Players or have a look at African talent on grassroots level and become pro for great deals. We will provide accommodation and security, throughout Nigeria. As we all known that African as a whole has good talented players, who need sincere and honest scout from European countries and Asia to help them show case there talent to the world. We are going to arrange for match, trials for the players in the present of the agent scout and managers to evaluate the players that suit such agent, scout and Manager Thanks to you all, God bless.

I know 20-year old soccer player who wants to be a professional soccer player in the world. If you need the player to introduce to professional soccer clubs, please let me know.

Have a great European Goalkepeer 1.12.95 looking for a UK academy can anyone assist!!

I have some young quality good players I want to sponsor for trial. Please, I need club to invite my players, I will buy their tickets to come over for trial. Please email me if you are in need of players. I have 2 strikers and 1 midfielder. And some others available play.

I am an English-born (mixed race Spanish, St Lucian and English) attacking player. My perfect position would be just behind the striker(s) and in front of the midfield. Football trials from a top company.

Taken individually, the messages had the troubling poignancy of a love letter from a fleeting acquaintance. Viewed collectively, they conformed to a pattern, a combination of spam and scam. These were shards of dreams, momentary insights into empty lives. They damned the system, and the sport which encouraged them. Demand for footballers was increasingly specific;

supply was inexhaustible. Recruitment, on the margins, was unregulated and unseemly. The better scouts, appreciative of their responsibilities as arbiters, were more comfortable with convention.

The Premier League and Football League outsourced exit trials, for young men released by academies and centres of excellence. Some were tailored to identifiable markets, such as the American College system. The majority were essentially a cross between a careers fair and a cattle market. These typically featured between 100 and 150 players, and were distinguished by certain rules and regulations. Scouts were forbidden from directly approaching players or their parents. Instead, they were required to lodge expressions of interest, which could be monitored appropriately.

The most intriguing initiative had commercial connotations, but was driven by altruism. The Nike Academy was unashamedly a marketing tool, but, as a human experiment, it had depth, credibility and value. It operated out of Loughborough University, and featured a fluid squad of around 18 players, under the age of 20, previously released by professional clubs. It was exclusive, and all-inclusive. The boys lived on campus, received cutting-edge scientific support, and had eight hours' contact time with tutors each week so they could continue, or resume, their education. They were supervised by Premier League staff, had the security of one-year contracts, and were expected to focus on a single objective, impressing visiting scouts, and getting back into the professional game.

Head coach Jimmy Gilligan, a former Watford and Cardiff City striker, also scouted for the England Under 21 squad. The Nike Academy was fed by two talent identification programmes: The Chance, a global competition featuring 100,000 players from 55 countries, and annual trials, which featured up to 200 players, released by British clubs. Twelve of the squad from the 2011–12 season were given professional contracts. The example they set was powerful, inspirational.

David Accam had gone from Evesham United, in Division One of the Southern League, to playing for Helsingborg in the Champions League. Tom Rogic, an attacking midfield player who won The Chance, was a full Australian international at 19, and had a four-and-a-half-year contract at Celtic. Alex Whittle, initially rejected by Liverpool, was a first team regular at Dunfermline. Exeter retained their faith in defender Jordan Tillson, despite a freak metatarsal injury which kept him out for five months. Other graduates were developing their careers in Scandinavia, South Africa, Belarus, Ireland and Italy.

The class of 2012–13 began to take shape on a windy day, under a weak sun, on a pitch set on a plateau behind the university's new stadium. Thirty-five survivors of the initial trials were split into two squads, yellow and blue, who would compete in three forty-minute matches.

They were evaluated by Gilligan, fitness adviser Jon Goodman, assistant coach Matt Wells and goalkeeping coach Mark Goodlad. 'We're doing due diligence,' said Gilligan. 'We're making assessments of players technically, tactically and physically, but also looking at them as young men and human beings.'

A couple of boys released by Chelsea had abandoned the trials that morning, preferring to gamble on their association with the club generating interest. 'They're in a bubble,' said Goodman, who was sitting on a blue plastic drinks box, as the hopefuls warmed up. 'It pains me to say it, but they've probably had their careers. These boys are all quite nice footballers, but we're looking for that little something that separates those who make it, and those who don't. Some struggle to understand this process. This is about the individual, not the team. We have somehow to identify the character of those who will work with us.'

This was a challenge to football's *modus operandi*, which involves choosing the most talented, and extemporising from there. It involved elements of the SAS recruitment strategy; Special Forces look beyond basic competencies and select on the basis of a candidate's capacity for self-improvement. David Goldsmith, a striker released by West Bromwich Albion, was asked, casually, to take the yellow team's warm-up. He didn't appear to realise his leadership qualities were being scrutinised, subtly, but the strength of his character, and his ease of command, shone through. He was a goal up, before kick-off.

'Everything that I've seen tells me there is a place for this type of academy,' said Gilligan, as he stood on a hill, surveying the scene. 'These kids need help before they get that ninety minute trial game, in front of a scout or a manager. They need time to develop. They need time to practise. They need time to be mentored. We've had twelve professional contracts, out of the door, in the last year. What would have happened to those players without something like this? Where would they have gone? Who would have seen them? Who would have picked them up?

'When I took this job I had to trawl around the country at a hundred miles an hour. I was saying to clubs, "You've got these scholars out there, these neo-pros you don't want. Send them to us." They are taking it on board now, but are still conditioned to ask what the catch is when they want someone. The catch is, we will give you a player. There's no baggage. You take him into your football club. He gets the best contract he can out of you, and hopefully he'll go on and do very, very well for you. He's a free agent. We want nothing. Not a bean. It simply gives me, my bosses at Nike, and the money people at the Premier League great, great joy when we get a player back into the game. That is, for us, the pinnacle of what we're trying to achieve.'

Fourteen spectators watched the trial unfold. Two

were scouts from American universities. Eleven were parents. They stood alone, imprisoned in an invisible force field of angst and apprehension. Their furrowed brows, furled umbrellas and Tupperware boxes, containing snacks, testified to the familiarity of the ordeal. The solitary club representative was David Dodds, assistant academy manager at Reading. He offered moral support to Jorge Grant, who had been released because of a numbers game, triggered by the desire of Anton Zingarevich, the club's new Russian owner, to replenish the academy with prospects from Europe, and beyond.

The folly of the decision was instantly apparent. Grant, known as 'Yellow Ten' for the day, was, at 17, one of the youngest triallists. Small but nimble, he moved with the fluidity of a fawn in flight across open country. He was billed as a central midfield player, but his game intelligence allowed him to operate wide, on either flank, or as a second striker. He had a great appreciation of space and an eye for goal. Gilligan reminded his brains trust, 'This is all about who we can get out of the back door, and into a club.' Giving Grant an opportunity to do so was a no-brainer:

'Talent ID, and scouting, is all about opinions. So when you're looking at a sixteen- to twenty-one-year old, you ask yourself: has the player got progression in him? Clubs will look to see how someone like the Yellow Ten can fit into the club structure: is he going into the first team squad, the development group, or is he just going to be a scholar for two years? A clever chairman and a clever director of youth or head of academy would weigh up his sell-on potential.

'We live in an imperfect world, in football. That boy, by rights, should be getting a contract. Someone should be working on him, on his development, physically, technically and tactically. If you gave him the right amount of coaching hours, and the right amount of advice, I can't see any reason why that boy wouldn't go and play in someone's first team in this country. But, and it's a huge but, with money coming into clubs, people look further afield. They are prepared to pay more. I don't necessarily have an axe to grind with that, but I would question the assumption that paying more for a young player means he will necessarily get better.

'Sometimes you just know. A lad like the one we are talking about might need to grow into what this programme is about. He's only a young one, remember. What that boy's got going for him, that everyone can see, is that he can play. He's got technical ability. But he's also got an unbelievable amount of potential, bags and bags of it. For a coach or a scout, that's a huge buzz. To be able to say "that kid sees it, he's got progression in him" is really, really exciting.'

Other decisions would not be so clear cut. Following the trial, Gilligan and his brains trust retired to a self-styled 'War Room' in the academy offices on the far side of the campus. An A4-sized photograph of each boy was placed, face up, on some tables, which had been pushed together. The coaches had their own notes, supplemented by physiological and biographical information. Video clips were available, from a laptop, if required.

'What's coming through the door, then?' said Gilligan, with a jauntiness which belied the gravity of potentially life-changing decisions which would be taken, over the next hour or so. 'Ground rules. We remove the people we all agree on from the table. Any question mark, they stay there. Those we are definitely not going to take, we turn over, face down. We will send official letters tonight, maybe phone a few immediately. No point in keeping them waiting.' The debate quickly gathered momentum. In true football fashion, it featured directness, bordering on cruelty, and subjectivity, laced with compassion:

'I absolutely hated him . . . Action Man legs . . . I expected more . . . I'm all over the Yellow Five . . . good talker, great weight of pass, super timing of runs . . . is he all hair flicks and no output? . . . liked how hard he worked, when the modern game tells them just to look good . . . he's buzzing for it, very polite . . . wants to score ugly goals . . . if we have to work with chicken shit, and turn it into chicken salad, we will . . . he's as ugly as fuck, can't run, but he's a battering ram . . . this kid is going to be a joy to work with . . . he's got a long drive back to Scotland, let's give him something to be happy about.'

Thirteen players were offered contracts, subject to passing a medical. In addition to Grant, the early stand-out was Cameron Edwards, an Australian also released by Reading. A technically accomplished central midfield player, comfortable playing on the left in a 4–3–3 system, he had an impressive range of passing and hidden reserves of character. 'He's been sick as a dog all week, and didn't want to tell anyone,' revealed Gilligan, after Edwards had been unanimously approved. 'Are we all happy? Lot of work to be done with that lot. Lot of work can be done with that lot.'

Once decisions had been taken, the mood eased, and the human dimension of the exercise became clear. Whittle and Tillson, two of the previous season's success stories, had attended the trial, hungover from the previous night's leaving party. Before collecting their belongings from the hall of residence, they asked Gilligan to pop into the room they shared. They were awkward, but handed him a bottle of wine, with the message 'We couldn't have done this without you.' The old pro, a survivor of a hard school, was touched:

'The simple act of saying thank you goes a million ways down the line for me. I don't want someone to shower me with gifts and cards and stuff like that, but I want them to be appreciative of everybody who has played a part in their lives. There are some terrific scouts out there. There are terrific managers, coaches and development staff. But no one individual makes a player. Without the component parts, without the human jigsaw, it wouldn't happen.

'For me, the biggest accolade is to have a player shake your hand and spend time with you. I never signed Jobi McAnuff at Wimbledon, but I did a little work with him there that had an impact. He's a terrific young lad, a very, very talented player who has been a credit to himself and the Premier League. I was doing some work for a specialist sports college some time back and needed a guest footballer to open a playground at a little junior school. He was playing at Watford, my old club, and I asked him if he would do it. He came out of his way, drove himself there, and spent two hours longer with the kids than he was meant to. I rang him up afterwards to thank him and he said, "No problem, absolutely no problem at all. I loved it." They are the kind of things for me, that matter.

'Modern players have so much done for them. I understand the principle of stripping everything else away so that they can concentrate on football, but we also need to teach kids how to speak to people. How to look people in the eye, how to shake their hands, say good morning. They will need people skills, because not all of them will make it. Is their agent going to get them a job when they are out of the game? Are Mum and Dad going to answer the interview questions for them? You can't grunt and groan your way through life. The fact you've been a footballer doesn't mean someone is going to give you a job.

'There are millions unemployed. These boys are in the rat race with everyone else. They need to match the skills their contemporaries have, coming out of college or university. Football is a fantastic vehicle and I don't want to take anything away from it; academies are a fantastic concept. But I also believe we can't underplay the morals and values of our young men. We must make them responsible for their own actions in life. If we do so, they will be better for it. There is a massively holistic aspect to what we do.

'The kids that come to us are broken. We patch them up and put them back together. We try to educate them, so that they have a Plan B. If I was to take a penny for every time I've said well done to a kid this year, I would be a millionaire. You have to build them up, but remind them about the bread and butter of the trade they want to enter. The real world, of professional football, involves making sure your manager doesn't wake up in a cold sweat, having selected you for tomorrow's team. I tell the lads the game has just let them out on loan. We're going to get them back in at some point. That might take two weeks, two months or two years, and first, they are going to have to help themselves.'

While Gilligan was preparing to entice scouts, by outlining a programme of 43 matches against development teams from the UK and Europe, smaller clubs were drawing up contingency plans to repel them. The probability of poaching was preoccupying Shaun O'Connor, in his role as Head of Academy Recruitment at Brentford. He intended to make life as difficult as possible for scouts from September 2012, when they were allowed unfettered access to training grounds as part of the controversial EP3 strategy. His idealism, however, was tempered by realism. He had little option but to acknowledge he was a product of the pitiless climate in which he was operating:

'It's getting desperate, absolutely desperate, out there. I've no doubt some of my boys have been tapped up. Let me find a piece of wood before I say this, but it looks as if we have done quite well. I left Arsenal's under tens with some outstanding young players, scouted at six and seven. I don't have their money, but I'm convinced we can be OK. Miguel's new academy group, the under nines, are great; sixteen boys, so we have two eight-a-side teams.

'We've studied Everton and Liverpool at that level. Both great clubs, but Everton are doing the better job, between the ages of six and twelve. They do it properly. They are sharper, ruthless. Chelsea are starting to do the same thing. I'm telling my club to get in there early, get the best boys we can between six and twelve. If we see an under seven that we like, we'll pull him out of his Sunday side.

'I know people will probably not agree with this, but we will bring him in for three days a week. We work hard to build a relationship with the parents, and hope they will sanction a pre-agreement with us. We will give him full technical training and a game each week, but will try to hide him. We will give him one game out of London each month. We'll play at least ten games in that sequence, against the likes of Liverpool, Wolves, Derby and Norwich.

'The problem from the club's point of view is that it is a big cycle. You are waiting for ten to twelve years for your work to pay off. I'd argue, though, that paying big money for fourteen or fifteen-year-olds is a much bigger risk. Take Sheyi Ojo, who has cost Liverpool two mill. I'd have wanted seven or eight exhaustive reports on him before doing anything. He's strong and powerful at the moment, but how will he develop? How will he deal with the physical and mental challenges?'

The question was pertinent, because O'Connor had something, someone, special to protect. He, too, was 14. Talent usually announces itself with a fanfare; all Courtney Senior required was an instinctive flick of a shiny black boot with fluorescent green studs. It came, one evening, towards the end of a small-sided Under 16 training game. His body had the pliability of plasticine as he received an overhit pass, to the left of the goal. He controlled the ball, feinted to his left in the same sinuous movement, and flicked the ball past the goalkeeper with the outside of his right foot.

The urge to make eye contact with O'Connor was overpowering, just as it had been with Mel Johnson, when Paulo Gazzaniga made The Save at Oxford. I mouthed a name: 'Jermaine Defoe'. Ose Aibangee, Brentford's head of youth development, was standing alongside us. He whistled through his teeth. 'That,' he announced, in hushed tones, 'is a centre forward. Pure instinct.' The barber's son, discovered playing in a park in Carshalton by scout Carl Davey, quickly became a rumour made flesh. Chelsea and Manchester City led the stampede to take a look.

Not for the first time, Brentford were in danger of being too good for their own good. Senior helped their Under 15 team win the Milk Cup, the most prestigious pre-season tournament in youth football. They beat a Liverpool side containing Oji 5–4 on penalties in the semi-final before defeating Everton, winners in four of the previous five seasons, 2–0 in the final. To put the achievement into perspective, Brentford finished 23rd out of 24 sides when they made their debut in the competition in 2010.

'Every club's looking at Courtney now' O'Connor confirmed. 'There has been talk at first team level about this kid, so we have to be very careful. Well, we can't be careful, to be honest. At the end of the day, if the biggest clubs want to get him, they're going to get him.

Their money tends to talk. I don't want to give a player away for any amount of compensation, because it doesn't really compensate, does it? But I have to accept the way of the world. If a Chelsea or a City come along after twenty games and say he's going to be a player, then we'll probably sell him.'

12

I'm Still There

Mark Anderson had played his last pop anthem, after two decades as an occasional DJ. He had handed in his hard hat along with his responsibility for a £1.5 million construction contract in Wandsworth. He was back in football on a full-time basis for the first time in 11 years, as Brighton's head of youth recruitment. His calling card was a letter, encased in a silver frame, which had pride of place in his new open-plan offices at the American Express Community Stadium:

On behalf of Academy Director Frank McParland and Kenny Dalglish I just want to thank you for your part in the signing of RAHEEM STERLING from Queens Park Rangers. As you know, there was a lot of interest from very big clubs in RAHEEM and this makes a massive statement on behalf of Liverpool Football Club, with regards to recruitment in England. Let's go and find the next one!

The letter, signed by David Moss, the former Luton winger who is the academy's chief scout in the UK, was inevitably a source of scorn and ridicule. The coaches and scouts with whom Anderson worked were conditioned to make fun of his artlessness and enthusiasm. It was the sort of perverse gesture of respect in which football specialised. The target of their stage-managed cynicism was so exultant he was beyond caring.

Liverpool's scouting system was imploding; though Mel Johnson persevered, other key figures, Steve Hitchen and Stuart Webber, had left, to join Queens Park Rangers, where Mike Rigg, Manchester City's former technical director, was working alongside Mark Hughes. Anderson, who had also been approached by Charlton and West Bromwich Albion in the dog days of the Dalglish regime, understood the dynamics of Brighton as an upwardly mobile football club.

He was a solicitous host, spending an hour on a tour of the £93 million stadium which was a monument to the ambition of owner Tony Bloom, a professional gambler and poker player who gloried in the nickname of 'The Lizard'. Anderson was eager to reveal everything from the contents of the home dressing-room refrigerator (cherry isotonic drink) to the number of industrial tumble dryers in the equipment room (four, in an Aladdin's cave of kit for the new season).

Brighton had been squatting at a municipal athletics stadium for twelve years, between 1999 and 2011. Players changed in Portakabins and fans sat, without protection from the elements, in temporary stands, borrowed from the golf Open Championship. They had moved from Palookaville to Paradise. Anderson's 18-hour days, juggling football with his day job, as a senior site manager for a construction company, were over. He merely devoted 18 hours a day to becoming the scout he had always wished he could be:

'There are not many hard core scouts out there. I have been doing this for twenty-seven years. I've got used to a culture of listening, observing and obsessing. I am going to produce. That's what I do. I got Raheem into Liverpool. They signed seven of my boys over the last three years. If someone tells me about a player I am there.

'I reckon I will bring someone into the first team here within eighteen months. I've done that wherever I have been. Bob Pearson, the great old chief scout at Millwall, used to tell me, "You've got to put your name on a player." I'm not scared to do that. I am forty-seven this year. I wanted to get back in, full time, before I settled for just ticking along.

'The building work was a means to an end, to be honest. Football was, and is, my passion. I was doing silly hours, getting on site at six in the morning so I could be off at games, later in the day. I'd be getting in gone midnight, doing two thousand miles a month on the road. It's so dangerous. There are so many times when you are sitting there behind the wheel, and you feel yourself starting to go to sleep. You can't stop it.

'But, once I knew this job was coming up, I took time to recharge. I will be full on. I will be focused. I will be at it from early morning to late in the evening, seven days a week. I won't stop. My family understands. This is about me now. It's a major life decision. I might have dropped money to do it, but this is all I ever wanted to do. I was at one of the biggest clubs in the world, but this one is growing, going places.'

News travels fast. Anderson's role, as outlined by Brighton's director of football operations, David Burke, had a rare scope. Scouts at clubs run on a shoestring could not conceive of the luxury of an academy with 55 full-time employees. They were quickly on the phone, confiding their availability. Shaun O'Connor was one of the first to contact him, but had a different agenda.

'Shaun was great. "I know what you are up to," he said. "I will not let you move an inch." I'm like him, another grafter. This will be done properly. The parents will be brought in for chicken and chips. The triallists will be treated well. The first night any boy trains with us he will be in full Brighton gear. I'm not the sort to be there one minute, and gone the next.'

Anderson stopped to take a call from a Ghanaian agent, touting a 15-year-old boy. It was a fleeting insight into another world. The agent owned 70 per cent of the player and his sales pitch was brutal: 'He was telling me the boy would cost me next to nothing, but he wanted a massive sell-on fee. I try not to get involved with people like that. I want boys without problems.'

Resentment scarred the landscape. The implementation of the Premier League's Elite Player Performance Plan at the start of the 2012-13 season prompted clubs in Brighton's newly enlarged catchment area of South-East London to treat visiting scouts with suspicion and ill-concealed contempt. At Crystal Palace's training ground, scouts attending youth matches were herded into a small, clearly defined area, and accompanied to the toilet by stewards to prevent them stealing away to speak to parents. At Charlton they were corralled in a ball court, away from the pitch, and forced to watch through a mesh fence.

'It has become very difficult, very personal. People want to make it as hard as possible for you to do your job. You are left outside, waiting, and are not allowed in before the whistle goes. They watch you as if you are some sort of criminal. You are taken into the stand, if there is one, and are followed everywhere. Once the final whistle goes you are marched out again. It is a very unpleasant experience.

'Look. I pride myself on my reputation. I work within the rules and consider myself a professional. I see some people cutting corners, but I do things the right way. I tell clubs, "I am not here to nick your players. But, if one of the better boys becomes available, give me an option, let me be in the race."

'Our best kids are highlighted by others. I'm not stupid enough to deny that. But we give them the best environment possible. We are creating a good model. There is an element of being out of the firing line down here, but we are going to be judged on the number of players who progress through the system. I know there is a lot of envy about. One of the worst things about football is the number of people who want to see you fail.'

Anderson was developing a scouting network, which included Jason Halsey, who had been released by Bolton. He was embedding the club in local schools, ensuring the effectiveness of 20 teachers, employed on a part-time basis to provide an early warning system for the best talent. Consistency and continuity were crucial; scouts were involved in technical meetings with first team manager Gus Poyet, whose broader influence was signalled by the presence of young Spanish coaches, such as Gerard Nus, a protégé of Rafa Benitez, in the academy.

James Baxter, who had spent six years at Southampton, was responsible for nurturing boys as young as six at pre-academy talent centres: 'If you go to an inner city club the kids are more streetwise. I've seen boys in the under nines at a London club turn up, on their own, in a black cab. You have to be attuned to the kid's welfare. We are producing technical dots, boys who, in terms of physicality, can be caught out. In the longer term they will flourish.'

Barry Lloyd was deployed in the search for undervalued or underdeveloped talent in the 17–19 age group. Murray Jones, lead development coach for boys between the ages of 12 and 16, was another of Anderson's key points of contact. He was worldly-wise and politically astute, the legacy of working in three of the better academies, at Crystal Palace, Reading and Fulham, over 14 years. Brighton had particular problems, in the demographic of the boys they recruited, but obvious opportunities:

'We had a lot of naturally talented boys at Crystal Palace, but there was a different culture there. Here the boys come from a middle-class environment. Parents tend to be more supportive, but it is natural to question whether their sons have the hunger of those kids from a working-class background, who see football as a way out, and up.

'Football isn't immune to social change. It is interesting how talent is beginning to dry up in Northern Ireland, which is a traditional hotbed, and how people are quite content to ignore areas like Sussex. Hardly any clubs have scouts down here. Arsenal have a guy, but he doesn't even have a car. There is no real point in worrying about losing players. We're a big club. Why can't we nick a kid from Chelsea?

'We're trying to change the coaching culture so that it is creative and inspirational, but we can only do so much. We can be the best in the business, as coaches, but we need raw material to work with. The bottom line is we all need the old school scout, in the cheese cutter hat, who stands on the touchline and writes it all down on the back of a fag packet. They've got my respect. They've put the time in. They know this business inside out.'

Anderson, who signalled his intentions by signing former Chelsea defender Rohan Ince on an 18 month development contract, appreciated the mechanics of power. Managers are creatures of habit; they develop tight professional networks which demand discretion and unconditional loyalty. They tend to sign players with whom they have worked, and rely on agents with whom they have done business. Senior scouts, trusted confidants, are part of the inner circle. Those left behind, in the chaos of transition, are exposed.

'It is a lot safer in the youth system, though you are still vulnerable from the ripple effect,' said Anderson, whose admiration of Mel Johnson at Liverpool was undiminished. 'Mel has been on a knife edge since Damien has gone. That's how it is. To be fair he has done a terrific job for Liverpool. He has been very good to me. I have got the greatest respect for his knowledge, and I hope it all works out for him. He is one of the good guys.'

The timeline was ominous. Damien Comolli was dismissed on 12 April 2012. Dalglish was sacked on 16 May. Brendan Rodgers was confirmed as his successor on 1 June. The impending appointment of Dave Fallows as Liverpool's new head of recruitment, and of Barry Hunter as chief scout, was made public on 15 June. Each was immediately placed on gardening leave by Manchester City until the end of the summer transfer window. Liverpool's remaining scouts were left in limbo.

Johnson's sense of isolation, shared by Alan Harper, his counterpart in the North of England, was understandable and acute. Yet he was a product of a generation which fostered a sense of duty above personal pride. He considered reactivating the family greetings card business, but continued to scout, on his own initiative, until Fallows and Hunter were in post.

Occasionally, a harsh light would be thrown on background machinations. Two more senior City scouts, Rob Newman and David Fernandez, reneged on an agreement to join Liverpool. Newman, the former Southend and Cambridge United manager, was promoted to a global role in City's scouting department, while Fernandez took his job, overseeing activities in Spain. Anfield was a place of rhetoric and rumour. The promotion of Michael Edwards, whose expertise in performance analysis mirrored that of Fallows, lent weight to suggestions Liverpool would place fundamental importance on analytical scrutiny of potential signings.

'I'm still going to games, and people are still asking me what is going on,' admitted Johnson, as he began to attune himself mentally to defining the type of player suited to Rodgers' system. 'I just tell them I'm still there. You will hear that phrase a lot in scouting. Football is an insecure business, and we all have to cope with change. We've all been through the mill, wondering what is going to happen. It is the way of our world.'

Maybe so, but the plight of a decent man who cared about his craft bit deeply. I was outraged on Johnson's behalf; it was a meaningless indulgence, because the supposed victim accepted circumstantial but strangely cathartic indignities. I realised I had completed the process of identification with the tribe. A Nowhere Man does not deserve to be treated as a Nobody.

A fly-on-the-wall TV documentary entitled *Being: Liverpool* was being made at the time. It was, at one level, a corporate video, designed to facilitate the club's brand-building strategy in Asia and North America. Rodgers, an engaging, sensitive and intelligent man, away from the cameras, came over strangely, as a cross between a folksy philosopher and a corporate automaton. The soft focus Shanklyesque acknowledgement of his working-class roots in Northern Ireland merely served to emphasise a paradigm shift in the club's structure and culture. A strategic decision appeared to have been taken to monetise tradition, and damn the consequences.

Those closest to Johnson could sense the strain. His son, Jamie, inevitably, had the greatest insight. 'He won't let on, but something like this does kick the enthusiasm out of you. All people want, in a situation like this, is to be told whether they are being kept on or not. Once there is some certainty, you can deal with it. Everyone, in whichever way of life, needs to feel appreciated.'

Steve Jones was still a slave to perceived opportunity and persistent disappointment. He had spent the early part of the summer trawling the Football League's list of released players on behalf of St Johnstone, who faced a hideously early Europa League qualifying tie against Eskisehirspor, the Red Lightnings of Anatolia. The Turkish club, who featured a Portuguese midfield player who dared to desecrate the name Pelé, won 3–1 on aggregate. That, together with the farrago of Rangers' demotion to the Scottish Third Division, was enough to deter the scout's latest would-be employers.

'The manager still wants me but the chairman won't do it,' Jones reported, sadly, as another trail went cold on the western bank of the River Tay. 'I'm doing a bit of *ad hoc* stuff with them, and others. I tried to help Leyton Orient get a striker today. I felt like Tom Cruise. It was Mission Impossible. It is getting me down, to be straight with you. I couldn't even bring myself to watch the European Championships.'

Yet, when the dominoes fall, things can change with disarming speed. Chris Hughton left Birmingham City to return to the Premier League with Norwich City, whose manager Paul Lambert had walked out to join Aston Villa. Lee Clark got the gig at St Andrews on June 26,

2012. His most trusted allies, Terry McDermott and Derek Fazackerley, were recruited as assistant manager and first team coach respectively. Fazackerley, who had worked with Jones under Sven-Goran Eriksson at Leicester, asked him to report to Malcolm Crosby, the new chief scout.

It was an imperfect opportunity. Carson Yeung, Birmingham's owner, was facing money-laundering charges in Hong Kong, he denied but would not be heard until April 2013, at the earliest. Money at the Championship club was tighter than anyone dared mention, but Jones was decisive. Before he knew it, he was holding a discreet meeting with Crosby, the former Sunderland manager who had been working for Oxford United as head of youth development, at the hotel which formed part of the stadium which housed the MK Dons.

'Clarkey doesn't know a lot about the Championship so he wants hundreds of match reports,' Jones said. 'I'm not one of those on the gravy train. I'm grateful to Faz for putting my name in, because it's hard for people like myself to get work. I nearly bombed it all out and did something else with my life, to be honest. There comes a time when you wonder why you put yourself through it. It's just going round and round in circles. It's never ending.

'If you are not with a manager it is really tough. I know people say follow your dream. That's true. I've said it myself. But sometimes you get to the point where you say enough is enough. What chance do you have when you hear someone gets a job because he is the manager's golf partner? That happens, I kid you not.

'Malcolm's a top bloke, a football man, but I've basically given him his database. I can prime you on every player at this level. That's how it works. You get to know your respective divisions, and I have built up a huge knowledge base over the years. I know who is on the way up, and who is on the way down, yet I still can't get a full-time job. I've had seven applications in and I've not had a sniff. You think to yourself: am I really a bad person?'

In another twist to the plot, Ewan Chester, Birmingham's former chief scout, was settling in to a hotel on the outskirts of Norwich, after moving there with Hughton, who was also living out of a suitcase. His wife, a teacher, remained in the family home in Glasgow. His days began at the training ground before 7.30 a.m. It was routinely midnight before the 'Do Not Disturb' sign was posted outside his hotel room. Even returning to a club he knew well, Chester had little time in which to operate. He was assisted in replenishing the squad by the team he had assembled at Birmingham, which included Eddie Presland, Mel Johnson's predecessor as Tottenham's chief scout, Asa Hartford and Colin Suggett.

'It's not ideal, but you are governed by the game. I'm lucky, in that my wife is self-contained. We've no kids. It is difficult to have a normal life. I am always the problem in a social situation. If someone asks whether I can come for dinner on such and such a night I can't give any guarantees. Football is full on, twenty-four seven. It evolves into a way of life. When you get to my age, and you admit to yourself you are nearer the end than the beginning, you become even more appreciative of it. I still haven't found a way to cut a corner. If you feel you are losing your edge it is time to get out, but as Fergie says, as long as the blood is still pumping you march on.'

Chester was 61, but looked a decade younger. Ironically for someone steeped in the heritage of Rangers – they won 15 Scottish League titles, 35 trophies and three domestic trebles in his 20 years at the club – his facial features resembled those of Kenny Dalglish. The blue-grey eyes were piercing, and his cheekbones were similarly sharp. His light brown hair was unfashionably long and swept back, behind his ears. Old Firm football had provided 'a fast track education', even if he was nonplussed by the ramifications of Rangers' fall from grace.

He laughed gently at a definitive childhood memory, being taken by his father to watch Dundee's 5–1 win at Ibrox in November 1961. The ground was shrouded by a dense fog and a Rangers side featuring the incomparable, tragically self-destructive Jim Baxter were swept away by four second-half goals by Alan Gilzean, who would be subsumed into legend at Tottenham. His first three goals were one-touch finishes. The fourth, a flick past a flailing defender, followed by a low left footed shot into the bottom left-hand corner, was reminiscent of Eric Cantona.

Chester's own playing career did scant justice to the quality of such tutelage. It never recovered from a bout of pleurisy, which disrupted two years at Workington Town. He played in Hong Kong, and formed a lifelong friendship with Willie Donachie at Oldham, where he was player-coach. Scouting was a natural extension to his career, and the complexity of the emotional challenge in Glasgow was intoxicating:

'I revelled in the intensity of being with Rangers. Plenty of good players are unable to handle that aspect of the club, but I was used to it, from an early age. You have to win. It is as simple as that. But the great majority of the fans don't realise the mutual respect which exists between Rangers and Celtic. When I go to Celtic Park I am treated magnificently. Walter Smith and Ally McCoist were pallbearers at the funeral of Tommy Burns.'

His spells at Ibrox were punctuated by two years at Fulham, and an association with Paul Lambert, initially at Livingstone in 2006: 'It looked pretty terminal. They were twelve points adrift, but we signed nine players and kept them up. You begin to understand the implications of success and failure in a situation like that. Avoiding relegation saved a lot of people's jobs. You saw the worry in their faces, and also the joy, when they realised they were going to be allright. It sounds a bit trite, but that gives you a great feeling.'

He linked up with Lambert at Norwich in May 2010, and, in 15 months at Carrow Road, helped fashion a side based on 'youth and hunger'. He had a slightly different brief on his return, when the strategy of continuing to cherry-pick emerging Football League players was augmented by the signings of defenders with Premier League pedigree like Sebastian Bassong, from Tottenham, Javier Garrido, from Lazio, and Michael Turner, from Sunderland.

Team building is an inexact science. Timing, opportunism and the certainties of first-hand knowledge are pivotal parts of the process. Memories are long and nerves must be strong. It took Chester four years to secure Alex Tettey, a naturalised Norwegian defensive midfield player. He failed to sign him for Rangers, on the recommendation of former Manchester United defender Henning Berg, but did so for Norwich, who paid Rennes £1.3 million.

Chester did not allow a lifelong allegiance to Rangers to deter him from taking advantage of their plight. Steven Whittaker, a right back signed from Hibernian in the scout's second spell at Ibrox, engineered a fractious move to Norwich as a free agent. Robert Snodgrass, the winger whose career Chester had helped launch at Livingstone, was signed from Leeds for £2.8 million. It wasn't quite Friends Reunited, but it worked: 'It is a tightly knit group. As scouts, we take our work ethic and philosophy from Chris. Over the past fifteen years most managers have stopped going to games. The fixture schedule is relentless, and the media and commercial side of the game has grown. Chris still gets out there, but we are given carte blanche. We follow up leads, see players in different circumstances, then come to a consensus.

'Managers do sign players you don't agree with, but you can't go around broadcasting that fact. If mistakes are made, I do my best to keep them out of the public domain. It is about trust and accountability. You can't fudge in this game. If I give Chris twelve names, I would be hiding behind him. If I give him two or three, I am helping him. We have a structured, computerised system. We keep revisiting our lists. It can be a long process, because we are not afraid to walk away and consider every aspect.

'It is far too simplistic to say the scout with flat cap and muffler has no part in a more technological era. I have an open mind, and will embrace new ideas if they add to our knowledge base, but I am there to find players, not to be a technical wizard. The first opinion I form when I go to a game is usually fairly accurate. It is an intuitive thing. I get sent a lot of DVDs, but they are mainly an encouragement to get out there, and see the player live.

'Value goes in cycles and scouting, like football itself, follows trends. Fifteen years ago we all flooded Scandinavia, in search of a bargain. Manchester United got Ronnie Johnsen and Ole Gunnar Solksjaer out of

Norway. Bolton were successful in Finland and Iceland, with Jussi Jaaskelainen and Eidur Gudjohnsen. Then we went to Europe to look for holding midfield players; the prototype was Michael Essien. I watched him at Bastia and Lyon.

'Everyone is now all over France and Spain. There's still value in Eastern Europe; a lot of clubs are starting to scout extensively in Poland. Udinese are very successful in South America but in general terms the biggest clubs, the Champions League clubs with the biggest budgets, have the biggest reach.'

Football might have infinite possibilities, but footballers are finite entities. Chester's relationship with Norwich chief executive David McNally, established when they worked together at Fulham, gives him greater influence than many of his peers. He has developed a professional sense of detachment, so that he can utter the fateful words: 'go and find a new home' to a player whose purpose has been served.

'Ultimately it is my job to recommend players. The manager makes the decision, and the chief executive closes the deal. If I can be helpful, by investigating the parameters of a potential agreement, I do so. I can instigate deals and if we want to move a player on, I would have enough clout to contact other clubs, to see if they are interested.

'Human nature being as it is, you need man management skills. Some players suspect you of having a decisive input into the decision to let them go, others are more philosophical. I try to help a player get the best possible move, but I am also selfish enough to know that my principal responsibility is to remove him from the wage bill. It is as clinical as that. My job is to generate as much money as I can for the club.

'In football you need to be strong-minded. There are more downs than ups. We've all been sacked at one point or another. When that happens, you go on to autopilot, waiting for the next chance. You feel it when you are on the outside, looking in. You miss that sense of involvement on game day. Enjoy it, because it doesn't last for ever.'

13

The Road to Perdition

Fulham's Human Resources department despaired of Barry Simmonds. The club's chief scout had taken four days off in four and a half years, and showed little inclination to respond to their suggestions that he should restore his work–life balance. They shared the communal shock when, one summer's morning, as torrential rain swept across the training ground in the South-west London suburb of Motspur Park, he decided he needed time and distance to gather his thoughts.

On impulse, Simmonds called a travel agent, with instructions to find the first flight to 'somewhere hot'. By that evening he was nursing a beer in a beachfront bar in Alicante. He had given himself a three-day break, though the battery life on his two mobiles would be tested as thoroughly as ever. He could stay in touch, and take stock. Pavel Viktorovich Pogrebnyak was still on his mind.

'I know, I know,' he said, through quiet, self-deprecating laughter. 'I am the saddest person. We move on, but this was a tough one. I am a cog in a wheel. I do everything I can, but if a decision is made above my head I just have to condition myself to the reality of it. Scouting is art, science, timing and mood. You can't let it get to you. It is difficult to live this life if you are not even-tempered. You see injustices and it can flip you over very quickly.'

It was a testing time. Clint Dempsey was agitating for a move, which would take him to Tottenham instead of Liverpool, as originally envisaged, hours before the transfer window closed at the end of August. Simmonds' fears that Fulham would be unable to retain Mousa Dembele were in the process of being realised. The European Championships were of limited value; he knew the players, and had organised a video scouting service, augmented by performance analysis. Those scouts who chose the alternative, £1,000-a-night hotel rooms and supposed VIP seats amongst the fans behind the goals, picked up little more than carefully slanted gossip.

It is not the recurring sense of betrayal which saps the spirit, or the butchery of a system that sells footballers like slabs of sirloin. It is the insistent whisper of the scout's inner voice, which struggles to be heard above the cacophony of conjecture, neediness and posturing. It asks a series of stark questions about relevance and respect. The answers can be intimidating.

The loss of Pogrebnyak, on a Bosman free transfer to Reading, hurt. The Russian was straight from central casting, an archetypal action movie villain, blond and blessed with a parchment-pale face which soaked up emotion. He was Dolph Lundgren in Adidas Predator boots. His muscularity was emphasised by skin-tight shirts, and even his nickname, 'The Cellar', had an ominous ring to it. Simmonds, though, had spent three years getting to know the man.

Simmonds had first heard the buzz about him when he played alongside Andrey Arshavin for Zenit St Petersburg. Fulham manager Martin Jol tried to sign him for Hamburg, at that time. Pogrebnyak held the ball up well, and, despite intermittent injury, developed his all-round game when he moved to Stuttgart, in 2009. He was Simmonds' principal target the following year, when the Bundesliga club staged its mid-winter training camp in Antalya, on the Mediterranean coast of south-western Turkey.

It was the perfect place for a busman's holiday. The resort, Turkey's biggest, has 300 grass pitches. It attracts clubs from Germany, Belgium, Holland, Russia and the Ukraine. When Simmonds was in town, it also hosted teams from Japan, China, South Korea, Kenya and Brazil. Football created its own subculture, in which scouts, coaches, agents and journalists collided gently, amicably. The training sessions were open, and the informality was instructive.

Recruitment is an intuitive process. Simmonds turned down one player whose mother-in-law had him on speed dial, because he sensed the dangers of external pressure on someone with a submissive personality. He has the authority to make decisions on loaning players, and matches personalities with club profiles. He had attempted to ferret for clues about Pogrebnyak's character:

'The stats wouldn't tell you he is a player, but you knew you were looking at one when you watched him in the Bundesliga. In Antalya I basically stalked him for four days, watching everything he was doing. One thing, a small incident, stood out. He tried a shot which went spinning into orbit, way behind the goal. They had two old boys there, whose job was to collect the balls. He saw them turn to go and fetch his shot, and stopped them. He waved them away and got his ball himself. It was a simple, selfless act. Very respectful. That taught me a lot about him.

'It was the same soon after he signed for us. I watched him in the canteen one day, after training. He carefully put his knife and fork down on to his plate, and carried it to the ladies serving behind the counter, so it could be washed up and put away. The other players, who let others do the menial stuff, got on to him about that, so he soon changed. But it told me a little bit extra about his character.'

So much for behavioural psychology. Simmonds was confronted by a classic clash between nature and nurture. Pogrebnyak had been in the Russian system since the age of six, when he enrolled at the Spartak Moscow school. He survived a season in Siberia, with Tom Tomsk. Like many of those emerging in post-Soviet society, he was conditioned to making materialistic judgements. His six goals in 12 games on loan to Fulham towards the end of the 2011–12 season were hard currency. Simmonds fretted as a three-year contract remained unsigned.

Scouting, like everything in football, reflects the cycle of boom and bust. Reading had decimated their scouting structure after relegation to the Championship in 2008. They had rebuilt it, in preparation for a return to the Premier League. Steve Head, who had been overseeing opposition scouting for Fulham, was their new head of scouting and recruitment. His inside knowledge was important but the drive of new owner Anton Zingarevich was decisive. When he visited Russia's training base during the European Championships, Simmonds knew the game was up:

'In my experience, as chief scout, it is your job to ensure the CEO or manager is not surprised by anything in the transfer process. You can't allow anything to trip them up. You get them as much information as possible. My due diligence on a player has to go beyond whether he can head or kick a ball. But when a Russian owner meets a Russian player with an agent who specialises in the Russian market you know you're in trouble.

'Your strategy has to be fluid, because of certain factors, like a change of coach, owner or status. But there are very few secrets out there. We live in a YouTube generation. People are everywhere. Drive, say, three hours outside Prague, and you will get to some cement stadium in the middle of nowhere. There will be eighteen clubs there, on the off-chance.

'It takes a special arrangement with the owner, CEO and head of recruitment to facilitate progress. Clubs live from hour to hour, not even from day to day. It can take so little time to completely destroy the work of six weeks, six months or six years. It's football's way. Things can change so quickly.'

Pogrebnyak duly joined Reading on a four-year contract, estimated to be worth anywhere between £45,000 and £65,000 a week. He received a seven-figure signing-on fee, thought by some to be close to £5 million. Dr Oliver Wendt, a Hamburg-based agent on the periphery of the deal, surprised absolutely no one when he admitted money was a determining factor. Simmonds understood the rules of the game: 'We all move on to the next one.'

Fulham had a frantic but successful window, despite high-profile departures. Dimitar Berbatov, perhaps the only footballer who could get away with playing in white tie and tails, signed from Manchester United for

£5 million, despite being courted by Fiorentina and Juventus. Strikers Mladen Petric and Hugo Rodallega were signed as free agents after leaving Hamburg and Wigan respectively. Former Real Madrid midfield player Mahamadou Diarra committed himself to a permanent contract, Iranian winger Ashkan Dejagah signed from Wolfsburg, and full back Sascha Reither agreed to a season's loan following Cologne's relegation.

'It was what I call a player recruitment window, rather than a scouting window. You don't need much scouting for players of that quality and reputation. We had a few get away, but we all have our fisherman's tales. Everyone has their running order of potential recruits, but it is ultimately determined by external forces and sources. That's why it is such a game of cat and mouse. Some clubs try and do their business early, but it is the English way to get the deals done in the last few hours.

'You never really know what is going on at other clubs. You don't know about the constraints so it is difficult to make judgements. For instance, the club might have a wonderful academy, but never produce a player because of internal politics. I am chief scout, but every club has specific duties regardless of the similarity of the title. We all get our coats on, and get out there and watch games, but I have more of a sporting director type of role, in that my key alliance is with the CEO, Alistair Mackintosh.'

The inclusive culture fostered by Mackintosh, who

arrived from Manchester City in the summer of 2008, suited someone of Simmonds' diverse background and innovative nature. In addition to scouting, he had managed in New Zealand, coached in non-league football and operated as managing director of Darlington before he joined Fulham.

His philosophy was summarised by a favourite phrase: 'The brightest gold is found in the murkiest rivers.' To prove the point, he had recruited Canadian striker Alen Marcina from Puerto Rico and Gao Leilei from China while in charge of New Zealand Knights, in the Australian A League.

Simmonds was inventive, tireless. He hosted a biannual scouting conference at Craven Cottage, and insisted each scout watch the Fulham first team, so they could benchmark regulars against potential signings. They took turns to liaise with directors, who were designated as a 'scout host' for each home game. He compiled a weekly scouting summary, in a magazine format, for senior management and board members, with detailed assessments and updates of principal targets.

'What the chief executive has done is promote and support the ethos that just because you are not based at the training ground it doesn't mean you're not part of the club. We can't afford to think of our scouts as Occasional Al. We promote the idea that they should talk to one another. A lot of people ask me "are you fucking mad?" and tell me that encourages them to talk about me behind my back. That just shows you the level of insecurity in the game.

'You have got to be more concerned about getting it right than getting it wrong. You can't afford to worry about the labels put on players when you pay a lot of money for them. Money has always been integral to the process. In 1925, Arsenal advertised in the *Athletic News* for a new manager. It stressed that the successful applicant would be expected to build a team, and not pay exorbitant fees. What was one of the first things Herbert Chapman did when they appointed him? Break the transfer record by paying Bolton ten grand for David Jack.'

Simmonds introduced the notion of 'stealth scouting', playing matches, featuring targeted players, on a video loop on a centrally situated screen in the office he shared with the coaching staff. The desks were close together, and signs of haste, half-empty coffee cups and scrawled session plans, were conspicuous amongst the common room clutter. His response to the inevitable teasing from the coaches about his belief in subliminal messaging – 'your work keeps me in work' – was predictable, shameless and entirely acceptable.

Satellite feeds ensured he had access to every French League game by Sunday evening: 'Everton were one of the first clubs to latch on to the possibilities. They had those big old satellite dishes at the training ground. It looked like Jodrell Bank. When I arrived at Fulham the only database we had was hand-written reports, in position order, in a filing cabinet.'

He insisted his scouts stay in hotels after night games: 'I'm not having one of mine driving his Mondeo up and down the motorways, past midnight, with only a Ginsters pie for company. I want them to feel valued. If they are family men, I try to ensure they are at home for the big holidays, like Christmas and Easter. If anyone needs to be on the way to Gatwick at five a.m., it's me.'

Tales from the trenches kept everyone entertained. Simmonds 'cried for four days' after being tear-gassed by riot police at a Paris St Germain match. A favourite fixture was the Athens derby between Olympiakos and Panathinaikos: 'Some bright spark in the marketing department decided to put a DVD of highlights of twenty years' worth of derby games on every seat. Fine, until some poor soul had to take a corner. He was pelted with about twenty thousand DVDs. Mad, absolutely mad.'

On this particular afternoon, when the muffled dramas of a development match against Aston Villa filtered through to the coffee station of a modern dining room, he was in the midst of another road trip. He had just spent three days in Turkey, where he took in four games, and assessed players with development potential. He was due to leave for a European scouts meeting in Holland, which he intended to use as a base for a swing through France, Belgium, the Czech Republic and Germany.

'We have this concept of legacy scouting, where we look for players with medium- to long-term value for the club, irrespective of who the manager or head coach is. Mousa Dembele is a good example of a legacy player. We purchased him, even though Roy Hodgson didn't fancy him when he was manager here.

'I have tremendous respect for Roy as a man, and as a football man. The way he was treated when he became England manager was disgusting. I have learned so much from him, but when he goes into one it is best to let him go. He has got a temper on him. Managers are ridiculously stretched, but I'd managed to get him to spend a rare night off in Holland, watching Mousa play for AZ Alkmaar against Roda JC. They used him as a winger.

'Roy was soon on the phone, and what he didn't call me wasn't worth knowing. He basically accused me of wasting his time. When his anger had blown itself out, I explained I saw Mousa playing through the middle, not as a wide man. Roy had obviously had enough. "No chance," he said. It was only later, when he was managing Liverpool, that he called, and said, "you were right weren't you?"

Hodgson was, with Bobby Moore, Malcolm Allison, Harry Redknapp and John Cartwright, one of the men Simmonds regarded as 'life mentors'. He had put him through his preliminary coaching badge when he was 16, though he was meant to be 18, and was a source of consistent advice, as well as occasional admonition. His failure to make the grade as a player at Crystal Palace was a blessing in disguise:

'I was always interested in coaching. Malcolm Allison and John Cartwright at Palace used to let me be a nuisance. They saw I was hungry for the game. I was very fortunate to meet Bobby Moore, through Harry Redknapp, so early. I was on an FA course with him and he ended up taking me to Oxford City. He recommended me as youth team coach at Fulham. I was twenty-three, and also did the reserves, but in hindsight it was too much too soon.

'I always wanted to coach and travel. My first manager's job was in Nelson, on the South Island of New Zealand. It was part time, but we trained each day from four p.m. to six p.m. I asked the club to improve the lights, because it was so dingy, but there was no money. One of the directors, a sheep farmer, came up with an alternative solution. He painted the goalposts in luminous paint, and also dipped the balls in it, in the way he dipped sheep.

'It was a strange one, but I got on with it. I'm in the centre circle with my assistant, checking through the session we had planned, when I notice the first two players coming out of the changing room. One gets the ball, the other wheels away. He wants it on his head.

Anyway, the guy kicks it, and collapses, screaming. The other guy heads it, and is knocked out. The paint had dried and it was like a cannonball.'

Like many in his trade, he had cause to be grateful for a twist of fate, and the paternal benevolence of John Griffin who, in his dotage, was operating as Wycombe Wanderers' chief scout. Simmonds was coaching at Dulwich Hamlet in 1999 when Brentford were owned by Ron Noades, and shared training facilities with Crystal Palace. Paul Kember, son of Crystal Palace's chief scout Steve, was playing for him, so they gravitated naturally towards clubs which had an intimate, almost incestuous relationship.

'I used to watch training as often as I could. John Griff would always be there, ready for a cup of tea and a chat. On this particular day, he mentioned that Stan Ternant had just left Palace. On the off chance they'd need a coach, I told Steve Coppell that I'd love to come back to the club. He said they needed some help on the scouting side, but I said "fuck that". Steve was persistent, though. He persuaded me to try it, and it grew from there.

'I spent more and more time with John in his tiny office, going through the box files behind his desk. He was so open with me, so generous with his time. Secretly, I was thinking: put up with this for three months and you'll be running the reserves, but we went through players together. Gradually I became intrigued. I began to ask John more and more questions: "What do you look for? How do you compare players? What am I doing wrong?"

'I was making classic mistakes. At half-time I would allow myself to be sidetracked. I'd be trying to imagine what the coaches were saying to the players in the dressing room or what I would be saying to them, instead of concentrating on my man or men. I realised I needed a completely different mindset.

'Now, if you speak to me ten minutes after a game, I can't tell you the specifics of what happened. I will only know that later, when I watch the DVD. I just don't follow the ball. Let's say I am watching a centre half. Providing he is on his game, I will know or sense, where the ball is by studying his body shape. Even though I have a team sheet, names and numbers are incidental to me.'

Simmonds was solicitous towards Griffin, before, during and after Fulham's development match against Villa. The old scout sat between his nephews, Gary Johnson, the Yeovil manager, and his brother Steve, who had claimed the scout's job at AFC Wimbledon. Simmonds had helped Griffin out the previous winter, by loaning Italian striker Marcello Trotta to Wycombe, where he scored eight goals in eight games.

Trotta, a product of the Napoli youth system, had not distinguished himself that afternoon, despite a smartly taken goal; there was a collective intake of breath from the 20 or so scouts, assembled in a small stand at the training ground, when he pulled out of a challenge with the goalkeeper. Such blatant self-preservation pandered to the stereotype. The B word – 'bottler' – was murmured, like an ugly secret.

The new season, in League Two, had not started well. The club was under the control of a Supporters Trust, whose responsibilities dispelled the romantic notion of a fans' buy-out. Steve Hayes, Wycombe's former owner, was on extended bail until May 2013, following his arrest by the Metropolitan Police as part of Operation Tuleta. In February 2013 Hayes stated that he was still co-operating with police in a protracted investigation – although he stressed he had not been charged with any offence and was confident he would not be.

Griffin was cordial, yet grim, and could not conceal his concern for his manager, Gary Waddock: 'It's an absolute nightmare. I promise you I am not exaggerating, but we have an entire first team on the injury list. We've had to play eight teenagers, and we are only five games in. We've had broken legs, cruciates, the lot. It's even happening in training. I could hear someone screaming when I drove into the training ground yesterday. It was our left back. He'd done his cruciate, turning quickly.

'We get the call at six p.m. Out for the season, quite unbelievable. I've never been at a club like it, in forty years in the game. It is in danger of falling apart. We're begging for loan players, pleading to pay them a hundred, two hundred quid a week. They're just players, not that good, but they are all we have got. The club is being run by the Supporters' Trust. They're fans, and behaving like them. There's been a lot of chatter about Wadds.

'Trust me, this manager is good. I've worked with Terry Venables, the best, and this guy is fantastic, an absolute diamond. The vultures are gathering. Managers looking for work are suddenly turning up to watch. I see them in the stand. I don't blame them. That's what managers do. I don't know what's going to happen, but we play AFC Wimbledon on Saturday. If we don't win that Wadds' days are numbered.'

The sadness of the veteran scout was telling; his prescience was equally poignant. Wycombe marked their 125th anniversary celebrations by losing 1–0 at home to Wimbledon on September 22. They were booed off at half- and full-time. Reserve goalkeeper Elliott Parish saved a penalty, but sustained a cartilage injury. Waddock was so upset he needed 45 minutes to compose himself before attending a press conference. He began by apologising, but his farewell speech was soured by empty defiance and bitter recrimination. 'The players have let the club down, let themselves down, and let me down,' he said, before going off to meet his fate. He was sacked that evening.

'All the people in the game are telling him he'll get another job,' reported Griffin, who took things too personally for his own good. 'They know what a terrific manager he is, but chairmen will only look at us getting relegated, and struggling this season. I don't know whether I've still got a job but that doesn't seem particularly important at the moment, to be honest.'

Employment news was bad, and didn't get any better. The obliteration of Watford's scouting staff, following the club's absorption into the empire of the Pozzo family, owners of Udinese in Serie A and Granada in La Liga, caused a surge of resentment. Headlines condemning Watford as 'a snapshot of all that is wrong with the modern game' found a receptive audience.

The ironies of the situation were galling. Gino Pozzo, the son of Giampaolo, who bought the Championship club for £15 million, paid homage to the art of scouting while culling an 11-man team headed by Brian Greenhalgh. 'There is no cosmic mix to enable us to win, but we understand what works,' claimed the Italian interloper. 'Fifty per cent is good scouting, fifty per cent is good management.'

No one could deny the effectiveness of his business model, dependent upon a core group of 50 scouts, trawling under-utilised markets for young players at a critical phase of their development. The poster boy for the Udinese project is Alexis Sanchez. Spotted as a teenager in Chile, playing for Cobreloa in the Atacama Desert mining city of Calama, he was nurtured in Argentina and Italy before being sold to Barcelona in a deal worth €37 million.

Yet this was a question of faith, a challenge to the belief that something as ultimately insubstantial as a football club has significance beyond the binary certainties of the win–loss column. Watford was the club which nurtured me, personally and professionally. It was where I discovered the illicit thrill of bunking in via the allotments, to stand on a shale bank on the bend beside the Rookery End at Vicarage Road.

My heroes were not household names, and were quickly assimilated into the communities which once worshipped them. A season spent as a ballboy at Watford was a formative experience, an insight into the game's splendour and cruelty. I began my career on the local newspaper, where I played darts with Watford's owner, who wore a pink satin suit and shape-shifted personalities between Reginald Dwight and Elton Hercules John. Forgive the indulgence, but these are two teams which matter to him, to me, and a few fellow travellers:

Walker, Welbourne, Williams, Lugg, Lees, Walley, Scullion, Garbett, Endean, Packer, Owen. Sub Garvey

Sherwood, Bardsley, Price, Taylor, Terry, Sinnott, Callaghan, Johnston, Reilly, Jackett, Barnes. Sub Atkinson

The former lost 5–1 to Chelsea in the FA Cup semi-final in 1970, on a moonscape of a pitch at White Hart Lane. They had beaten Liverpool 1–0 in the previous round with a bellyflop of a diving header by Barry Endean, a centre forward who was bought for £50 and became a builder in his home town of Chester-le-Street. It was 14 years, two months, and five days before the latter team represented Watford in their first FA Cup final. I still cannot bring myself to watch a recording of the 2–0 defeat to Everton.

My alienation with the club, which once espoused family values and rallied around a ringmaster named Graham Taylor, was complete. A minority of Watford fans were concerned about a loss of identity under the new regime, but the majority were as spellbound as natives blinded by the sheen of a silver penny. They didn't care about Greenhalgh, and the brutality with which he had been despatched.

I remembered him as a underwhelming forward in an underwhelming Watford team. He played 18 times, scored a solitary goal, and promptly ended a journeyman's career, which had encompassed spells at Preston North End, Aston Villa, Leicester City, Huddersfield Town, Cambridge United, Bournemouth and Torquay United. 'I wasn't enjoying it,' he recalled. 'I was thirty, my legs were going, and I thought "what's the point?" It was time to get a proper job.'

Greenhalgh worked as a sales rep, sourcing orders for biscuits, cheese and butter in North London, while he dabbled as a part-time coach. He was introduced to scouting at Everton, initially for petrol money, and eventually spent nine years as chief scout to Howard Kendall, with whom he had been an apprentice at Preston. He returned to Watford, to work under Graham Taylor, before his instinctive fears were realised.

'I'd been at the club that long, I saw it coming. When the previous owner was looking to sell I thought: hang on, there could be trouble here. When it became clear the Pozzos were taking over I said to myself: that is it. Game over. They are bringing in an entirely different system. They'll do the job their way, and let's see how they come to terms with the mentality of the English game.

'What worries me is that Watford has been seen as a very good example of how to run a football club for football reasons. Now there is a completely different business model. That ignores, totally, the club's stature in the community, and its history. You walk into these scenarios with the best of intentions, but they treat you as a piece of paper. It is a tick box mentality. I have come through the old school. I have a certain feeling for the game. These people want a different club.'

If Greenhalgh was reconciled to his fate, others were prepared to take up the cudgels on his behalf. Simmonds was unequivocal: 'I have had a fantastic relationship with the Pozzos in the past. In fact we nearly took Yohan Mollo, a French winger, from Granada last year. But I had an agent, highly connected to them, ring me yesterday. I told him I was not the only one unhappy with the way Watford have conducted themselves. People are talking about not helping them.'

Solidarity, in the shadow of the sack, had an obvious relevance and resonance. Simmonds was acutely aware of his longevity at Fulham; only three other chief scouts in the Premier League – Robbie Cooke at Everton, Steve Rowley at Arsenal and Jim Lawlor at Manchester United – had longer service records. It was no coincidence that each worked for dynastic managers. Simmonds accepted his relative vulnerability, and harboured no illusions:

'It'll be a black bin liner job. It might be next week, next month or next year, but these things usually end one day. The only inevitabilities of life as a scout are birth, death, taxes and the occasional bin liner to clear your desk. As long as you accept that you will be allright. What do they say about the drowning man? The third time he goes down is the most peaceful.

'The more I live this life the more I see the parallel with the foot soldiers, the poor bloody infantry. They are acceptable casualties. It is the sort of job which chooses you. You tell yourself it'll only be a month or so, until that coaching job comes up, but you blink and you've spent years in the game. I'll always remember that line, by Paul Newman, in the film *The Road to Perdition*: "This is the life we have chosen." That's us.'

It was a great line, but the quote was slightly inaccurate. Newman's character, Irish mob boss John Rooney, actually said: 'This is the life we chose, the life we lead. And there is only one guarantee: none of us will see Heaven.'

You will be able to spot the football scouts, if you reach the celestial gates. To merge Hollywood images, they will be the angels with dirty faces.

14

The Loneliness of the Long-distance Walker

There is a profound poignancy about a footballer dying before his time. The cause may be medically mundane, but premature loss is the stuff of legend. It confers an intimate form of immortality; the stricken player leaves a legacy of images in a multi-media age, but continues to exist, most powerfully, in the imagination of those who watched, and wished they could be him. At Arsenal, one word is sufficient to stir the soul.

Rocky.

David Rocastle was just 33 when he passed away on 31 March 2001, a month after being diagnosed with non-Hodgkin's lymphoma, an aggressive form of cancer which attacks the immune system. He died on the morning of a North London derby against Tottenham at Highbury. Most fans heard the news just before kick-off. Despite the tribal tensions of the fixture, the minute's silence was broken only by the unmistakable sound of weeping.

Rocastle had Everyman qualities. His audacity allowed him to chip Peter Schmeichel from 25 yards at Old Trafford. He was born a generation too early: his pace and technique, strength and nimbleness, were suited to the modern game. He won two League titles and a League Cup for Arsenal, but is loved for who he was, rather than what he achieved. He was precious because he shared so readily the deep joy he derived from his game. His name is still chanted at the Emirates, where he is one of 40 club legends depicted, arm in arm, in groups of four on huge murals which circle the stadium's exterior. His image is reproduced on countless tee-shirts, printed on basement presses.

He played 14 times for England. The shirt he wore on his debut, a 1–0 win against Denmark on 14 September 1988, is framed, and dominates the neat, narrow dining room of an unprepossessing pre-war house in North London. An angular grass stain, faded to a faint lime-coloured smear but unmistakable across the bottom left-hand corner, proves it has not been washed. The inscription above the Three Lions badge, in capital letters, appears to have been written in black felt tip pen. 'To Terry,' it reads. 'Top Scout'.

Terry Murphy lingers. Silence stimulates the senses. I'm aware of a faint aroma of furniture polish, evidently applied to a small oval table, and a glass-fronted cabinet containing other items of football memorabilia. Murphy, a courtly, gracious man in his 73rd year, is lost in momentary contemplation. 'I told David to keep it, or give it to his family,' he says, quietly, 'but he wanted me to have it.' He leads me into the kitchen, where two cups are ready on coasters beside a modern, tubular kettle, without breaking the spell.

We progress through to the lounge, where a symmetrical arrangement of biscuits, Digestives, Ginger Nuts, Garibaldis and Rich Tea, await on a plate on the coffee table, alongside a bowl of mint imperials. Memories well up, like a child's tears. Murphy remembers the first time he saw Rocastle play, on an astroturf pitch on Market Road, where Holloway, the school at which he was a PE teacher, were hosting Roger Manwood Secondary from Brockley Rise in South London. The visiting boy was 13, and the scout sensed, immediately, that he was exceptional:

'David was the difference between the sides. He was so comfortable on the ball. He had tricks; even as a youngster he would do his step-overs and drag-backs. He was a talent, but it wasn't just me who knew how good he would be. There were other clubs around. I quickly spoke to his mother and brother. This is when it comes down to selling your club to the family. It wasn't hard in those days to sell Arsenal as a club, because you could talk about good training facilities, good coaches, good players to play with. You could talk about opportunity, and point to the first team. At times we had eight players in the first team who had come through the youth squad.

'David was easy to talk to. Some youngsters won't come close to you at all, they're distant. But David was very friendly, talkative. We just got on well. Sometimes, if your characters are compatible, it helps with a relationship. I don't try to butter anybody up. I always believe in speaking the truth and whatever I would say to David I would say to other people because that's the way I am. Players react differently to conversations, some players listen, some players don't.'

Rocastle listened, learned, and never forgot. His bond with Murphy sustained him throughout a career hampered by injury, and was renewed on his death bed.

'When David was in hospital, no one was allowed to see him. I didn't realise that when I went up there, but he said, "No, I want to see him." This was two days before he passed away. It's very difficult to say how special the relationship was and why it was special. It was just the personality that he was. We seemed to click together.

'You like to feel that Arsenal is a family. Once the boys are there you don't just say "right, we've got the player, that's it, forget him" and go on to someone else. I would always maintain contact with the parents and the players themselves. I can go back twenty or thirty years and I'm still in contact with them. But David was special. Yes, very special.'

He paused, and refocused. A celebratory DVD, a compilation of Rocastle's greatest moments, was stacked neatly beside the television, to the left of the deep, high-backed peach-coloured armchair which enveloped him. The house contained fragments of a football life. Two brass cannons, symbols of Arsenal's heritage, faced one another in the grate. The walls were studded with small photographs, taken in moments of private exultation.

A dressing-room scene at Anfield, where the League title was won with incomparable drama in 1989, captured Rocastle and Paul Merson wide-eyed, as if in awe at what they had just done. Another photograph shows the stern features of Martin Keown softened by satisfaction. The glint of sun, off the Premier League trophy, illuminates his angular face. Rocastle and Keown were his boys, his men.

Murphy joined Arsenal in 1973, along with Terry Burton, who had also supervised PE at Holloway, the school which produced Charlie George. Holloway flourished under an unconsidered visionary named Alan Wright, who brought in contemporary players, such as Arsenal goalkeeper Bob Wilson and Wales captain Mike England, to conduct coaching sessions.

Wright's staff, which also included Peter Shreeves, who would go on to manage Tottenham, taught football, cricket and badminton. The communal goal was to follow another Holloway alumnus, Tommy Coleman, on to the coaching staff at Highbury. They took the school motto – 'Aspire. Achieve. Succeed' – seriously.

'We were coming up to the summer holidays and Terry Burton suggested writing to the Arsenal, to ask if we could go and watch one of their training sessions. He got a reply from Bertie Mee, because he had been there as a youngster. We were watching a match involving some thirteen-year-olds with the then chief scout, Gordon Clarke. Suddenly he blows the whistle, stops the game, and out of the blue he says, "Right, you talk to that team, you talk to that team." We'd only gone in to watch, so we were in at the deep end. We said a few words, blah, blah blah. This went on about half a dozen times, with Gordon stopping the match, and telling us to go in and have a chat.

'There's luck in everything in life, isn't there? We were in the right place at the right time. The first team training had finished and Bertie Mee came over with Bobby Campbell, his coach. We must have been doing something right. About a week later Terry got a phone call, asking if we'd like to do a bit of evening training at Arsenal. We took sessions twice a week. That was really the start of it all. Terry and I went on a full badge course together, he passed and I didn't.

'Terry went from strength to strength as a coach. Arsenal had a fella called Ernie Collett, who was chief scout at the time. He'd been at the club man and boy.

He got me going out to watch games, and I eventually took over some of the schoolboy duties from him. Unfortunately, he got run over and killed by a fire engine in Finsbury Park. He was a lovely bloke, but always rushing around. That's how I came into scouting. Strange, but true.'

Murphy and Burton, who became first team coach under Don Howe and eventually returned to Arsenal in August 2012 to oversee the development group and reserve team, embody social history. Each came from a culture of street football, in which they played games like three-and-in and Wembley. It was a time of grazed-knee innocence, when footballs were plastic, gossamer-thin, and required rescue from railway lines, or back gardens guarded by mongrels who raged with Pavlovian excitement whenever an intruder appeared. They played other street games, such as Tin Tan Tommy, a form of hide and seek which involved throwing a can, and hopscotch.

Murphy was born in Islington, and walked to watch Arsenal, but his first love was Wolverhampton Wanderers. They enraptured him in the immediate post-war years, when radio amplified the achievements of such players as Billy Wright, Jimmy Mullen, Johnny Hancocks and Jessie Pye. As he grew up, and studied Arsenal from the terraces, opposite the Highbury clock, he developed a new group of heroes. Little Joe Baker, an effervescent centre forward signed from Torino for £70,000 in 1962, became a particular favourite when he floored Bill Shankly's cherished enforcer, Ronnie Yates.

Murphy is unashamedly old school, and will not use email. Yet his humanity is timeless. He represents a distinct group of football men, drawn not from the abrasive, impulsive world of the dressing room, but from the more reflective, aspirational environment of the classroom. David Pleat, who was Tottenham's care-taker manager on the day Rocastle died, employed Murphy in later years because of his depth of knowledge, and his innate sensitivity.

'Alan Sugar always used to say of scouts "What is he? Is he a spotter or a closer?" I knew exactly what he meant. Some can get the younger boys. They can schmooze the parents. They can go and knock at their flat, on the seventeenth floor in a high rise in the East End. They might be facing a single mother, who doesn't know football from Adam. She's got to be convinced that Arsenal are better than Tottenham or Tottenham are better than Arsenal, or whatever. That's a job, in my opinion, for an ex-school teacher, someone with well-developed social skills. Many scouts are expected to have those, and not many are capable of doing the job.'

Murphy diverted personal praise, but agreed with the sentiments. He regards lateral thinking as an essential element in football's intellectual challenge. 'I think that way of thinking comes from Don Howe,' he said. 'What he did in the game, for all the peaks he reached, he always had an open mind. He acknowledged he didn't know everything. There was always something else to know, to learn and discover.

'I think it is the same with scouting. You can't be dogmatic and say if you see this or that, you've got a player. It's difficult to know where to start, because you go to matches for so many reasons. Sometimes you are there as a match assessor, or just to see if there is anything special. Other times you go to see someone who has been recommended, or to have a look at your own player, on loan.

'Football intelligence is different to normal intelligence, and there are so many factors. Some people, I believe, are born with a gift. Footballers are like musicians; in every aspect of life there is someone who is born with something that's a bit special. There are a number of players probably like that, the Georgie Bests and the Paul Gascoignes of this world.

'What catches my eye is someone doing something that's a bit different. I concentrate on him, to see if it was a one-off. Then I consider the opposition. You want to know whether he could do well, given less time, against better opposition. There are so many variables. Over time I've seen so many people who've looked a bit special, only for them to peak and fade away.

'Nothing is certain. I remember one boy, having a trial to go to the old FA national school at Lilleshall.

He was a good player, on the day one of the best in the group. The coach sat them down to talk to them, and he just moved away. He wasn't interested in what the coach was saying. I thought: hello, attitude isn't quite what it should be, but he went on to be one of the top ones. It was Andy Cole. It's funny. I was with him recently, watching his son Devante in a Nike tournament. He's a player, doing well at Manchester City. Andy and I started talking and he remembered that trial. We had a laugh about it. He told me, "my lad's like me, he doesn't listen to anybody."

'This is where scouting, seeing players and making decisions, gets real. You have to be honest, and question yourself. I keep notes and records. I look back and try to work out why someone I thought was going to be a good player didn't come through. What went wrong there? You don't know everything as a scout, no way. I always think that as a professional, you've got to be seventy per cent right. You're never going to be a hundred per cent right. A normal person would get it right ten per cent of the time.

'You're always looking at the good ones who made it and at the ones who were better than them, but didn't. In one good group at Arsenal we had two players in the same position at thirteen, coming up to fourteen. We just wanted to keep one. This one was sharp, good movement, got forward. He was a full back. We decided to keep him and he bombed, captained the reserves, but nothing more. He hit that peak where he needed to work harder to get through it. He didn't or couldn't do it. The lad's name was Robbie Johnson. He's a taxi driver now, I believe.

'I had to say no to the other one. No matter how many years I did it, I always found it difficult. To tell the boy and his parents, sorry, you haven't made it, is not enough, on its own. I used to say, Well, it's our opinion at this moment in time. It's really up to you. You can either go away from here and say I've finished with football, or you can say I'll prove him wrong. Well, this particular boy was quite a big-set fella. He put his foot in but didn't appear to have a lot of pace. Nobody was interested in him. He went out and played Sunday morning football. Then he got into non-league, and then he became an England player.

'It was Stuart Pearce. He was the sort of character who just got on with the game and played it. I've spoken to him about it and he understood. He said, "Well, that's what makes it difficult doesn't it? You can never be certain with a player." Everyone has their own character, don't they? We could have easily made the same mistake with Martin Keown. I can remember seeing him as a thirteen-year-old, playing in a district match in Oxford.

'What stood out was his pace and his aggression when he went in to win the ball. I was Arsenal's youth development officer, so I had the chief scout look at him. He said not for me. I respected his opinion, but it was my decision. I kept Martin because he had basics that other people lacked, and he was a winner. OK, technically he might have lapsed occasionally, at that stage in his development, but no one else had his qualities.'

Just as the relationship with Rocastle and his family acquired tenderness and longevity, the bond between Murphy and Keown has blurred personal and professional boundaries. The scout attended Keown's wedding, and remains close friends with his father. He has followed the progress of the former England defender's son Niall, who has balanced his football career, as a defender in Reading's Academy, with academic work.

'Arsenal could not have a better role model or ambassador,' said Keown, with unashamed affection. 'Terry was my first point of contact with the club. I can still see him coming to my school, to meet the headmaster before I signed schoolboy forms. Arsenal blazer. Collar and tie. Impeccably presented. You knew here was a man of great dignity. Terry was loyal to us because we believed in the dream.'

Keown used to board with Murphy and his wife Pat on Friday nights, when he slept in the study after taking two trains and a bus, from Oxford to Muswell Hill. The scout drove himself to distraction, unsuccessfully attempting to match the boy's three-minute mastery of a Rubik's cube, but he also shared life lessons. Old match programmes were scrutinised, and wisdom was dispensed without pretension or condescension.

'Terry and his wife were a fantastic partnership. Pat was an absolute diamond of a person, a polar opposite in character, but so kind. She used to do all the cakes and sandwiches for the trial matches. There was quite a bit of interest in me from other clubs. They kept calling me, promising me that I'd be their captain, but I couldn't bring myself to let Terry down. He taught me that, if you play for Arsenal, you need to love the club.'

The educator in Murphy is never far from the surface. He unzipped a leather folder, which had been perched on the arm of his chair, and handed me a single piece of paper. There, in landscape form, was the Arsenal way, fashioned over 40 years of siphoning boys into a business which eats its young. Scouting may seem a disconnected, haphazard calling, but he had transcribed its most sacred tenets. The tone was set by a single word, in capital letters, on the top left of the sheet: 'PRINCIPLES'.

An old-fashioned image of a footballer was set in the centre of the page. Four basic elements of the game Physical Attributes, Character, Technique and Understanding – were at the centre of a web of inter-connectivity which highlighted 32 qualities found in a successful recruit. They ranged from mental toughness to controlled aggression, athleticism to adaptability. The document encouraged a series of questions, covering the quality of decision-making, intensity of commitment and awareness of responsibility. In the bottom right-hand corner, Murphy had written a fundamental truth, in copperplate handwriting, which testified to the disciplines of his youth: 'Players reach peaks, and the higher they climb, the harder it is to take the next step.'

Roger Smith, another of scouting's tribal elders, who remained at Charlton, was familiar with the contents. He, too, was a product of the Arsenal system, despite playing for six seasons at Tottenham. He forged a close relationship with Terry Burton after starting at a regional centre of excellence with Steve Rowley, who went on to become the club's chief scout. Roger's son, Gary, who was attempting to maintain his impact as Stevenage manager, after losing in the previous season's League One play-offs, spent several years in Arsenal's youth system before joining Fulham, on his release.

'Essex is always a good hunting ground for Arsenal,' said Roger. 'Steve was more the eyes, to recruit players. I coached them, because initially that's what I wanted to do. Whenever Steve wanted another opinion, he'd ask me. That was my first venture into looking at schoolboy players. I was working for Kerrygold, the Irish dairy produce company that later became Adams Foods, but I had a burning desire to get into football full time.

'That's where my direction changed. There were a

lot of people in the queue at Arsenal, and Terry Burton had moved on to become youth team coach at Wimbledon. They had just won the FA Cup, and wanted to set up their youth team properly. Terry asked if I was interested in becoming what was then a youth development officer. There were no academies at that point, and that role involved responsibility for a scouting network. I was satisfying my coaching needs in training, but gradually became recognised more as a recruiter. It was a slow process and maybe I didn't even realise it myself, but my coaching ambitions were receding.

'I was always wary when I went to games. I wasn't being anti-social, although quite a few people probably thought I was, but I avoided that big group of scouts who were often standing on the line, chatting to each other. They were having a laugh. Some of them even had their back to the game for half of it. I wanted to find my own space. I'd mix with them, of course, but not get engulfed in the social activity. I didn't want to have a game go by, and wonder what I'd seen.

'There is a strange phenomenon involving scouts, where a name might start to get bandied about. It's like one of those Christmas games where Chinese whispers get passed on. Suddenly this boy's been built up to be the best thing since sliced bread. Everyone ends up watching him, merely because his name's been touted around. That's why I try to keep a little bit of distance.

I try to take in everything, because I might need to speak to the team manager, maybe even the parents.

'In those days it wasn't difficult to find out who was little Johnny's dad, especially if he was quite decent. They're normally quite happy to let everyone know who they are. Parents, Christ. Some of the scouts also want to tell you why they're there. They're decent, well-meaning people. Maybe they've only played in parks football, but have just wanted to somehow be involved in the professional game. A lot of them are doing it for next to nothing, apart from a ticket and a jacket to wear at the weekend.

'You don't need to have been a pro to be a good scout. Take Steve. To the best of my knowledge he's played nothing but parks football. He's chief scout at one of the biggest clubs in Europe. He's got some very good people who are his eyes and ears around the world, so you're going through them first before he gets involved. But he's clearly a very good judge of a player. I've seen that. Football is about personal contact. I went to Cardiff as chief scout when Terry was assistant to Dave Jones.

'We had a decent three years, got close but not quite close enough, and the Malaysians who'd taken over about a year before moved Dave on. Malky Mackay came in, and everyone I knew had gone. What he said at the time was correct; he was left with only twelve in-contract players. I would have thought the first person he would have rung in that situation would have been his chief scout, but he didn't. There are not many advantages about getting older but one is that you don't have to put up with things. I put my notice in. Clearly Malky was going to go with his own guys. It would have been quite nice if he had told me, but sadly people deal with things in their own way . . .'

There was no surprise, or even particular sadness in Smith's tone. Just as many servants of the Pharaoh in Ancient Egypt were entombed with their king, so they could assist in the afterlife, the fate of the chief scout tends to be determined by his allegiance to a particular manager. Everyone accepts the recurrent absurdities of the situation; Dave Bowman left Wolves with Mick McCarthy, and joined him at Ipswich when they sacked Paul Jewell, whose faithful retainer David Hamilton spent more time with his allotment, and did some mileage work for Millwall while he waited for the wheel to turn.

Football's throwaway society lacks logic. Any industry which diminishes the self-esteem of its contributors, on a systematic basis, has major fault lines. Murphy, an idealist, was taking stock, literally and metaphorically. A compulsive hoarder, like many scouts, he was in the process of clearing out his attic. He smiled at a yellowing press cutting, in which Sir Alex Ferguson was promising to protect a 1,000-match tyro named Ryan Giggs. He pored over half-forgotten treatises on physiology, conditioning and the principles of talent identification. He cherished knowledge for its own sake. His report on a scouting trip to Brazil in the late 1990s intrigued him:

'I watched training over there. They do a lot of work in water. They run through sand, through stones, through different grades of material. I've come across stuff that I've had for donkey's years, and I'm now filing it all. Because I've been so busy it's been "put it here, put it there" and it needs putting together. I'm keeping it but I don't know what's going to happen when I go. Who's going to be interested in it?

'It's funny that I should come across that bit on Alex and Giggs. It proves there's nothing new in this world. The reason I say that is because people are having a go about Alex Oxlade-Chamberlain, asking why Arsène Wenger doesn't play him this way or that. The great managers have got a reason for doing things. I don't think I could ever be a manager. I'm not sure I would withstand the pressures they go through.

'Jobs in youth football are becoming much more pressurised, because money is playing such a role within it. There was money in my day but my philosophy was that I only wanted people to come to me because they wanted to, not because you bought them, or you had to pay someone something. The game's changed, in so many aspects. It's not the game that I used to know. I don't enjoy it so much. The job hasn't changed, in essence, but the expectations of the parents have changed.

'Unfortunately nowadays it all comes down to money. That puts a different emphasis on management, influences the way things are run. It's the deciding factor. It makes it difficult for clubs when there are one or two prepared to pay the big money, and not only pay big money but through agents. With one thing and another, your best players are whisked away. Unless you change, you can start to be left behind. We have problems lower down in football that no one seems to worry about. I mean look at Portsmouth and Rangers. I mean Rangers!'

This was not the last bellow of a dinosaur at an approaching meteorite that was destined to block out the sun. It was the authentic voice of football's conscience, a fastidious man of principle attempting to prevent the erosion of everything in which he believed. Would the technocrats and barrow boys, conspiring in an irreversible change in culture, care about an old man who cared about others? I doubt it, but they are lesser men, arid characters lacking depth and humanity.

'I played, but not at any level. Barnet was about the highest I got. I wasn't the best, but I'd always give a hundred per cent. There's a dreamer in all of us, you know. I started off in the old days as an outside right, and I can still remember one game, as plain as anything. It was over at Wanstead Flats and I was about sixteen. The ball came over from the right and I just leaned back and volleyed it in the goal. Fantastic! I can still see it now. But that was it. I never did it again. That's why I tell my scouts, you've got to be careful of the one-offs, because everybody can do it, at every level.'

It was good to see the years fall away, and the old man laugh without restraint. The void left in his life, by Pat's death, was easy to detect. I had been told, quietly, he was fretful about my visit. He was not a man for idle conjecture or manufactured controversy. I liked him immensely, but also trusted him implicitly. I would have happily given him responsibility for my son's welfare in a game which preys on naivety. I chanced one final question, about whether he could ever imagine a life without football. The answer was revealing:

'What I like about football now is that I'm meeting people that I've known for thirty, forty years. And because we've known each other, we actually help each other. By that, I mean, someone from a lower Division club might ask if I've seen a centre half or a left back. I might be able to point out someone who is not Arsenal material but who would do someone a job, lower down. Likewise, they might tell me about a really good centre half they could never afford. But, to answer the question, I can imagine walking away, because I'm a walker. I love it. I will spend more time travelling the world to walk mountains.'

I thought, at that moment, of the young man who was destined never to grow old, the daydream believer who wore the shirt displayed in the dining room. David Rocastle was once recorded talking to a group of younger players. His advice echoes down the years, from beyond the grave. He told the boys: 'Remember who you are, what you are, and who you represent.' Terry Murphy represents Arsenal, an imperfect institution, and football, an immodest game, with rare and unqualified distinction.

15

Hunger Games

A rsenal's representatives at Broadhall Way, home of Stevenage Football Club, resembled hit men, diverted en route to a Mob funeral. Each was dressed casually, yet uniformly, in black. Terry Burton carried off the turtle neck look with rather more aplomb than Steve Rowley, who chose an open-necked ensemble, and sat in the back row of the main stand spooning chips into a puddle of tomato ketchup with impressive gusto.

Burton was infinitely more approachable. We shared an interest in John Wooden, the doyen of American college basketball, whose integrity and insight into the human condition, forged as an Indiana farm boy and lavished on such iconic athletes as Magic Johnson, made him one of the most revered coaches in world sport until his death, at the age of 99, on 4 June 2010. Wooden's conviction, that his duty was to produce rounded human beings rather than athletic automata, had unspoken relevance.

Not for the first time, one of Wooden's most quoted maxims – 'It's what you learn after you know it all that counts' – rang true. Burton, like his friend and colleague Terry Murphy, understood the implications of the external issues complicating his work. Young footballers were becoming more precious, in both senses of the word. The night's scouting mission had a reassuring simplicity, compared to aspects of the development cycle of many emerging players, or ballers, as they preferred to be presented.

These social, emotional and economic issues had been placed into perspective by Liam Brady, Arsenal's head of youth development, in an intervention which hinted at the strains which would eventually signal his determination to stand down from the role. He bemoaned the distortions of the modern celebrity culture, which turned schoolboys into trend setters and a certain type of football follower into a cyber-stalker. He pointed the finger, without equivocation, at over-exposed and over-indulged English players, without revealing what he intended to do about it:

'We don't lose many of the Italian boys or any other of the boys we bring over from abroad at a young age because of lifestyle. They're here because they want to be footballers, and have another twenty years in the game. With a lot of the English kids, it's a battle to get them to see it like that, to get them to take their football as seriously. That's hard, a real challenge. Technology does us no favours in keeping players' feet on the ground. You've got guys writing blogs about them, how they're playing in the under fifteens. You've got our players tweeting, giving these people information about their lives, telling them what they're up to. They think they're celebrities.'

Such candour was anathema to Rowley; when Mel Johnson, Liverpool's principal scout in the South of England, introduced us, and the reason for my presence became apparent, he had the look of a startled fox and excused himself as soon as he could without causing offence. He has, to my knowledge, only ever given one extended interview, an anodyne summary of Arsenal's philosophy which failed to offer any insight into why Tottenham and Chelsea were rumoured to be ready to pay him up to £2 million a year to defect.

His associates were respectful of his work ethic, and in awe of his uncanny ability to find a McDonald's burger restaurant in football outposts which barely had running water. He was wedded only to life on the road, and valued his anonymity. Yet the invasive culture to which Brady referred could not be ignored; Arsène Wenger, and by implication Rowley himself, was vulnerable to increasingly tart and unsolicited observations about the nature and effectiveness of Arsenal's recruitment policy. The word in the tea room was that they were indecisive, over-cautious.

Everyone knew the identity of the evening's target,

Southampton full back Luke Shaw. He was 17, and had been watched, with increasing ardour, for three years. Yet two bids had been rejected, and the sight of Rowley and Burton, in tandem, meant one of two things. Arsenal were either steeling themselves to pay silly money, or they were in danger of succumbing to paralysis by analysis. The scouts who joined them, to assess the potential of a typically callow League Cup team, were split.

It would be several days before the ultimate irony, that Shaw was physically depleted by a virus, became apparent. Johnson, who was developing a long-distance relationship with the new regime at Anfield, quickly sensed something was wrong. 'He's a baby. Do we expect too much of him?' he asked, rhetorically, as the latest product of Southampton's Academy was uncharacter istically wasteful and ill-focused. 'I saw him in a game against Ajax and he was at it. He looked a great modern football back. Now he looks tired, and he's playing tired. I want to give him the benefit of the doubt, because I've seen him do so well.'

It was good to find Johnson so engaged. The difficulties of transition at Liverpool, under Brendan Rodgers, were being worked through; he had reignited the spark I feared had been extinguished by a worrying summer. It helped that scouting is a process of constant renewal; this was the first time he had seen Paulo Gazzaniga, perpetrator of The Save, since that afternoon in Oxford in April. Southampton had signed him from Gillingham for £1.25 million, and were emboldened by his promise. The young Argentine was trying to adapt to a new system, which involved building from the back. Flashes of his reflexive shot-stopping ability had to be balanced against the occasional positional lapse. He was a work in progress.

James Ward Prowse, another precocious 17-year-old, diverted the scout's attention. He reminded me of Frank Lampard; he was continually available to accept possession, and played with his head up. For someone of his youth to have such positional sense, vision and stamina was remarkable. 'He's the first one I've seen this season who looks a Liverpool player,' said Johnson. 'I've got to get a different head on, and work out what Brendan wants. He would certainly fit into the system, in that circular midfield three he likes.'

Dean Austin, sitting two seats down, spoke from experience. 'Brendan would be good for him,' he said. 'He'll teach him tactical discipline.' The authority with which he spoke was generated not only by his background, as Rodgers' assistant at Watford and Reading, but also by the rigour of his approach to a game which was doing him few favours. His brevity, earnestness and realism were convincing. If Brady needed someone to remind cossetted youths of their good fortune, Austin was his man. Whenever I saw him on the circuit, and felt the force of his personality, I mentally recited another of Wooden's homilies: 'Things turn out best for the people who make the best of the way things turn out.'

Austin had survived the summer cull, which halved Bolton's scouting team. He was working towards his Certificate in Applied Management for Football Managers at Warwick University, and applying for management jobs, usually without response. The course, effectively a finishing school for progressive young managers such as Chris Hughton, Malky Mackay, Nigel Adkins, Chris Powell, Sean O'Driscoll and Michael Appleton, was simultaneously stimulating and frustrating, because it confirmed his readiness to make a move, if the opportunity arose. He was 42, and had the indomitable spirit of a well-adjusted 20-year-old.

To understand where he was going, it was essential to appreciate where he had come from. Austin's career, like that of many footballers, was an assault course. He failed to make the grade at Watford, joined St Albans City, and impressed sufficiently to earn a second chance. He was signed for Southend by Dave Webb before Terry Venables invested £375,000 in his long-term value as a combative full back. Though he spent six years at Tottenham, the club he supported as a child, and had four years at Crystal Palace, his career was blighted by serious injury.

Austin played his final game, a 5–0 win over Telford which saved Woking from relegation from the Conference, on his 33rd birthday, 26 April 2003. He could have taken the easy option on retirement, and concentrated on a successful restaurant business in Spain, but his restlessness pushed him forward. He spent the next nine years completing his coaching badges, and fulfilled his ambition of getting his Pro Licence before he was 40. His back story explained why scouting was a means to an end:

'People say to me, why scout? I look at different elements when I watch a game. I'm trying to look at it as a scout but with a coach's eyes. I went to watch Bolton last year because I needed to know how the team functioned, so that I could find players to fit into their system. I needed to know their remit. There is no point me putting a report in on a player that I know they can't afford. This is part of a process. If I don't go out and watch games, how the hell is anyone going to know about me? You've got to have something a bit extra about you, nowadays.

'I think it is key for any young coach or manager to watch games, know the players and know exactly who's who and what's what. The way the game is evolving financially, you've got to go out there, and do the graft. You've got to know exactly the type of player you need. OK, you've got your foot soldiers to come to you and say, "gaffer, I've got this player. You have to have a look." You have to check it out, because you're the one that's ultimately accountable. If you're not watching the games, not getting the players, what are you going to do? Blame your chief scout? You can't do that. It's your job, you know.

'I decided I wanted to be a coach, or a manager, when I was twenty-eight. That was really through the encouragement of two people who believed in me, Terry Venables and Steve Coppell. I've gone through nine years of process to get my badges. I enjoy being on the grass, coaching players and helping young players. I enjoy that far more than I remember enjoying playing. But that was probably because of the injuries. They took over my life, really. From the age of twenty-four, I had eight knee operations. I broke my leg, broke my foot and had a hernia. I was popping tablets, having injections. You do what you have to do because you want to play.

'I've had experiences that you wouldn't believe. People don't understand. Imagine yourself in this position: a man in his prime at twenty-seven years old gets told by a surgeon that it's all over, finished. I was at the height of my career at Tottenham, well I should have been, but because of the injuries I was struggling. The surgeon says he is prepared to perform an operation, but it's never been done on a professional sportsman before. He doesn't know if it's going to work. People like him helped save me from the depths of despair.

'It was 1997. My contract at Spurs was coming to the end. My agent was trying to negotiate a new contract with Alan Sugar, who is never the easiest person to deal with, and we couldn't agree a deal. I had a couple of clubs abroad interested in seeing me, but I went back to Spurs at the beginning of pre-season believing we'd get the contract sorted. After a week we go to Norway. In the first game I sustained this horrific knee injury. My foot basically got stuck in the ground and my cartilage severed in three.

'The surgeon said to me, "we either whip the whole thing out and you'll be done in eighteen months to two years, or I take one part of it out and staple the other bits back together and save a vast chunk of your cartilage. I know it'll work on an everyday person, but I ain't sure it will work on a sportsman. It could be all over anyway." Imagine being confronted by that. You can see why players get depressed. I was in a dark place, I've got to say. I was in a very, very dark place.'

Austin learned that, in football, even the bad times are good. He sustained his playing career at Palace, where his natural leadership qualities came to the fore as club captain. When the club entered administration in 1999, he liaised with corporate recovery specialists and acted as a spokesman for a dressing room which contained fretful family men. Lives were put on hold; players were up for sale, contracts could not be fulfilled and 46 staff were sacked. Austin survived to see the funny side of one of the most bizarre missionary exercises undertaken by any British football club, a two-week trip to provincial China:

'Anyone who earned over sixty grand a year had to take a sixty per cent wage deferral. Eight of us did so. We all had kids, the club had no dough, and then they told us we were off to China. Virgin sponsored the trip, and they upgraded the eight players who took the hit on their money. Fourteen hours to Shanghai, and the boys are lording it. We've got the old beds out. The champagne is coming round and the sleep suits are on. It was absolutely the bees' knees, but when we got there, oh my. Shanghai was unbelievably humid, playing in the Olympic stadium in Beijing was weird, but the last place we went to, Daqing, was unreal. It was about a hundred and eighty miles from Siberia, and to get there we got on this internal flight that was simply horrendous.

'I'm sitting there, next to the window, and this old woman just cleared her throat and spat on the floor. It was just like, oh my God! Did I just see what I thought I saw? There are chickens in the aisle and a kid in front of me with no nappy, and a huge hole in the back of his trousers. I'm praying he doesn't have the problems some of the boys are having, because the food is kicking in. The only one of us who didn't mind it was Lee Bradbury. That was because he had been in the army and he was used to eating anything and everything to survive. Everyone else was like, no.

'We got this minibus from the airport. It took about two hours to get to the hotel, and you know you're in trouble when your itinerary says "local best". Basically, it was the Chinese Table Tennis Institute. The rooms stank. There were fag burns on the bed, stains on the carpet, all sorts. When we walked down the corridor we saw this guy, obviously a coach, with a kid who couldn't have been more than five or six. He looked like a little Buddha, with that little skinhead haircut. I've never seen a table tennis ball fly like it did over this table. The boys stood there, three or four of us. We were just in awe of this kid. The young lads were coming out of their rooms, and going "Skip, this is unbelievable."

'They told us tea would be at four. Well, we went down, and they brought out this part-cooked chicken still with the head on it. I said, "fuck this, this is enough." I went over to Steve Coppell and the administrator and said, "gaffer, we cannot stay here. This is below human standards and the boys ain't having it. We ain't staying here, I'll tell you now." Steve's telling me to calm down and I'm like, "No gaffer, there's trips and there's trips. This is a fucking hole. We ain't staying here so you'd best find out where we can stay." About two hours later he came to me and offered a deal.

'The stadium was just across the way. We'd play the game against this select Chinese eleven the following day, but no one would play for more than a half. It was like a hundred and twenty-five degrees on the pitch, silly humidity, no wind, nothing. Then we all piled on the minibus and got out of Dodge. It was unbelievable. I'd met my wife about six months before I went out there. When I was away, she went to Ayia Napa with her mates. I was away fifteen days and she was away fourteen days. I got on the scales and I'd lost sixteen pounds. She got on the scales and she'd put on fifteen!'

His laughter was spontaneous, prolonged and infectious. 'You miss stuff like that,' he reflected, needlessly. Football's fatal attraction might not have been enough to keep Rowley and Burton occupied for more than 70 minutes that night, but Austin gladly succumbed to it. It was a life choice, a life force. He used a coffee shop near his home as an office, nursing a phone, a laptop and a succession of skinny lattes. Leads were followed up, brains were picked, favours were granted and accepted.

He covered 23 games in August and in September it seemed his background work had paid off. A chairman called, and confided he was mindful of sacking his manager. He promised Austin a place on the shortlist for his successor, and asked for his help in sourcing a striker on loan. The manager was duly discarded, Austin's recruit scored on his debut, and the club appointed an internal candidate to save money. It was a casual betrayal, typical of its kind, excused by the cruel conformity of an apologetic phone call. Austin sought solace from peer recognition:

'This guy comes up to me in Warwick, at the uni, and asks who had impressed me on the course. There wasn't anyone in particular, but I wanted to be diplomatic so I just said sometimes you don't see people for what they are in that environment. They might be holding a bit back, or they might not be as confident in a group as they are in familiar surroundings. Take Lee Bradbury. I played with him at Palace from 1998 to 2000 and coached him at Southend in 2006. If anyone had said to me that he'd be a manager, I wouldn't have seen it. But he's had a go, and he's done allright at Bournemouth.

'Anyway, this guy says to me, "I've watched you, and I've spoken to three people on this course. I've asked them who out of this group of sixteen, eighteen people would go on and become a top manager. They've all said you. You're a bit different. You've got something about you, a drive, a determination. The way you conduct yourself stands out." They were kind words. It was a really nice thing to say, and he didn't need to say it.

'I actually believe that I will get an opportunity, because I believe in myself. If I allow myself to be convinced that the situation is hopeless, because the system is seriously flawed, then I'll never get an opportunity. It only takes me to meet one person, one chairman, one potential benefactor. I may sit down with him, and discover he thinks along the same lines. We may share ideas. He may be impressed by how I talk and by what I say. That's all you need, a little opening to persuade people to give you a chance. It's a brutal game, absolutely brutal, but I believe good things happen to good people. You've got to keep going, you've got to keep fighting, and scrapping through.'

Austin's hunger was insidious. He had worked at every level in football, from Watford's Under 13s, through non-league management at Farnborough, and a range of senior coaching and recruitment roles at developmental and first team level, yet the game was being reshaped by fear, penury and expedience. His application to manage Coventry was ignored, and he was unsurprised to learn, through a friendly agent, that nearly half of 55 supposedly serious candidates seeking to return to the game had offered to work for nothing. He was back on the chain gang, and headed for Barnet.

The NextGen series was going from strength to strength in the autumn of 2012, much to the horror of UEFA who, with characteristic cynicism, hastily unveiled plans to launch a rival competition, run on near identical lines, in the 2013–14 season. Arsenal, coached by Burton, were playing the previous season's beaten semi-finalists, Marseille. It was sufficiently intriguing to attract Wenger and Ivan Gazidis, his ascetic American chief executive, to the front row of the stand. It had been a wet evening, but as kick-off approached the rain stopped, and back-lit clouds sped across the suburban skyline.

The scouts' seating section was delineated by yellow tape, as if it were a crime scene. The usual suspects had turned out: Austin, Allan Gemmell and I squeezed into a row containing Steve McCall, from Ipswich, Brian Talbot, from Fulham, Jason Halsey, from Brighton and Phil Chappell, from Charlton. Ted Buxton, the Duke, sat on the end, interpreting individual patterns of play in what appeared to be a schoolboy's notebook. Mel Johnson had gone native, and sat amongst the fans, one of whom, a lady of indeterminate age, indulged in a solitary, monotone chant of 'we love you Arsenal'.

Ibrahima Sy, the Marseille goalkeeper, was rather more entertaining. He had the sangfroid of a man whose shorts were on fire, and the random movements of a mouse, attempting to evade the clutches of a tom cat. He treated his penalty area as if it were radioactive. Austin released the frustrations of a difficult journey from Warwick – the M1 roadworks in the Milton Keynes area were becoming the bane of his life – by yelling 'Bomb scare!' when Sy bounded out of the box on a particularly clueless rescue mission.

Gemmell permitted himself a rather more restrained 'oh, my God'. It was a phrase with which he had become familiar during a turbulent period at Nottingham Forest, after the Al-Hasawi family had purchased the club from the estate of the late Nigel Doughty, Forest's former benefactor and chairman. Omar Al-Hasawi, regarded as a frontman for his cousin Fawaz, set the tone by sacking Steve Cotterill, and suggesting the Kuwaiti owners would oversee recruitment policy, with a special emphasis on the Gulf.

Three Kuwaiti players were parachuted in for a month-long trial which ended when they were refused work permits. Khalid Al-Rashidi was a tolerable third string goalkeeper in the extended squad of a Championship club. Defender Hussain Fadhel and Bader Al-Mutawa, a second striker who was supposedly the best Kuwaiti player of his generation, would have struggled to make it in the Conference North. The owners' ostentatious announcement of a 'three-to-five-year' strategy missed the point. Forest's needs were immediate and acute.

'Two weeks before the season started we had no manager and no players,' Gemmell recalled with unconvincing insouciance. 'The owner was persuaded to interview Sean O'Driscoll, because he knew the setup inside out. The owner asked the players about him, and away we went. We had a few deals lined up, but it was a case of having two eyeballs, two earholes, and getting out there. Everyone knows everyone's business in football, and some of the calls have been interesting.

'Paul Sturrock phoned from Southend, asking if we were going to take Kane Ferdinand. We were strong on him, liked him a lot, but decided to pass. They had a tax bill to pay, and needed to sell him to pay the wages. That's what it is like in football, financially at the moment. I guarantee at least fifty per cent of Championship clubs are up for sale. Everyone's overspent. I'm not sure where all this is going.'

Nevertheless, 14 players arrived on 'a conveyor belt'. O'Driscoll had been employed for his acumen as a coach, and played a marginal role in the recruitment process. As Gemmell, whose protégé Jamaal Lascelles signed a new four-year contract after attracting interest from Manchester City, explained: 'All Sean has to do is shake hands with the players, and get them out on to the training field.'

Gemmell, like many around us, was impressed by Serge Gnabry, a German clone of Alex Oxlade-Chamberlain. Arsenal won with ease, 3–0, but could easily have doubled the score, given the paucity of the French resistance. Chuba Akpom, an England Under 19 striker who would sign his first professional contract on his 17th birthday in October, scored twice. He led the line intelligently, held the ball up well, and linked play thoughtfully. Wenger praised his 'personality and quality'. Akpom was diligent and responsive, a model student in football terms, but the noises off were worrying. The cultural problems, to which Brady referred, resurfaced when Pat Holland lasted only six weeks as coach of Arsenal's Under 18 squad. He was popular, admired by his peers, and was quickly reintegrated into Rowley's scouting team, but the brevity of his tenure as a coach was ominous. Holland had been disrespected by a strong-willed group of young players, who resented his disciplinarian approach. The honest pro took on the hoodie generation, and lost. Austin was not particularly close to Holland, but, like many, was appalled:

'When you are a professional sportsman, especially at a higher level, people think money is a substitute for everything, and it's not. The money I was on as a player wasn't bad, but it is not like these boys now. One year and they'll never need to work again. I've realised in the last eighteen months that I'm fortunate I've got a real good family around me. I've got four kids, three young ones with my current wife and my eldest boy, who is eighteen. I lost a bit of perspective on life. Because you throw yourself into this game so readily, you forget the things that are really important to you.'

Gemmell, too, had long-term plans. Scouting had changed, irreversibly, in the 37 years since his career had begun by watching Windsor and Eton play Aylesbury as a favour to his brother-in-law Peter Taylor, Dartford manager at the time. Gemmell intended to base himself in Vilamoura on the Algarve, to search for undervalued talent in Spain and Portugal. 'It's only a hundred and fifty kilometres from Lisbon, and a lot of Portuguese clubs don't pay their players,' he reasoned. 'When they go three months without being paid, they become free agents. That's when we can dive in.'

There was only one blemish on what appeared to be the perfect scenario: football's ex-pat community already had the 'No Vacancies' sign out.

16

The Good, the Bad
and the Ugly

The class warrior selling the *Socialist Worker* newspaper outside the New Lawn Stadium in the
Cotswold village of Nailsworth never stood a chance.
Doughty matrons, collecting for the RSPCA, protected
their patch, and ushered him to the end of the driveway.
Stewards stationed there were studiously indifferent to
the Range Rover driver who slid his window down and
said 'Wigan Athletic' as if the words were the key to a
magic kingdom. 'Sorry, mate,' he was told. 'No concessions. Three quid.'

Gary Penrice shrugged, paid up and parked on a
patch of grass sodden by mid-winter rain. Forest Green
Rovers, his nearest professional club, was certainly
different. Dale Vince, an eco-friendly owner, refused to
have red meat on the premises, and aimed to produce
football's first organic pitch within two years. The grass

was cut by a robotic mower controlled by a GPS positioning device and fuelled by 180 solar panels on the roof of the main stand.

Sheep grazed on a hillside overlooking the ground, and three Union flags, tattered and faded, flopped wearily in a gentle breeze. It was a snapshot of a contrasting culture. Penrice had taken a break from a sequence of three-day weekends, watching up to six games in the Low Countries or Southern Europe. He lived just down the Stroud valley, and it was a rare chance to catch up with a friend, Jamie Johnson.

Millwall's chief scout needed a left back, and was watching Chris Stokes, Forest Green's player of the year. A former England youth international, who once captained Bolton's youth team, he was a decent size, assured on the ball, but had a disconcerting habit of drifting inside under pressure. Johnson, whose three year pursuit of West Bromwich Albion striker Chris Wood had been rewarded with a mutually beneficial loan deal, concluded: 'Maybe more of a central defender. He keeps you interested, but he's not ready for us yet. We'll keep an eye on him over the next few months.'

Penrice looked at a broader picture. He was a prolific striker, who made more than 400 League appearances for Bristol Rovers, Watford, Aston Villa and QPR before becoming assistant manager, under school friend Ian Holloway, at Bristol Rovers and QPR. He acted as chief scout at Plymouth and Leicester, but moved into European scouting with Stoke. He was combining a similar role at Wigan with a portfolio approach, suited to stringent times.

An increasing number of clubs were rationalising their scouting programmes, effectively cutting out the middle man by dealing directly with agents. Penrice had anticipated the trend, setting himself up as a freelance scout, and establishing a strategic association with the Wasserman Media Group, which represented more than 400 players in La Liga, Serie A, Ligue 1, Bundesliga and the Premier League. He had created a European talent-spotting network for them and a unique niche for himself.

It didn't make for a quiet life. His mobile ringtone, Ennio Morricone's theme from *The Good, the Bad and the Ugly*, was the soundtrack to his working day. His Bristolian burr was accentuated by the speed of its delivery, which occasionally made him sound like Hagrid on helium, but his instincts were sharp. When he was in the car with his children, his Bluetooth headset protected them from the 'effing and jeffing' which constitutes normal football conversation.

Europe was a goldfield, inundated with prospectors. Each sought to emulate Graham Carr, given the unprecedented security of an eight-year contract as Newcastle United's chief scout because of his ability to exploit the French market. The fever was spreading across the continent, fostering the illusion of riches for all. For every Paulo Gazzaniga, the goalkeeper Penrice had found on the fringes of Valencia's third team and propelled into the Premier League with Southampton, via Gillingham, there were a thousand hard luck stories. The pathos of players without hope or, in extreme cases, even a passport highlighted recruitment as a cold, methodical business. Penrice knew the game, in all its forms:

'I took Paulo to Gillingham, where I knew Andy Hessenthaler, the manager. I said, "He's a good lad, good attitude, very cheap wages, free transfer, no money, have a look at him." Well, Paulo is six foot five, and he always wanted to play in England. I knew that, see? We've got an Argentinian under 18 international, at a top club in Spain, who's getting a maximum of thirty thousand euros a year. You wouldn't find that goalie in England, in my opinion. Not at that wage, at that age, and that size. Hessy can't afford a scout in England, never mind a scout in Spain. How is he ever going to hear about that player?

'They had no way of knowing him. So you've got a situation in England where a club like Gillingham, good club, good stadium, all the fundamentals, have a manager who has got to run the team and also find players. How does he do that? He can't, because scouting is an expensive thing. They've done well out of the goalie, and he's in the Premier League with Southampton.

We've all benefited from the "look after your mates" culture. English players are massively overpriced. Do they care any more? I'm not sure they have the character. The reason I went the agency route is that the game's gone global now.

'We're a small island, with a million teams, and there's only a limited amount of talent. The pressure of people trying to nick each other's players is ridiculous. You have to go to the agent, especially at Premier League level, and maybe at Championship level. I know people knock agents but they can come to you with good deals. Say, as a scout, you go to Spain. It's a lot of effort to watch one game. You might catch your player on the best day ever. You come home, you say to your manager "fantastic", but where do you go from there? You watch him again, but you still need a point of contact.

'You don't know him. Does he speak English? Does he want to come to England? You invariably learn that the agent is the one who knows the player really well. You establish a bit of trust with him. Even if you agree a fee with the club, you still have to deal with the agent because the club will contact him. There's no way round that. A scout only sees the player from the stand. Sometimes, the first handshake is when he blinking signs him. I knew Paulo. I knew his dad. There's more of a relationship.

'If you're at a specific club it can be very frustrating. It's exciting because it is result-driven, but if the manager says "I need a right winger" you can spend a whole year looking for one. It doesn't matter that you see a hundred good left wingers while you are out there. Even if you find your player, he has got to meet certain criteria to fit the way the manager wants his team to play. People have this thing about the mystique of scouting, but I think that only really works in youth departments or development situations. Then you are buying players to work with, to shape. At first team level it is not actually scouting, but realising what a manager wants in a player for a specific position.

'The ideal situation for a Premier League club is if you believe you've got a team that's good enough to stay in it. Then you can look for your nuggets. Stoke are probably in that situation now. Tony Pulis has done brilliantly to establish them, and he might be able to take the odd chance. It is still difficult, because it can be hard for a foreign player to adapt to a specific coaching style. Communication is a massive thing within a team, so it helps if they're not fighting for their lives.'

Football men are patchwork quilts of experience, often bitterly acquired. Penrice was ahead of the curve in terms of recruitment trends, but at heart remained a traditionalist. He underwent apprenticeship as a plumber before working his way up, as a player, from Mangotsfield United. He drove the bus for the reserve team at Bristol Rovers despite periodically injuring his shoulder because it lacked power steering. Little wonder he considered academy products, sheltered from reality in a self-perpetuating system, increasingly unfit for purpose.

'Without the Mangotsfield experience, non-league, regular football against men where you get kicked and there's a result and a crowd, I don't think I'd have mentally adjusted to the professional game. They're giving lads five year contracts straight from school. That's great in theory, but the problem is, when you get released, you actually are no use to society. You're twenty, and there ain't too many jobs at the Job Centre for a footballer.

'Don't get me wrong, good facilities are important. But they don't make a player. Brazilian players play on the streets and kick a can around. There is a balance to be struck. An elitist world has been created, but ultimately a young footballer needs to be hungry. I came from non-league. Ian Wright came from non-league. Stuart Pearce came from non-league. Peter Beardsley as well. They've not come from brilliant situations but they've played games. Now when Man United under nineteens play Arsenal under nineteens it all looks great. They've got a perfect pitch, a lovely restaurant after the game, but that is not what the real world is like.

'Get thrown out of some of the foreign teams, and you've literally got nothing. Survive, and you are brought up with the culture of your club. Take Barcelona. You've got players like Thiago, Montoya and Bartra moving up from the B team. They've played against men, in the equivalent of the Championship. They have to win. They must chase the game if they're losing. It's real. They identify with the club, and the demands of the game. It's different here. Take Scott Sinclair. Ollie and me signed him at ten years old. Then he went to Chelsea, but was loaned out to a lot of different teams, all with a different culture. He didn't know where he was for a while. It wasn't until Swansea bought him, believed in him, and played him, that he did what he's capable of.'

There were no short cuts. Carr was respected by his contemporaries because he had learned his trade. The new breed of numerate, dispassionate technical scouts lacked his earthiness and authority. Newcastle had been paying inordinate sums for substandard players on the strength of a promotional DVD, and needed some tough love. Carr was helping to reinvent a club once defined by the infamous Xisco, a seventh-choice striker who cost an initial £5.7 million and earned £12.5 million playing nine times in five years before returning to his natural level, the Spanish Second Division.

John Griffin, the sage of Wycombe Wanderers, remembered Carr fondly, 'ducking and diving' in non-league management with the likes of Dartford, Nuneaton Borough, Maidstone United, Kettering and Weymouth. David Pleat eased him into scouting at Tottenham because 'he was such a hard worker and didn't mind jumping on the Eurostar every weekend'. Carr contemplated retirement after a turbulent spell working for Sven-Göran Eriksson at Manchester City and Notts County, but is now contracted to Newcastle until he is 75. By the time the transfer window closed, at 11 p.m. on 31 January 2013, they had signed 11 players from Ligue 1.

Carr was stealing Arsène Wenger's clothes, which would have endeared him to his former employers at White Hart Lane. One of Pleat's observations – 'never waste a flight' – stuck with Carr, whose work ethic and affinity with his boyhood club gave him a head start with conscripts to the new model Le Toon army. 'People know me,' he admitted. 'I'm from Newcastle, so if I bring in a bad player, I know I'll get stick. We go for realistic targets, and we're not able to pay big fees.' The frisson of interest created by his son Alan, a camp comedian who, according to his father, 'had no co-ordination and couldn't trap a bag of wet cement' was not sustained.

Carr looked for players with pace, youth and sell-on potential, but the process was often complicated. The career of Demba Ba, lost by Newcastle to Chelsea when the European champions exercised a buy-out clause, was an instructive case study. The sixth of seven children born to Senegalese immigrants who settled in Normandy, Ba played junior football for Montrouge FC 92 in the south western suburbs of Paris before undergoing unsuccessful trials at Watford and Barnsley in 2004.

Penrice detected him scoring 22 goals in 26 games for Rouen the following year, monitored his progress at Mouscron, and, like Carr, took a detailed interest in his development at Hoffenheim, whose chief scout was active in the French market. No one doubted Ba's goalscoring talent. His knees, unfortunately, had the consistency of digestive biscuits. A €14 million move to Stuttgart was abandoned when he failed a medical; Stoke were similarly cautious when Penrice thought he had his man, for £7 million.

Carr kept his nerve when West Ham took the calculated gamble of offering a pay-as-you-play contract, and pounced when Ba exercised a clause allowing him to leave for free in the summer of 2012. Timing and good intelligence are the essence of modern scouting. Yohan Cabaye was, according to Penrice, 'never an off-the-radar sort'. He was the star of a championship-winning team at Lille, and Newcastle merely moved fastest when it emerged he had a bargain buy-out clause of £4.5 million.

The nuances of the market are important. Newcastle's cachet in France grew because of the standard of care lavished on Hatem Ben Arfa when his first season on Tyneside was decimated by a double break of his left leg. Flattery has its place; it was no coincidence Carr should choose to tell *L'Equipe*, the French sports daily: 'I love France and the French players. Yohan Cabaye and Hatem Ben Arfa are real quality players, very professional and indispensable. Both of them are intelligent and understand quickly what you want, they also have a very good tactical brain. It is because the French youth academy system is so good.'

It can take years to create an overnight sensation. Carr and Penrice both began watching Papiss Cissé, Ba's Senegalese striker partner, when he was at Metz, between 2005 and 2009. He was ineligible for a UK work permit when he joined newly promoted SC Freiburg in the Bundesliga for £1.4 million, but once he had acquired the necessary international experience, his price soared to £15 million. That dropped to £12 million. Once the asking price dipped below eight figures, a reflection of Freiburg's sudden concern about the financial impact of relegation, Newcastle's club secretary Lee Charnley did the deal, on Carr's recommendation.

It was strictly business. Penrice didn't take it personally. As he pointed out: 'I know Graham well. He's a good lad, you know. We've been on loads of trips together. We both knew those players for a while. He is very good at scouting for a position. He knows what the team needs, and the manager wants.'

All scouts have tales of the ones which wriggled off the hook. Penrice watched Cheick Tiote seven times before recommending him to Stoke City in 2009, more than a year before the Ivorian midfield player signed for Newcastle. Pulis was dissuaded by a telephone call to Steve McClaren, Tiote's manager at FC Twente at the time. Steven N'Zonzi, signed by Stoke for £3 million in the summer of 2012, had been identified by Penrice in a poor Amiens side, three years earlier, when he was available for £500,000.

When Stoke sought to stabilise after their first season in the Premier League, in 2009, Fernando Llorente and Javier Martinez, who were emerging at Athletic Bilbao, were on Penrice's wish list. The scout was also impressed by the discipline and defensive versatility of Laurent Koscielny, who was available on a free transfer following the expiry of his contract at Tours, in the French Second Division. Koscielny opted to join L'Orient, who sold him to Arsenal for £8.5 million the following year.

'I don't blame any of the managers for saying no. We all talk about the good ones we've put up, but don't kid yourself. We've all come up with crap ones as well, the ones we forget about. If you're a Premier League manager earning a million pounds a year why do you want to take a chance on a bloke from Chateauroux Reserves? It's easy for us scouts. He's the one that's got to sit on the touchline, get beat three-nil and go in front of the press. They'll ask him why he didn't sign so and so instead.'

Some people chart their lives through holiday photographs, birthday cards or glowing annual assessments which lead to promotion at work. A series of ring folder files, stored haphazardly in an office at his home in the Gloucestershire countryside, are central to Penrice's existence. These contain thousands of team sheets, accumulated across three continents in the previous decade. Each player is given a mark between A and E. Those with an S against their names were recommended as signings. Those with an M were monitored further.

Pick a file at random, and the names spill off the pages. Mesut Ozil, a callow substitute for Werder Bremen, 18 months before he starred for Germany in the 2010 World Cup. An A and an S. An 18-year-old Eden Hazard, who would eventually cost Chelsea £32 million, playing for Lille. An A and an S. A 17-year-old Raphael Varane, playing for Lens, two years before a £10 million move to Real Madrid. An A and an S. David Luiz, playing for Benfica in a Portuguese Cup tie two years before Chelsea signed him for £21 million. An A and an S.

'You can't hide from it, can you?' said Penrice, with the reverence of a true believer, going through the scriptures, line by line. 'The letters are there, aren't they?' He was on a spiritual journey; my questions were incidental, ignored not through disrespect but because he was consumed by a latent sense of wonder. The players lived a double life in his imagination; he envisaged them as they were, savoured the memory, and placed them, lovingly, in the context of what they had become.

'You can't buy this knowledge . . . no scout would have this knowledge . . . I've got book after book, hundreds of them . . . can you see what I mean? . . . this stuff don't lie . . . it's true, ain't it?' In those ethereal moments, that sacred stream of consciousness, Penrice had unwittingly answered one of my central questions. Why do scouts embrace the privations of a fractured lifestyle, and the frustrations of a disposable football culture? I suspect they dare not admit this, even in solitary moments of self-doubt, but they do so because they exist in a parallel universe where schoolboy sticker books come to life. They bear witness to the game's central struggle, between talent and ambition. They exist on the cusp of cynicism and idealism. They don't need to be indulged; it is sufficient to be intimately involved.

Penrice is a garrulous man, not given to quiet contemplation, but struggled to articulate what he felt, as he flicked through team after team: 'It's a funny, stupid thing. I don't get any satisfaction, me, out of the business side, to be honest. I get my satisfaction out of seeing the players do well. It's very rewarding. This job has a fair amount of longevity. When you find somebody you can watch their career progress. It's quite nice. I get more joy out of that than anything else, you know?'

Emotions are inevitably suppressed, because economics are more important. The Spanish market, though inflated at the top end, can still produce bargains like Michu, a £2 million revelation at Swansea, following Michael Laudrup's arrival as manager. The relative impoverishment of Portuguese football offers opportunities, as do underdeveloped systems in South and Central America, but the complications are onerous.

Eligibility for UK work permits is a recurring problem, because of the stipulation that a player must have appeared in 75 per cent of competitive games for a nation ranked in FIFA's top 70 over the previous two years. This leads to some players being parked at feeder clubs in Europe and Scandinavia. Third-party ownership is rife, but prohibited in England following West Ham's signing of Carlos Tevez and Javier Mascherano, who were owned by anonymous investors represented by Iranian-born businessman Kia Joorabchian. It is also outlawed in France.

Luiz is a case in point. A quarter of his so-called economic rights were owned by the Benfica Stars Fund, run by Banco Espirito Santo, Portugal's biggest bank. The fund received £5.25 million from the £21 million Chelsea paid to Benfica for the Brazil defender, a profit of £1.38 million over 14 months. It still has a stake in 18 Benfica players. Transparency is assured because, like Porto and Sporting Lisbon, Benfica are listed on Portugal's Stock Exchange. The sale of footballers' economic rights must be publicly declared.

Third-party ownership is seen as beneficial by some, because it allows clubs to share the risks of producing young players, and to manage their debts. It is endemic in South America, where clubs effectively use investment funds in the way overstretched householders use pay-day loan firms. However, UEFA announced in December 2012 they opposed the practice on principle, and would seek to pressurise FIFA to ban it, globally. If FIFA did not do so, they would take unilateral action.

Michel Platini, the UEFA president, chose a conference in Dubai to renew the attack: 'I sincerely believe that such a system poses unnecessary risks to football by creating improper links between agents, financial speculators and clubs that could ultimately affect the fairness of competition while promoting abuses such as money laundering which can only harm the integrity of football.' He was answered by Portuguese agent Jorge Mendes who, like Joorabchian, is also involved in the partial ownership of players' economic rights. He insisted: 'If we do this, we put an end to football for small clubs.' Former Manchester City defender Ray Ranson, whose fund had invested £50 million in a pan-European portfolio of 20 players, argued clubs needed the third-party system because 'the banks are shut'. Fund profits averaged 50 per cent over two years, and though Ranson insisted he had no influence on transfer policy, risks were managed through contractual inducements for clubs to sell.

Pressure, applied also by Richard Scudamore, the Premier League's chief executive, flushed out others from a secretive world. Traffic Sports, an arm of a Brazilian sports marketing company, was raising $100 million for its third football investment fund, in conjunction with a Dubai-based buyout firm, Cedar Bridge Partners. Jochen Loesch, Traffic's head of international business, suggested, in a filmed interview with Bloomberg TV, that third-party ownership 'doesn't exist'.

Such semantics were strange, because he then outlined 'a billion dollar market' in football, in which a single investment of $6,780,362 in Brazilian striker Kerrison, who was sold to Barcelona for $19,310,067, produced a 114 per cent profit for Traffic in eight months. He also warned that any legislative strictures from UEFA or FIFA would be 'widely ignored by the market'. It was an unmistakable signal that the facts of football life remained unchanged.

When the agent has more power, the scout, by defini-tion, has less influence. Clubs planning their transfer strategy for the summer window in 2013 had started to circulate South American agents with their require-ments the previous autumn. West Bromwich Albion were especially thorough, and were looking to repeat the success of the previous summer, when they signed defensive midfield player Claudio Yacob on a Bosman free transfer.

Albion were a progressive, stable club. Their strategy was sufficiently robust to sustain the loss of Dan Ashworth, their highly regarded sporting and technical director, who was replaced by Richard Garlick in January 2013. Ashworth stayed at the Hawthorns during a two month transitional period, before he joined the Football Association as director of elite development.

Albion's shopping list for the 2013–14 season, in the

initial form of a request for suitable CVs and recommendations, was extensive: they sought a young goalkeeper with development potential, a right sided centre back, with pace, and a right full back, with extensive experience. Another holding midfield player, in the mould of Yacob, two wingers and two central strikers were also required.

It was a measured, businesslike and professional process. Such adjectives cannot always be applied to the mayhem of the Primera División of the Argentine League, which Yacob had left in bad odour in the summer of 2012. He was marginalised after refusing to sign a new contract at Racing Club, who stripped him of the captaincy. This ensured Ashworth was unable to see him play when he visited Buenos Aires in late February and early March in 2012. He made his choice on the strength of a DVD, peer testimonials and an instinctive assessment of his character. He passed on his other principal target, Mariano Pavone, a British-style centre forward, who subsequently moved from Lanus to Cruz Azul, the Mexican club.

The attractions of the Black Country were brought into sharper focus for Yacob during the April derby against Independiente, who also represent the port city of Avellaneda. Racing led 1–0, but lost 4–1 after having midfield player Bruno Zuculini and goalscorer Teo Gutierrez sent off. Yacob sparked a media firestorm by being pictured wearing a pair of Independiente shorts, and the Racing Club dressing room resembled something out of the Wild West. Gutierrez pulled what he later claimed to be a paintball gun on goalkeeper Sebastian Saja, with whom he had swapped punches in a brawl which also included defender Lucas Aveldaño and Gutierrez's fellow Colombian Gio Moreno.

Boing Boing, indeed.

It was so much simpler in Penrice's world. He had immersed himself in the memories of an Under 16 match between Den Haag and PSV Eindhoven, one morning in 2009. He had never forgotten the PSV winger, a waif blessed with searing pace, quick feet, adhesive control and an eye for goal. His name was Zakaria Labyad. He was subsequently spirited to Sporting Lisbon, and great things were expected from this 18-year-old.

'One last thing,' said Penrice, as he steeled himself to close a blue loose-leaf file. 'See this one here? Labyad. I put him down as an S. Just you wait and see what happens. They're already talking about him going to Barcelona or Real Madrid. That's scouting!'

The dream was still alive.

17

Glue Guys and Bad Buys

S hane Battier is football's missing link. That is an odd accolade for a multi-millionaire basketball player whose employer admits 'he can't dribble, he's slow and hasn't got much body control', yet it offers a tantalising glimpse into a future shaped by human chemistry and applied mathematics. Battier, the Miami Heat forward, is the No Stats All Star of the NBA. They call him 'Lego', because when he is on the court the pieces start to fit together.

His job is to harass, block, steal, dive and draw fouls. He needs acute peripheral vision, anticipation and intestinal fortitude, to take a charge from the best offensive players in an aggressive, relentless sport. So far, so obvious; but every team in which he has played, even supposed basket cases like the Memphis Grizzlies, acquired an uncanny ability to win. The Heat, NBA Champions in Battier's first year, 2012, secured one of the great bargains when he signed a three-year contract worth a minimum $9.41 million.

Superstars such as Kobe Bryant lose their edge when Battier guards them, and ushers them into areas of statistically proven inefficiency. The contagion of uncertainty, when a marquee player is diminished, triggers collective ineffectiveness. Statistics provide an instant insight into what is happening, without allowing coaches immediately to understand why. Bright young things in basketball's back offices regurgitate such phrases as Battier being blessed with 'the IQ of where to be' but are constantly in catch-up mode.

The mystique of the process is enhanced by the impact Battier has on his teammates, who suddenly become more productive. It can be condensed into a single statistic, the plus–minus. In short this quantifies fluctuations in the score when any given player is on the court. Anyone who crystallises such magic in football, and finds the equivalent of what basketball identifies as a 'glue guy', would make a *Moneyball*-style impression.

Emile Heskey seems the footballer closest in spirit to Battier, because his credibility amongst coaches and teammates defies popular disdain and perceptions of weakness, but his career is petering out in Australia. The search is inherently difficult, because football is a low-scoring game and, according to Blake Wooster of Prozone, 'the most important things are the hardest to measure'.

New data is invaluable, and influential. Football's progression is reliant upon a quantum leap in thinking. It needs a man like Matthew Benham to be appreciated, instead of being feared and mistrusted, like a medieval witch. Brentford's owner is an Oxford graduate, a former financial trader who has become one of the world's leading professional gamblers. Smartodds, his consultancy, provides statistical and quantitative research to football punters, and executes bets on behalf of clients. A team of 17 graduates, all holding PhDs, initiate and develop sophisticated probability models, which incorporate theories, trends and anomalies.

Benham is a close friend of NBA legend Steve Nash, the LA Lakers point guard. He senses the significance of Battier's admission that 'when there's any question, I trust the numbers. The numbers don't lie.' Benham has accumulated a substantial personal fortune at the age of 43 because of his nerve, and faith in the nuances of arithmetical logic. It has enabled him to secure Brentford's future, by buying the land for the new stadium they hope to build by 2016–17 season, and given him a healthy scepticism about football's innate conservatism:

'I am quite alone in this belief, to say the least, but Shane Battier and the plus–minus principle is the way forward for football. Basketball informs us players' individual stats don't tell you much. The whole thing about Shane was that they looked at him in relation to the team. To define that in football terms, I am not just talking about whether a team wins or loses or scores or not, because there is a huge amount of what we call noise in that statistic. I want to look at the number and quality of the chances they created.

'If I am looking at a striker I absolutely do not care about his goalscoring record. For me, the only thing that is interesting is how the team do collectively, offensively and defensively, within the context of an individual's performance. To give an example, back in the day, I always thought Alan Shearer gave his team an amazing outlet. He'd be up there on his own. The team would be under pressure. You knew if you hoofed it in his general direction there'd be a high chance that the ball would stick, and he'd win a foul. That is a great defensive service Shearer is offering. The fact that a front player can hold the ball up means you are not going to concede another attack.

'We're working towards a new football model, but we are pretty far away. It really is not straightforward. It is a computational issue. Say you've got a Barcelona reserve, Tello for instance. To appreciate his value and potential you need to identify the players he has played with. Has he come on when Barça are 3–0 up and holding on to the ball? What is the context? Who were they playing? Similarly, you would look, for instance, at what happens on the few occasions Messi is absent. What impact does that have on Xavi and Iniesta?

'I know people's brains will fuse. They will tell us we are talking absolute bollocks. We are almost operating in a parallel universe. The thing about bogey teams is bollocks. If I tell that to anyone who has played the game they will tell me it is because I haven't done so. I don't dispute football people believe in the concept, but it doesn't stand scrutiny. Many things which people think are important are not. Let's take this idea that a player is "on fire". If I choose a player at random it doesn't matter if he has or hasn't scored in ten games. It makes him no more or less likely to score in the upcoming game. People perceive confidence, or otherwise, where we simply do not see it.

'If you look at any striker, at a random point in his career, and you want to know whether he is going to score in the next game, knowing how many he has scored in the last ten, twenty, forty games tells you very little. Similarly, the notion of "Hot Hands" in basketball is a myth. They used to think that a player with hot hands, one on a streak, was more likely to sink baskets. But then they did a bigger study and realised it wasn't true. This didn't go down well with certain people.

'They tried to explain it away by saying that a hot player would take more risky shots, or be marked more tightly. Nonsense. It is the same with free throws. It doesn't matter if the guy is hot as fire or cold as ice. If you have a guy like Steve Nash, who has taken several thousand free throws in his life, and you want to know what the percentage is he will get the next one, you need to know his percentages over the last five or ten years. If you only look at how he has done in the last five or ten games there is a huge amount of noise.'

An observation by Billy Beane, the *Moneyball* pioneer, sprang to mind: 'The idea you would not rob good ideas from other sports and apply them is crazy. You would have a hard time finding any major sport in the world which is not using metrics in some way. Performances in baseball are much more easily measured than in soccer but each sport has a metric which is relevant. Identifying it is the trick. Basketball is much more similar to soccer and many NBA teams are using metrics.'

Benham is an intriguing, reclusive character. He is softly spoken for someone so dependent on, and comfortable with, the strength of his convictions. Few Brentford fans would recognise him, though his formative gesture, bunking off school to catch a Football Special to a fourth round League Cup tie at Nottingham Forest in December 1982, has entered club mythology. Like any supporter, he relishes landmarks, such as winning the old Third Division at Peterborough in 1992, and such eccentric achievements as coming back from 4–1 down, with ten men, to draw 4–4 at Doncaster in 1982–83. The idiosyncrasies and inadequacies of any small club mask the potential which his wealth has unlocked.

When Brentford resorted to taking bucket collections to ease cashflow problems, he took on outstanding loans approaching £10 million. Within ten days of assuming ownership, in June 2012, he ended eight years of procrastination by buying the site for the new Community Stadium in Lionel Road, less than half a mile from Griffin Park. He is anxious not to be bracketed with the tangerine-hued self-publicists, vulpine opportunists and imported control freaks who inveigle their way into club ownership, and his allegiance to Brentford is genuine. He funded the upgrade in the club's academy, despite his understandable reluctance to trust the Premier League and FA to govern youth football equitably.

We conducted this, his first major interview, in a small, glass-walled meeting room set on a landing above the trading floor at Smartodds, on the third floor of an unprepossessing industrial complex close to Kentish Town tube station in North London. His visibility to his staff, uniformly responsive and largely employed straight from university, was indicative of an open management style in what is, by its nature, a secretive environment. He padded around the office, where lines of video monitors and computer terminals played out an array of live matches from around the world, in white towelling socks, combat trousers and a lightweight hoodie.

Football is the primary focus, although Benham also works in basketball, baseball, American football, ice hockey and tennis. It is an arcane world of parameters, probability theory and pseudo likelihood, which has a human dimension. Benham orders each recruit to read *Thinking Fast and Slow*, a book by Nobel prize-winning psychologist Daniel Kahneman, a professor emeritus at Princeton. Two chapters, 'The Illusion of Validity' and 'Intuition Versus Formula', are deemed particularly relevant:

'In the fifties, Kahneman was helping the Israeli Army on a leadership exercise. Six trainee officers, in the blazing sun, had to get a log over a wall. They and the log couldn't touch the wall. Very difficult, but you should be able to spot leadership potential. He was looking to see who was calm under pressure, who was respected by his peers, who was not respected, and who was flustered. He then made predictions on who would make officer material.

'It turned out his predictions were terrible, no better than chance. He was astonished because he had huge certainty that his predictions would be good enough. They were absolutely useless. What was especially interesting was that when he watched another batch of people do exactly the same thing, he couldn't help but feel incredibly confident in his predictions, despite previous experience. He concludes that experts in so many fields are ludicrously overconfident in their own intuitive ability to make predictions.

'That's why I make all our traders read those two chapters again and again. We have very sophisticated mathematical models, rating teams. What was constantly happening was that our traders, like everyone else, thought of themselves as football experts. I've done the same thing, and given my muggish public judgements much more weighting than a model that's been put together by loads of Maths PhDs and extensively back-tested.

'It is a phenomenon I see again and again in football. If I want to know how good a player is I want to speak to a person who has seen that player play one hundred times, in all conditions. What tends to happen is so many people in football will see that player for forty minutes and decide they are the oracle. They absolutely know. A typical example involved Gerard Houllier, when he signed the United States midfield player Michael Bradley from Borussia Mönchengladbach for Aston Villa.

'He was asked whether he had scouted him, and replied he had watched him in the World Cup. He said "he played four games. That was enough for me." Four games is a tiny, tiny sample. Anyone can play particularly well or badly in that timeframe. Perhaps most importantly, those four 'live' games in South Africa were for the United States, against England, Slovenia, Algeria and Ghana. England are OK, but the others are Championship-level teams.

'What tends to happen with human beings is once they form an opinion, it is very hard for them to shake that opinion. The best player we have ever had at Brentford was Wojciech Szczęsny, on loan from Arsenal. He was outstanding but in one game towards the end of his loan spell, against MK Dons, he dropped two and was responsible for two goals. Anyone seeing him in that game would have said dodgy keeper, flapper, but we knew otherwise. You might see a full back have a horrific game, but what are the variables? Is he playing injured? Does he have personal issues? Is it not his fault? Is the midfielder in front of him not giving him cover?'

Football engages and elevates; it bestows bogus authority and excuses crass ignorance. The average crowd is swayed by the power of perception and prejudice. Loyalists look for the unjustified alibi, while cynics cherish a glass that is perpetually half empty. Throw in regurgitated clichés from the golf club bores on *Match of the Day*, and it becomes clear why scouts, coaches, managers, players and even professional gamblers are routinely second-guessed. Benham smiles at the eccentricity of the court of public opinion:

'It's a funny one. Fans, and the media, see something in everything, when it is actually randomness. For example, if a team goes on a lucky or unlucky run, there is nothing really more to say than they have been very lucky, or otherwise. People feel obliged to say the lucky team ground out a result. They embellish the story by saying they showed character and commitment. The old lines – "the sign of a good team is when you win when not playing well" – are trotted out. It is all bollocks.

'Within every single move in football there are hundreds of small actions, little pieces of luck and skill, good and bad play. In professional gambling you try to strip out the element of luck. You are left with the signal after you have got rid of the noise. The more low scoring the sport, the more randomness there is. If the better team always won in sport then no one would watch it. There needs to be some element of randomness but not much. I'll quite often watch NFL games when one team wins 35–0 and they are the inferior team. Maybe the other team had double the yardage, but couldn't convert.'

As the season evolved, Damien Comolli surfaced intermittently to justify his legacy at Liverpool. Charlie Adam had been sold to Stoke, and Andy Carroll was enduring an injury-interrupted loan spell at West Ham. Yet, to be fair to the Frenchman, Stewart Downing had revived his career after being informed he was surplus to requirements. Jordan Henderson was maturing, appreciably, in a team energised by the pace and vivacity of Raheem Sterling.

Comolli's rumoured interest in succeeding Dan Ashworth as sporting and technical director at West Bromwich Albion remained unrequited, but his profile caused Benham to pause. He had not forgotten a clandestine meeting with Comolli, orchestrated by Frank McParland, whose stock as Liverpool's academy director had risen as Sterling had become an England international, and the most coveted young player in the Premier League:

'Is a statistical model useful in scouting and recruitment? Absolutely, without a doubt. The problem, however, is that too many people in football are running these computer models without having a maths or science background. If we had a hundred of the best maths PhDs we could find and they were working for the next ten years, there would still be loads of uncertainty. We'd probably have five different models. Ask them to spit out a number on a particular game, and they might well come out with wildly different numbers.

'The thing about modelling is that it is an inexact science. You are constantly running into lack of data versus relevance. If I want to model home advantage in the Premier League for instance, and I only look at one year, I don't have enough data. If I look at the last hundred years I have loads of data but little is relevant. There is a constant offset involved. For instance, do I look at other top leagues in Europe, or lower leagues in England?

'Frank took me up to Liverpool to meet Comolli. The idea was "we've got a model, you've got a model, maybe we could talk about ways in which we could work together". It was extraordinary. He just said, "my model is correct." Anyone with a pure maths or science background simply wouldn't have said that.

Science, in particular, is all about uncertainty and the limits of human knowledge. He was laughably overconfident.

'Looked at logically, it is easy to see how a club could end up paying £35 million for Andy Carroll. That would need reliance on a model which didn't correspond to the reality. In those circumstances there is a temptation to tweak the parameters, mix them up, until it starts to get sensible answers. Carroll had an exceptional six months in the Premier League with Newcastle before Liverpool signed him. A model might tell you he won a high number of aerial duels but only over a handful of games. We have to accept there might be some noise in that.

'Valuing new players is always a tricky one. A lot of models used by clubs seem to create what I call over-parameterisation. They have far too much in them. As I said, if I am looking for a striker I am not interested in his scoring record at all. All that is important to me is the team creates more chances, and offers fewer, when he is on the pitch. If there is a gun to my head, and I really have to include a scoring record in the model, it would be as long term as possible. That means his record over five or ten years.

'The key thing to understand about analytics is we are talking about a model. It is not reality. It is a model of reality. Too many think models are the truth. You absolutely a hundred per cent still need the old school input from scouts, just not on its own. There is room for subjective judgement, as long as it is part of a bigger picture.

'Everything we do is a mix of the subjective and objective. I might trade five games at once. The most I have done simultaneously was fifteen. I wouldn't be watching the games in that situation. We have people who do that, watching and inputting the stats as we request. We have various formulae which work out targets. The screen beeps and goes red if a bet is there. It goes grey if the bet is far away. Then it goes yellow and through the shades to red.

'We grade the quality of chances on ten different levels. Let's suppose a player runs on to a through ball and is wrongly given offside. If that decision hadn't been taken you'd have a man running straight in on the keeper. We can put that in as a really strong chance. Or maybe the decision was correct but marginal. We can still say that was less of a chance, but a chance nevertheless. All grading of chances is completely subjective but once we have the number and quality of chances for each side we can crunch it and put it into the models.'

It is a process of constant recalibration. Rule changes and refereeing standards are factored into the equation. Pythagorean Expectation, the mathematical theory originating from baseball, where it is used to estimate the number of wins, based on runs scored and conceded, is popular in the NFL and NBA, but cannot translate to football. Draws, regarded as a cultural aberration in North American sport, get in the way.

The boundaries between sport and academia are blurring. In February 2013, the NFL introduced a player assessment module designed by Harold Goldstein, professor of industrial and organisational psychology at the City University of New York. This test, applied on potential recruits from College football, measured learning styles, motivation, decision-making skills, ability to respond to pressure and core intellect.

Kahneman and Amos Tversky, a cognitive and mathematical psychologist, published a series of seminal articles on judgement and decision-making, culminating in the publication of their 'Prospect Theory: An Analysis of Decision under Risk'. This paper suggested human beings are naturally risk-averse when making a decision which promises gain, but risk-seeking when making a decision which will lead to a certain loss. The eminent academics could have been speaking about Queens Park Rangers and their traumatic 2012–13 season.

It was a case study in short-termism, unexpected näivety and ruinous expedience. The underpinning five-year strategy was sound, the personnel were experienced, but there was a disastrous disconnect between basic philosophy and best practice. Mistakes multiplied and, when Mark Hughes was replaced by Harry Redknapp on 24 November 2012, they were repeated. Misjudgements of players' character, and the perceived influence of agents who were paid £6,818,688 between 1 October 2011 and 30 September 2012, added to a toxic mix.

When the transfer window closed, on 31 January 2013, QPR had signed 29 players in 17 months under the ownership of Tony Fernandes. Redknapp was raging at 'gang warfare' being conducted by unnamed agents. Christopher Samba, a club record £12.5 million signing from Anzhi Makhachkala, was on a four-and-a-half-year contract worth £100,000 a week. Unsustainable gambles were being taken at a club with minimal match-day revenue, and an atmospheric but limited ground which held only 18,000. The club's culture was in tatters.

QPR's training ground, which lies under the flight path to Heathrow, has changed little in the 20 years or so since it was first rented by Chelsea. The offices, glorified portable buildings, are cramped. A small video room, with tiered seating, is one of the few concessions to modernity. But outside, there is a car showroom a petrol head would kill for. Bentley Continentals are parked haphazardly alongside Porsche Panameras with European plates. Customised Range Rovers flank a Ford Mustang. The place reeks of new money and Premier League pretensions.

This was where Mike Rigg had to develop and implement the strategy in conjunction with Hughes, in the summer of 2012. His credentials were impeccable. He had left Manchester City a month before they won the League title, after four years overseeing a recruitment programme which depended on a global network of 35 scouts. His inheritance from QPR's previous regime, under Neil Warnock, was non-existent:

'I walked through the door here and thought Oh my God. This is a Premier League club. What's happened? How can a club be like this? We'd spent money on scouts, but didn't even have a scouting department. There were zero, and I mean zero, scouting reports and targets. Who are we looking at? Who is our target? Right, we need a right back, what's our list of the top five right backs? Where is it? Nothing. There wasn't even a filing cabinet, and that in itself is a system which is thirty years out of date. At least in other clubs I have been at there was some record of where everybody had been.

'Everything we've done this summer has been catching up. We've had thousands of names thrown at us. "Go and get this kid from Belgium, Portugal, this lad from France." I said to Mark, "We are doing this and we have no idea. We have done no due diligence. We have no idea who they are." I guarantee you now the day I walk out of here the next person in will be able to click on a button and source information from all around the world. That's exactly what I left at City. It's an industry that's like no other, and I know what it is like. When I do go it will be "thanks, Mike". A week later it'll be "who's Mike?"'

There was a terrible foresight in his words. It would be easy to use hindsight to score points, and denigrate certain individuals. That is football's way, because it helps to dissipate the blame. No one sets out to fail, and events offer a perfect opportunity to reverse engineer the Rangers project. A lot of what Rigg said was uncomfortably close to the truth:

'The problem with the football business is if it lurches from crisis to crisis, and you have no fundamental principle or philosophy, every time there is a change at the top of the organisation, the whole organisation changes. On my first day, I went to see Caroline our PA, and asked how long she had been here. In her fifteen years at the club she's worked with thirty-three managers. I guarantee you that every time a new manager comes in there's change.

'They try to implement new methods and systems, but within two, three or six months people are saying "we have got to get him out". Frenzy is generated. Everyone in football wants it and wants it now. No one is prepared to wait for anything, any more. If the club decides to make changes, there's not an awful lot you can do about that, but surely there should be a consistent set of principles to work on.

'At City it was like living in the most luxurious palatial mansion. From the outside everyone sees this wonderful building, but you open up the doors and inside are the most dysfunctional family you'll ever come across.

When I came here it was like someone said to me, "there's a field, and a caravan for you to live in. For the next couple of years there's going to be a bit of mud and shit and holes and dirt, but you can actually build something." This, for me, is not just going through the motions of the job. It's a passion, it's my life, it's what I spend seven days a week thinking about and doing.'

He pushed his laptop across the desk, at an angle, and scrolled through a 56-page dossier he had compiled on Alexis Sanchez, when City considered signing him from Udinese. It was ultimately futile, because Barcelona did the deal, but it represented the sort of template he wanted to implement at QPR. Recruitment was a haphazard process, because football is a haphazard business. The intelligence operation he had carried out, in conjunction with Barry Hunter, who had subsequently moved to Liverpool, was revealingly indiscriminate:

'Barry was my Italian scout. We went out and spent four or five days, on the back of two years' worth of work, watching Alexis. We saw Udinese train, looked at his house, met family and friends. We went into town at one point, sat down and had a coffee, and we actually followed him walking around with a mate of his. We weren't trying to be private investigators but it's only a small place. We were noticing who he was with, what he was doing. At one point we went into a hotel and pretended to be fans. We asked for an autograph to see what the reaction was like.

'We should be doing psychometric testing with people to find out what makes these players tick. But the rules state you've got to go and spend fifty million on someone on whom you are not allowed to do any due diligence, unless you get permission from his club. And if the club want to sell him, because there are problems, they are going to prevent you from doing that.'

Rigg led me across to a whiteboard, on which players were split into first team and development groups. Their names were on magnetic strips. Those who were surplus to requirements and out on loan, like Joey Barton, were turned over to face the wall. The names of those who had left the club that week, like striker Tommy Smith, were removed and thrown in the bin. Rigg then drew an organisational flowchart, in which his function was linked to that of Hughes and Fernandes.

'My role is to balance the football and the business. I need to pay attention to the here and now, but formalise the future. Succession planning should never stop. We have a four-tier system, in terms of recruitment. Number one is a top Premier League player, who can come and fit straight in. Number two is a senior squad player, who may be coming towards the end of his career. There's minimal resale value but determinable risk. Number three is a development player aged between seventeen and twenty-one. Number four is a schoolboy. We have a global target list for each tier.

'What you don't want to do is throw the baby out

with the bathwater. You don't want to throw good people away, with good knowledge, but the whole concept of scouting has changed. Absolutely everybody is a scout. It's not so much what you see, but how that information is communicated. If there's a player out there, and he is seen by a parent, or the man on the street, it's on Facebook and Twitter. The information is with an agent. It's on the internet, on video, on DVD, on YouTube.

'It's on people's phones; someone stands on the side of the pitch and sends a text to someone, which is shared. Technology means communication is no longer reliant on a scout on the touchline. That's come about because a lot of people realise that there are vast sums of money to be made from players who have talent. That may be a Mum or Dad who sees their son as being the next Ryan Giggs, or it could be an agent who wants to snap up a player at the age of thirteen or fourteen because they want him for life.

'It's not hard to come by who the best players are. I could literally pick up the phone now, and say to someone, "do me a favour. Just email me a list by one o'clock this afternoon of the best twelve-year-olds in and around London." You can get that information very quickly, because there are so many people out there. Yes, you do need people who have good eyes, but you've got a new culture of people coming into the game.

'They are hard working, enthusiastic. They are

graduates, sports scientists. They are intelligent, articulate. There is also a new breed of professional footballer, who doesn't have to think about what he is doing next because he is so well off, financially. He doesn't have to stay in the game. That leaves the boys in the flat caps.'

All are dependent on the men in the boardroom who are prepared to fund flights of fancy, but begin to panic when others lay the blame at their door. Hughes was sacked because QPR bought rashly, placed undue faith in experience, and failed to recognise the character flaws of players like Stéphane M'bia, Jose Boswinga and Esteban Granero. Injuries to such senior pros as Bobby Zamora, one of the few footballers with the honesty to admit he dislikes football, were disruptive.

An embedded recruitment programme would have picked up the danger signs of indolence, complacency and culture shock. Rigg made the fatal mistake of believing 'this group should be brilliant for us for one or two years' and left Loftus Road just before Christmas 2012. Redknapp spoke archly of QPR's owners having 'their pants pulled down', but proceeded to staple their underwear to their ankles by sanctioning another round of recruitment. Change meant a new batch of casualties.

Stuart Webber, lured from Liverpool in August, quickly jumped ship, to become head of recruitment at Wolves. Hans Gillhaus, another senior figure appointed by Rigg, was sacked. Paul Dyer, who had watched Jack Butland at Southend with Mel Johnson and myself, was another victim of the dismantling of a scouting system that had only just been ratified. Redknapp's long-time chief scout Ian Broomfield, gave Dyer the bad news that he was out, and asked how long he had been in the game.

'Forty-five years.'

18

Smelling the Tulips

Friends and family, football men and little boys, gathered at the Royal British Legion in the West London suburb of Parsons Green to commemorate the Golden Wedding of John and Gloria Griffin. It was a celebration of a life shared and of a flame which flickered and refused to die. The years melted away into a mist of remembrance, a reaffirmation of faith and fidelity.

Parallel worlds collided gently. Football had obsessed John Griffin, Wycombe Wanderers' chief scout, since he was a boy in post-war London, when he turned left out of the council estate on the fringes of the Fulham Road, and headed to Craven Cottage. Had he turned right, and taken an equidistant walk towards Stamford Bridge, he would have matched his twelve grandchildren, and supported Chelsea. The prospect amused and appalled him.

'My whole family warned Gloria about me,' he said, his face illuminated by soft, ruminative laughter. 'She didn't listen, thankfully. I know I am stupid about football, but there is nothing more important than family. I see the kids in their Chelsea kits and I shudder, because I was brought up to dislike that club, but I love each and every one of them to bits. They remind us of what is important, don't they?'

The temptation to take stock was irresistible. More than 100 guests had come to pay their respects. Griffin was surrounded by managers he had worked for, scouts he had worked with. The trade to which he had dedicated himself was supposed to be on its death bed. Everyone knew its vital signs were weak, but prayed they would remain viable. Too many good men were being sacrificed in the name of innovation, and their names were recited, like a lament for a lost legion.

Steve Gritt, sacked as Bournemouth chief scout, and replaced by a video analyst. Russ Richardson, sacked as Bristol City chief scout, and effectively replaced by Jon Landsdown, the owner's son. Brian Greenhalgh, surviving on mileage rates at Huddersfield after Watford's new owners decimated their scouting department. Keith Burt, sacked as Nottingham Forest's head of recruitment by Kuwaiti owners who also seemed set on operating a manager of the month policy. The list went on and the word went out. The Nowhere Men had a duty to help their own.

Mel Johnson was the first to respond. He successfully recommended Mike Robbins to Gillingham manager Martin Allen, a fellow guest of the Griffins. Robbins was another victim of the cull at Queens Park Rangers, a former army cook who had also scouted for Exeter and Norwich. 'He called me as soon as he was topped,' said Johnson. 'He didn't know what to tell his missus. Mike's a nice guy who wants to get on, and Martin told me he was looking. It's good to get him fixed up.'

Johnson's empathy was understandable, because he had benefited similarly, by being offered a lifeline by Newcastle when released by Tottenham. Graham Carr gave him breathing space and a broad brief, working in France and England. He respected Johnson's experience, liked him as a man, and appreciated why he eventually chose to move on to Liverpool. Newcastle's chief scout offered the same respite to Greenhalgh, whom he asked to work the Northern circuit. They were of comparable vintage and character. Greenhalgh insisted: 'I like a laugh, but I will not be compromised on integrity. The younger ones, with their numbers, don't know what it is like to listen to that voice in your head when you see a special player.'

Meanwhile, the analysts were taking stock. They gathered at a conference on the Eastern seaboard of the United States, on March 1 and 2, 2013, in which the keynote debate was entitled 'The Revenge of the Nerds'. They were addressed by Nate Silver, the so-called 'Dork Jesus', who made his name in baseball sabermetrics before morphing into a political blogger who correctly called all 50 States and the District of Columbia in the 2012 US Presidential election.

They weren't having things all their own way. The NFL's 'anti-technology rule' banned coaches from using any electronic devices – iPads, laptops, phones or calculators – during matches. Offensive co-ordinators were forced to use pen and paper to calculate in-game statistics. A forum bemoaned the short-termism of English football, the difficulty of proving a return on investment, and the challenge of creating trust. In the words of Chris Anderson, a behavioural political economist from Cornell University who was one of the pioneers in the field of football analytics, 'going 0 to 100 in data is scary to lots of clubs'.

Anderson reinforced his message at a Sports Analytics Innovation Summit, held in London three weeks later: 'In many ways, I think football analytics has stalled. Inside football clubs, analytics has sort of ground to a halt. There was a lot of excitement about Moneyball but I don't think we've got super far with that. That's a truth we have to face. Football analytics is in danger of becoming another fad.'

Little wonder, given the conservatism of the British game, and the flights of fancy undertaken by the likes of Daniel McCaffrey and Kevin Bickart. They were neuroscientists, who suggested future recruitment policies in sport would be shaped by analysis of heart rate synchronicity amongst teammates. In layman's terms, they argued players who enjoyed playing together, played more effectively together. Their affinity could be measured through motion charts and biological data, assuming privacy issues could be overcome.

It was, of course, tempting to dismiss this as rom-com drivel, in which the eyes of the protagonists, a hulking centre half and a demure second striker, met across a crowded dressing room. Yet McCaffrey and Bickart supported their case by citing an experiment involving married couples and their ability to co-operate to solve a puzzle. Partners whose heart rates were most in sync experienced lower levels of conflict, solved the puzzle faster and, perhaps with a nod to Griffin, were more likely to have long and happy marriages.

The only interpersonal dynamics which concerned Griffin involved the relationship between the Supporters' Trust, which ran Wycombe Wanderers, and the League Two club's bank manager. The sale and lease back of their training ground, for a knock-down price of £350,000, promised to ease the immediate threat of administration, but the trust were still asking fans to donate £10 a month to a fighting fund. Griffin had been on the verge of retirement when Gary Waddock was sacked earlier in the season, yet remained to help Gareth Ainsworth mould a successful team out of veterans, loanees and teenagers. Fourteen first team players earned a total weekly wage of £3,000.

'No one really knows how bad it is,' said Griffin. 'I was very, very down when Wadds left, and I thought about jacking it in. I'd known him since he was thirteen, when I tried to take him to Brentford on schoolboy forms. You build up relationships with your managers. I've known Gareth since he was a kid of seventeen. That was the reason I stayed. I did say to him that I wouldn't have had a problem if he wanted to bring his own man in. But if he wanted me, I felt I owed it to him to stay.

'You feel for young kids trying to make their way. I'm not going to lie to you. Sometimes I wonder what I am doing, still in the game. I ask myself, why? The problems here are serious. But then I look at the young players, and their eagerness to get a life. I look at Gareth, still playing at thirty-nine. He can be a hard man, because football is a hard business, but he is so bubbly and infectious. It's a love affair. I think it helps that he comes into the team and does everything he asks the young lads to do. He tells them: "As long as you do it for me you will always be in my side."'

That sense of mutual trust and respect bred an affecting intimacy. Football was a strange fusion for Griffin, a surrogate family which included his own flesh and blood. His nephews Peter and Steve were scouts. Their brother Gary was renewing his managerial reputation at Yeovil. He revered his uncle's knowledge, and had never forgotten his gesture, in leaving Crystal Palace to assist him when he secured his first managerial job at Cambridge United. Griffin, too, remembered:

'I left Palace for eighteen months. Ron Noades let me go, and he promised to take me back. He knew what Gary meant to me, and was as good as his word, the day it went wrong for Gary at Cambridge. I enjoyed it there. I was never afraid to look for players at the lowest of the low. I went to watch a boy play for Christchurch. He was seventeen, ginger hair, a spotty college boy playing in the Wessex League in front of four men and a dog. The next day I said to Gary, "I've just found you your centre half for the next fifteen years. This kid might be out of the ordinary."

'And he was. It was Jody Craddock. I'll always remember him coming to see Gary. He was very much the student. He had cut-down shorts and a pony-tail. After we'd signed him and all the formalities were done, he walked out of the room. Gary said, "What have you done to me? Are you sure this is right?" He was in our first team within four weeks. He's had a great career in the Premier League with Sunderland and Wolves. He's doing some coaching now, though they tell me he wants to paint for a living.

'Gary always tells me, "You're such a mug for not getting a percentage of everything." People say I should go for the money, because everyone else makes money out of the deal, but I enjoy looking at a player progress and saying to myself: yeah, I started him off. Not too many of the players keep in touch, and they don't realise the boost to your ego it is when you see them doing well. I follow every one of them really closely. If I bump into them, which I frequently do, they will always make a fuss.

'I remember a few years ago I saw Stan Collymore at the football writers' dinner. He was way across the hall. He saw me and walked through thirty or forty people to throw his arms around me. That was nice. I'll always remember that. Things like that stick. I think they all spoil me if they see me. A couple of scouts I helped along the way do it, as well. One of them, Alan Watson, works for Manchester City. A very well educated man, who worked for me for about ten years. When he went to City he sent me a wonderful box of wine. He sent a note which said: "This is just to say thank you for everything you do. Other people don't realise how I got this far in my career." That was lovely. That was brilliant.'

Commercialism was continuing to accelerate change. Scout7 attempted to increase their market penetration by offering clubs free video scouting packages for the second half of the season. The major data companies, Prozone and Opta, were responding strategically to the needs of technical scouts like James Smith at Everton by offering statistics of greater depth, sophistication and relevance. These involved the timing of high-intensity sprints, the location and number of shots on goal, and the metrics of a killer counter attack. The pursuit of legitimate business aims threatened jobs and livelihoods of men who lacked an ability to fight back.

'It is all anyone talks about at the moment,' admitted Griffin. 'It's absolutely impossible for an analyst to do the same job as an experienced scout. You can't see players on a screen, and have an appreciation of what's going on thirty, twenty or even ten yards away. You couldn't possibly take a player just from the internet. Someone's eyes have to be involved. What happens to that trust you need between a chief scout and a manager? How can he go to him and say, "This one is worth a look, gaffer" if he is not certain himself?

'Facts and figures have their limitations, but I know the world is changing. I had a phone call recently asking me to find a chief scout for Crystal Palace. They wanted a younger man, an IT specialist who could also go to games and scout. I helped them find Tim Coe, who is a good lad. He's very bright and has been out on the circuit. They sent me a dozen bottles of red wine, which was nice, but it was worrying that they should insist IT skills were more of a priority for them than a scout's eyes.'

The complexity and consequences of change were familiar to Ray Clarke. We had first met on Valentine's Day, 2012, in a lounge on the 38th floor of the Gherkin, the iconic skyscraper based on the site of the former Baltic Exchange in London. He was off to West Ham with his wife Cindy, whose champagne lunch was an apology for an evening spent waiting in the car park, because someone had reneged on the promise to supply her with a match ticket.

She smiled indulgently, and would while away the game reading. He was on crutches, following a hip replacement operation, but when he talked football, with his glasses pushed backwards through a full head of grey hair, he was bright, youthful and expectant. The ball was out, the delicately presented beef and duck wraps were pushed to one side, and the capital, spread beneath us like an architectural and historical textbook, was reduced to a peripheral blur.

Clarke was a pioneering player, a striker whose career began at Tottenham and encompassed successful spells in Holland with Sparta Rotterdam and Ajax, and in Belgium with Club Brugge. He returned to England to play for Brighton and Newcastle, before moving into coaching, initially as reserve team manager at Southampton under Graeme Souness. He was one of the first scouts to work extensively in Europe, holding international roles at Coventry, Southampton, Newcastle, Middlesbrough and Celtic.

He had spent two years attempting to set up a Football Scouts Association, under the auspices of the League Managers' Association. A constitution had been prepared. Clarke liaised with the Football Association, and supervised ticketing arrangements for scouts at the

Olympic football tournament, before the dead hand of bureaucracy threatened to throttle the life out of the idea. It was an opportunity missed, because the welfare of scouts was regarded with increasing indifference.

'Scouts are treated with no respect,' said Clarke, more in sadness than in anger. 'We don't matter to too many people. There's no security. No one knows what we do, and no one cares. There are a lot of people out there struggling. They're doing it for the love and no money. The old school chief scouts are getting bombed out. I can see a lot of errors being made in recruitment because of that. You can't just push numbers at people.

'In Holland the scouts have a saying: "you have to smell the tulips". Statistics are all very well, but they don't give you what the traditional methods give you. You are out there, looking at everything from a player's movement to his mentality. You sniff the good ones out. People might listen to that, and turn round and say "oh, you're just one of those old farts" but we know what to look for in any given situation.

'Sometimes it is a question of body language. Rio Ferdinand isn't a natural defender, Nemanja Vidic is. He puts his head into a challenge, while Rio turns his away. The head is so important, because it determines body shape. Sometimes it is about gut feeling. You can see the pictures in a player's brain when he receives the ball. It can take less than a minute to make your mind up about someone. Once you are sure about him, you get in there early. We did that at Newcastle with Tim Krul, the goalkeeper who cost us only two hundred and twenty thousand euros as a sixteen-year-old.

'Sometimes it comes down to basic background work. Players work at certain clubs. Fernando Torres was successful at Liverpool because they were brilliant on the counter. Once Steven Gerrard had the ball, Torres was on his bike, hitting the channels. The ball invariably arrived. The reason why Torres is failing at Chelsea is that they do not play with a high enough tempo and the ball doesn't come quickly enough.'

So much for logic, and the eternal verities of the scout's trade. Clarke's appointment as Blackburn Rovers' head scout, in September 2012, was compromised by the arrival of a new head of recruitment, Luke Dowling, the following January. The apparently arbitrary usurpation was a response to the arrival of Blackburn's third manager of the season, Michael Appleton, who called Dowling 'my right arm'. It was, at the very least, a criminal waste of knowledge and experience, but it proved to be a temporary aberration. Appleton was sacked after 67 days in charge, together with Dowling, on March 19, 2013.

Dean Austin was utilising his knowledge and experience as assistant manager at Notts County. The break he had been seeking so persistently arrived suddenly and unpredictably. He was out with his young family in Radlett, a large prosperous village in the Hertfordshire commuter belt, when his mobile rang. He saw it was Chris Kiwomya, realised that Keith Curle had just been sacked at County, and turned to his wife. 'He's got the job,' he said, impulsively. The decision to abandon scouting duties at Bolton, who had lured Dougie Freedman as manager from Crystal Palace, was a foregone conclusion.

'It was quite bizarre,' admitted Austin. 'Chris and I are not best mates. I played against him for Southend and Tottenham and we'd seen each other on the development circuit over the last couple of years. We'd talk about football, and how we'd want to do it properly, given the chance. He left a development job at Ipswich, and we hadn't spoken for three or four months when he called. I waited until I'd got the kids in bed that night before calling him back.

'To be honest I'd been really looking to get out of Bolton. I was not enjoying it, and people I respected there had been topped. I didn't want people to say there was a problem between Dougie and me, because there wasn't, but I knew if I took another scouting job I'd be accused of sour grapes. Coaching is different. When Chris asked me to work with him there were no guarantees. He was a caretaker, but I believed in what we could do. I just thought that, even if it got me out on the training field for only a week or two, it was worth it.

'It's been a bit of an eye-opener. I have never worked

in an environment like this before. There's no running water or changing facilities at the training ground. The lads come to Meadow Lane, get changed, drive five miles, train, and then drive another five miles back to the ground in soaking wet kit before they can have a shower. It is what it is, I suppose. It has got me back on the horse. Let's see where it takes us.'

His deadpan delivery disguised his excitement. Austin is not an expressive man, but I had become attuned to his earnestness. We had talked about the alchemy of the appointment process, and how the force of his convictions could unnerve a potential employer. I admired his relentlessness, his determination to allow hope to triumph over experience, but doubted whether his diligence would find due reward. I was wrong. The discomforts defined and inspired him:

'I've had a really good response from the lads to my sessions. Quite a few of them got on really well with Keith Curle, so there was some hangover from that, but this is what I do. I'll do the scouting stuff, anyway, as part of this job. I have tried to take everything I have learned over the past twenty months in there with me. I've realised sometimes people don't want intensity. They merely want to understand what they are doing, and why.

'After the first week my wife asked how it was going. I told her Chris reminded me of myself six or seven years ago. Very keen, very professional, very passionate.

If he had a fault perhaps he talked too much. I have learned a lot about footballers, and their attention spans. You lose them in any meeting which lasts longer than twelve to fifteen minutes. Preparation is everything. At half-time, if Chris asks me to contribute, I am short, sharp and concise. I want them to work off a few points.

'I go round to a few individuals and talk about simple things, like passing with a purpose, or strikers running beyond the back four. When you are signing players in League One or Two it is about mentality. They have a different outlook. There's not much money about, but the good ones put everything into it. Some will try to mug you off, but you can recognise that and deal with it. We've got two months to get as many good results as we can. I'll just throw myself into it, and see what comes around in the summer.'

Steve Jones had reached yet another crossroads. He was working on a monthly consultancy contract at Bristol City, his seventh club in 15 months, and had been promised a place on the shortlist for the head of recruitment's role in a department remodelled in response to debts of £41 million. The need to slash a wage bill which had spiralled beyond £18 million, ruinous in the lower reaches of the Championship, preoccupied owner Steve Lansdown. His dissatisfaction was expressed tersely and with revealing candour:

'In the past we have been plagued by a football hierarchy who want you to believe there is some form of black art to finding players and those secrets should never be shared. I suspect it is a means of protecting their position and trying to show their importance, but I am pleased to say that our recruitment policy has now moved into the twenty-first century. We have two people working full time on compiling the statistics and information on players, while we are establishing a team of scouts around the country to watch these and report back.'

Jones had been alerted by Richard Shaw, who was scouting on an ad hoc basis after being dismissed by Coventry, following a short spell as caretaker manager. The strategy had been set by the owners' son, Jon, the club's managing director. It survived the almost immediate sacking of manager Derek McInnes, and his replacement by Sean O'Driscoll. He was an exceptional coach, but a dour, taciturn man. Jones had to read his moods, and relate to his ambitions, while meeting the demands of a club in transition.

'I've got a clean sheet of paper, and first dibs at the job. It is a big opportunity for me to get back in full time. I've worked through the lists, and it is clear some players have been nicking a living. I've got to help the club make the most of their assets. Twelve are out of contract in the summer; only four will be staying. Five of the other eight have already been told they're going. It is a simple brief, but a difficult one: slash the wage bill, and find young players with sell-on potential.'

Jones found time to observe tribal custom, and successfully eased Steve Gritt into his old job, on a retainer at Birmingham City. He also employed Brian Owen, the cabbie who had been let go by Hibernian during the implosion of Scottish football in the aftermath of the Rangers scandal, on a part-time basis in London. Gary Penrice gave him leads in Portugal, with Belenenses, in La Liga, with Las Palmas, and Holland, with Ajax. A throwaway line, delivered on our visit to Forest Green – 'some of the best scouts I've seen are the forty-pence-a-milers who are struggling for their lives' – acquired sudden clarity.

'I don't pretend to know it all,' said Jones, who was putting 5,000 miles a month on the clock of his old Mercedes. 'They might end up giving the job to someone else. I've spoken to the owners' son, who has told me to stop worrying about it, but there's no back-up. I talked to my wife about things, before I gave it a go. This is my last chance. I am not going to mug myself off. It can be a horrible game, and if I get rolled, I'd rather become a plumber, or go van driving.'

The tone was familiar, valiant. I hoped for the best, feared the worst, and decided my journey, started that night at Staines Town, was coming to a close. Just enough light had been directed on the nooks and crannies of a shadowy world for attitudes to be struck and conclusions to be reached. Football scouts are an imperfect breed, but their instincts are sound. They are unfashionable, encouraged to believe in the myth of their built-in obsolescence, but have *cojones* and credibility. The best work at their craft, but don't take themselves too seriously. They are strong-willed and built for the long haul.

I had been primed to amplify whispers about financial impropriety. Though there was the occasional unsubstantiated rumour about the relationship between a manager and a scout who was known, acidly, as 'The Bagman', his story did not belong here. Tales of sweeteners, of shady practices involving nameless agents and faceless players were simple to concoct, and impossible to disseminate, without funding the winter tans of m'learned friends. Bogeymen doubtlessly lurk under the bed, but let us leave them to the darkness.

Scouts are not stereotypical scallywags; they have a rare generosity of spirit. Jamie Johnson, Mel's son, took my son, a sports coaching science graduate who had worked within football for two years, under his wing when he expressed an interest in technical scouting. The first lesson was of the futility of hiding behind the computer console: 'You don't see people then, and people talk. You know what we are like; we're a bunch of old ladies who like a natter. People can't help themselves. They want to tell you what they are up to. That is the essence of our game.'

Technology has its uses in recruitment, but was being implemented blindly, often for its own sake. There was little scrutiny of its benefits, an assumption that, in isolation, it was infallible. Analytics will evolve, and eventually justify the inordinate faith placed in it, but the link between a scout's optic nerve and his brain will never lose its value. You can't create a love letter out of numbers, or express beauty in an algorithm. There's no sensuality in a sine curve, or warmth in a heat map. The neuron boogie, which causes tiny hairs to elevate on the back of a scout's neck, is a timeless tune.

It's time to 'fess up. Scouts remind me of my own tribe.

Journalists become inured to the absurdities of an insanely competitive profession, but remain vulnerable to perceptions of progress. As a breed, we are being assailed by accountants, who relate hi-tech methods to low cost bases. Too many good men have been stripped of security and self-esteem because of financial expedience. Too many mistakes have been excused by advances in technological expertise. Those of us who remain in the trenches tend to care, even though we disguise our commitment with gallows humour and guttural laments for what we once had.

I came to identify with Mel Johnson, my guide and tutor. I had feared for him as his, and our, story unfolded; the interregnum between the sacking of Damien Comolli and the bedding down of the Brendan Rodgers regime was ominous. Johnson would have been forgiven for losing his faith, but he retained his professional perspective , and continued to do his job to the best of his ability, in difficult circumstances. He was not blind to its cost, nor unappreciative of its eccentricity:

'We always put football first, before family. That's wrong, but it is why we do what we do. I can remember once having tickets for Dionne Warwick at the London Palladium. She is one of my favourite singers. Then I got a call to go and do Atletico Madrid against Athletic Bilbao. What do I do? You've guessed it. I'm on the plane to Spain. I put football first. They are killing us, but nine out of ten scouts would have done the same.

'I really must find time to clean out the garage. I have condensed everything in my life, but not football. You can't move in there for boxes and suitcases full of stuff. I keep everything; match programmes, team sheets, match tickets, even plane tickets. I tell you, if I go to a match and I can't get a team sheet I am positively suicidal. Silly, I know, but that is the way we are.'

There was a soothing familiarity to the conversations he had with Gary Penrice in the Mona Lisa café on the Kings' Road, before a sequence of Chelsea games in March. Luke Shaw's price had soared, beyond £10 million. Dave Philpotts and Ronnie Moore were achieving minor miracles, in maintaining Tranmere's challenge for promotion to the Championship. Brentford were making inroads into the immigrant community, because of the sensitivity of the scouting of Miguel Rios, their park-keeper.

On a broader level, the irony of Stoke City's signing Jack Butland for a cut price £3.5 million, from Birmingham City, had not gone unnoticed. Mark Cartwright, the goalkeeper's erstwhile representative, was Stoke's newly-appointed technical director, and memories of that Friday foray to Southend remained vivid. 'A bad game will always be with you,' said Mel Johnson, sympathetically.

He was invited to Melwood, to be briefed on the renewal of Liverpool's recruitment strategy. He watched the first team train, and saw Jordon Ibe, his protégé, score twice as Liverpool reached the quarter-finals of the FA Youth Cup at the expense of Leeds United. Together with Alan Harper, the other principal survivor of the Dalglish era, he was extremely impressed by the intellectual rigour and detailed vision of Dave Fallows, the new head of recruitment. Johnson's diligence had also been noted.

The potential of analysis and experience became apparent when he was asked about Isaiah Brown, a 16-year-old prodigy who had been an unused substitute for West Bromwich Albion at Chelsea that weekend. The scout had done his homework: 'He's a Kit Carson boy. I met his stepfather at an under twenty-one game recently. He told me the boy had changed agents.' Such information was invaluable and unavailable online.

Rodgers had resisted the introduction of a Director of Football at Anfield, but accepted a collegiate approach, in which transfer policy was dictated by collective wisdom. Fallows, Michael Edwards, the head of analysis, and Ian Ayre, Liverpool's managing director, all helped to shape the strategy. Senior scouts like Johnson were their eyes and ears.

Since Liverpool's business plan was based on the detection and development of young players. Griffin was quick to push the potential of Wycombe's full back Charles Dunne – 'he's getting some interest from Celtic, and will play in the Premier League one day' – and gave an honourable mention to Kortney Hause, a 17-year-old centre half.

Johnson smiled, knowing his friend had been told by his club to generate a loan fee, to help cash flow. He had heard of a prospect in Plymouth, 17-year-old striker Tyler Harvey, and had been given additional responsibility for scouting in Poland, the Czech Republic and Austria. 'I'm so excited,' he said. 'I can't wait to do it.'

There was a plane to catch, a player to assess, and a dream to pursue.

Index

Abramovich, Roman 132, 176
academies, football youth:
  budgets 5, 8, 336
  categories of 8, 71, 76
  drop out rates 5, 128–9
  Elite Player Performance Plan (EP3) and
    7–9, 71, 73–4, 75–6, 132, 226, 234
  exit trials and 210–26
  failure of 132, 133, 255, 317
  French 321
  importance of 41
  NextGen Series and 78–82, 89–99,
    305–6, 308
  Nike Academy 216–26
  poaching/'nicking' kids from 7–8,
    75–6, 80–1, 226, 234–5, 236, 315
  release of players from 86–7, 210–26
  see also scouts *and under individual*
    club name
Accam, David 217
Accrington Stanley 192
Achterberg, John 151, 160, 163
Adam, Charlie 26, 340
Adkins, Nigel 297
AFC Wimbledon 167, 208, 262, 264
agents:
  appearance/character of 1–2, 9–10
  approach players 76
  assessment of players 28
  baseball 173–4
  clubs dealing directly with 313
  coaches operating as 174
  French 94
  media-savvy 91
  Redknapp criticises 345
  Russian 254
  shady practices 370
  South America and 51–2, 326, 327
  third-party ownership and 233–4, 326
  usefulness of 313
  using as scouts 75
  ages of players, false 174

Aibangee, Ose 59, 66–7, 70, 71, 75, 76, 79,
  228
Ainsworth, Gareth 357, 358
Ajax 81, 82, 130–1, 295, 362, 369
Akinde, John 207
Akpom, Chuba 308
Al-Hasawi, Omar 306–7
Al-Mutawa, Bader 307
Al-Rashidi, Khalid 307
Albert, Florien 138
Aldridge, John 204
Allardyce, Sam 104
Allen, Clive 14
Allen, Martin 200, 355
Allison, Malcolm 259, 260
Alvechurch 202
American College system 216, 292
American Soccer League 191
Amiens 322
analytics 2, 143
  analysis of heart rate, recruitment and
    356–7
  baseball and 21, 36–7, 170, 172–5, 186,
    187, 335, 336, 343, 355–6
  basketball and 182, 292–3, 330–1,
    332–3, 334–5, 336
  Bill James and 36, 172–3, 187
  Billy Beane and 21, 27, 36, 37, 335
  Charles Reep and 171–2
  Damien Comolli and 12, 13, 20–8,
    33–7, 340–2
  driven by bloggers and statisticians
    185–6, 187–8
  Everton/Moyes and 38–56
  football and 2, 20–8, 33–7, 38–56,
    175–88, 332–44, 356–7, 360–1
  future of 370–1
  limitations of 360–1
  Liverpool and 20–8, 33–7, 340–2
  Matthew Benham and 332–43
  Moneyball and 21, 26, 36, 171, 172–3,
    176, 184, 188, 331, 335

analytics and 175–7
EP3 and 8
feeder clubs 52
culture at 175–6
FA Youth Cup, 2011/12 4, 10–12, 110
reserve team 108
scouting network/youth teams 10, 11,
12, 17, 29, 31, 69, 76, 104, 110,
131, 151, 175–6, 177, 218, 226,
228, 229, 236, 237, 294, 318, 319,
323, 325
Torres and 364
*see also under individual manager, scout
and player name*
Cheltenham Town 149, 150, 151, 157,
158
Chester, Ewan 154–5, 242–8
Cissé, Papiss 321
City of London 59
City University, New York 344
Clark, Lee 240, 241
Clarke, Cindy 362
Clarke, Gordon 276
Clarke, Ray 361–4
Cleveland Indians 174–5
Club Brugge 82, 362
coaches:
anxiety of 179
attitude of players towards 280
bad player habits and 213
badges 260, 276, 298, 299
change of 254
changing culture of 236–7
complain about scout approaches 63
data analysis and 331
differences from scouting 365
directors ask scouts about 153
emotional attachment to job 180
FA syllabus for 58, 60
foreign players adapting to British 316
inspirational qualities of 88
lack of foresight 5
lack of knowledge in some 135
Moyes as 45, 47
operating as agents 174
performance analysis and 179, 180
players challenge 16
respect of players for 99
rotated around age groups 73–4
scouts as 6, 59, 129–30, 140
Spanish 235
spot players 32

teams reflect 61, 62, 64
wedded to winning 66, 178
Coe, Tim 361
Colchester United 101, 107, 110, 118–24,
155, 156, 198
Cole, Andy 280
Cole, Ashley 32, 91, 214
Cole, Devante 280
Coleman, Tommy 276
Collett, Ernie 276–7
Collymore, Stan 198, 202, 203, 360
Cologne 255
Colorado Rapids 111
Comolli, Damien:
appearance 21
Arsenal, career at 21
attempts to justify legacy at Liverpool
340–2
character 21–2, 33–4, 35–6
Dalglish and 24–6, 37
data evangelist 21, 24, 25, 26, 27, 28,
36–7, 341–2
dedication 20, 22
Liverpool Sporting Director 12, 13,
20–8, 29, 33–7, 55, 91, 95, 151,
161–4, 170–1, 205, 231, 237–8,
257, 340–2, 371–2
Martin Jol, relationship with 21
Matthew Benham on 341–2
Mel Johnson and 12, 24, 33, 91, 161–3,
170, 207–8, 231, 237–40, 371–2
Moneyball and 21, 26
Robert Pires, remembers first impres-
sions of 35
polarising figure 20–1
poor transfer choices and 26, 340–2
Raheem Sterling, scouting of and 29,
33
Ronaldo, remembers first impressions
of 34
sacked from Liverpool 161–4, 170–1,
237, 340–2
Saint Etienne, career at 21
Tottenham, career at 21, 23
Van Persie, remembers first impres-
sions of 34–5
Coney, Dean 201
Conference 4, 6, 87, 202, 203, 205, 297, 307
Convergence Capital Partners B.V. 52
Cooke, Robbie 43, 44, 47, 269
Coppell, Steve 206, 261, 298, 302
Cornell University 356

Queens Park Rangers 14, 29, 31, 58, 64, 84,
150, 152, 155, 230, 231, 312, 344–52, 355
Quayle, Andy 190

Racing Club 328, 329
Rangers, Glasgow 115, 154, 240, 243, 244,
245, 289, 369
ranking players 119–24
Ranson, Ray 326
Rastrick, Dean 67
Reading 6, 140, 197, 204–5, 206, 220, 223,
236, 251, 253, 254, 282, 296
Real Madrid 28, 91, 184, 255, 323, 329
Redknapp, Harry 12, 102, 133, 259, 260,
344–5, 351, 352
Redmond, Nathan 17
Reep, Charles 171, 172
Reid, Peter 165
Reither, Sascha 255
Rekik, Karim 149
release of player 85, 102, 157, 166, 189–96,
205, 208, 211, 216–25, 235, 240, 284,
317, 355
Rennes 245
resale value 6, 41, 50, 53–4, 133, 221, 349,
368
Richardson, Russ 354
Ridgeway Rovers 12
Ridgeway, Mark 67
Rigg, Mike 231, 345–51
Rios, Miguel 57–61, 62–5, 77, 78, 80, 226, 372
River Plate 166
Road to Perdition, The (film) 269–70
Robbins, Mike 355
Robinson, Karl 29
Rocastle, David 'Rocky' 271–5, 278, 282, 291
Roda JC 259
Rodallega, Hugo 255
Rodgers, Brendan 6, 237, 238, 239, 295, 296,
371, 373–4
Rodriguez, James 52–3
Roeder, Glenn 17
Rogic, Tom 217
Ronaldo, Cristiano 34
Rooney, Wayne 41
Rosenberg 82
Rösler, Uwe 80
Rouen 320
Round, Steve 46–7
Rowe, Terry 202
Rowley, Steve 34, 83, 111, 126, 141, 269,
284, 286, 292, 294, 295, 303, 309

Sabermetric Revolution 170, 186, 355–6
Sage, James 91
Sagers, Hans 152–3
Saint Etienne 21
Saja, Sebastian 329
Samba, Christopher 345
Samper, Sergi 82, 83
Sanchez, Alexis 265, 348–9
Sansom, Kenny 200
Santa Cruz, Roque 40
Santos, Georges 93–4
SAS 218
SC Freiburg 321
Schmeichel, Peter 272
Scout7 110, 184, 360
scouts:
allegiance to their own 93, 269, 354–5
analytics and see analytics
anonymity 2, 3, 294
attitude of players and 42, 150–1,
157–9, 168, 179, 203, 280, 314
background of players and 11–12, 28,
30–1, 33, 86
boom and bust, reflect cycle of 253
character of players and 12, 28, 41, 42,
85–6, 87–8, 137, 153–4, 193,
252–3, 293–4, 308–9, 315, 328,
348–9
competitive nature of 93
conversation between 127–47
cycles of (changes in fashionable
nations of interest) 246–7
decision to let players go and 247–8
dedication of 20, 35, 155, 249–50, 256,
294, 354
disciplinary issues with players and 35,
85, 87, 99, 135–6
discovering 'the one'/discovery, feeling
of 3–4, 29–35, 59, 67–9, 83, 84–5,
150–1, 152–3, 144–5, 202–3,
230–1, 273–4, 321–4
dismissal/sack and 10, 12–13, 92, 103–5,
111–12, 113, 114, 130, 141, 155–6,
161–4, 207–8, 237–8, 248, 264, 269,
286–7, 300–1, 303, 307, 351–2, 354,
357, 364, 365, 368, 371–2
don't need to be a good pro to be 286
DVDs, watch players on 43, 144, 162,
246, 258, 262, 275, 318, 328, 350
emotional intelligence and 23, 108
emotional investment in 74–5
as an endangered species 172